MW00783711

The Coming of Democracy

The Coming of Democracy

Presidential Campaigning in the Age of Jackson

Mark R. Cheathem
CUMBERLAND UNIVERSITY
LEBANON, TENNESSEE

Johns Hopkins University Press
Baltimore

© 2018 Johns Hopkins University Press
All rights reserved. Published 2018
Printed in the United States of America on acid-free paper

2 4 6 8 9 7 5 3 1

Johns Hopkins University Press
2715 North Charles Street
Baltimore, Maryland 21218-4363
www.press.jhu.edu

Library of Congress Cataloging-in-Publication Data
Names: Cheathem, Mark Renfred, author.
Title: The coming of democracy : presidential campaigning in the age of
Jackson / Mark R. Cheathem.
Description: Baltimore : Johns Hopkins University Press, 2018. | Includes
bibliographical references and index.
Identifiers: LCCN 2017046427| ISBN 9781421425979 (hardcover : alk.
paper) | ISBN 9781421425986 (pbk. : alk. paper) | ISBN 9781421425993
(electronic) | ISBN 1421425971 (hardcover : alk. paper) | ISBN 142142598X
(pbk. : alk. paper) | ISBN 1421425998 (electronic)
Subjects: LCSH: Presidents—United States—Election—1840. | Harrison,
William Henry, 1773–1841. | United States—Politics and
government—1837–1841. | Jackson, Andrew, 1767–1845—Influence.
Classification: LCC E390 .C47 2018 | DDC 973.5/8—dc23
LC record available at https://lccn.loc.gov/2017046427

A catalog record for this book is available from the British Library.

*Special discounts are available for bulk purchases of this book. For
more information, please contact Special Sales at 410-516-6936
or specialsales@press.jhu.edu.*

Johns Hopkins University Press uses environmentally friendly book
materials, including recycled text paper that is composed of at least
30 percent post-consumer waste, whenever possible.

For Alli

Contents

Acknowledgments

This book was written during a period of transition at Cumberland University, which witnessed my undergraduate alma mater beginning to fulfill a potential unrealized since Cordell Hull's days as a law student. I am grateful for the leadership that Board of Trust Chair Bob McDonald, President Paul Stumb, VPAA and Provost Bill McKee, and Dean Eric Cummings provided our institution during the past few years and for their support of my research.

In 2001, I had the opportunity to publish a piece expressing my appreciation for librarians and archivists, the unsung heroes of academia. At Cumberland University's Vise Library, all the staff deserve thanks, but I want to single out Ashli Wells in particular. Every library has an invaluable staff member who goes above and beyond, and for Cumberland, that is Ashli. I also want to thank the staff at the American Antiquarian Society, the Library of Congress, the Richmond (Virginia) Library, the River Campus Libraries at the University of Rochester in New York, the Arthur and Elizabeth Schlesinger Library at Harvard University, the Tennessee State Library and Archives, and the Virginia Historical Society.

I imposed on several people in asking them to read this book in part or in whole. As always, John Marszalek was my primary critic and cheerleader. If I had not seen his C-SPAN talk on the Eaton affair in 1998, the last two decades of my life would not have been as rich professionally or personally. Tom Hilpert is my toughest critic, but as long as he respects my knowledge of commas, I will keep subjecting myself to his edits. Miles Smith IV and Kenneth Owens read one of my earliest drafts of the book, and I think all three of us agreed then that the quality could only go up from there. Two of my students, Jennifer Allen Erickson and Josh Williams, kindly tolerated my request for feedback on another early draft. One of my former Mississippi State officemates, Tim Vanderburg, provided a primary source that I could not easily access, as did Andy Moore, whom I admire and respect more than he knows. John Belohlavek avoided being drafted into reading another manuscript this time, but I want to acknowledge here that I appreciate his professional generosity and personal interest in my career.

I began directing the Papers of Martin Van Buren during the review stage of this book. Co-editor James Bradley and the following students and volunteers who have contributed to the Van Buren Papers made it easier to tell the Little Magician's side of the story: George Allyn, Daniel Barr, Bill Claydon, Jennifer Allen Erickson, David Gregory, Adrienne High, Ally Johnson, Zach Morgan, Christian Noland, Carrie Ordiway, Jordan Russ, Jazmine Smith, Sarah Tiger, Alyssa Walker, Josh Williams, and Kayelee Young.

My thanks to Bob Brugger for overseeing this project before his retirement from Johns Hopkins University Press and to Elizabeth Demers for shepherding it to publication. Lauren Straley was a pleasure to work with as the book went through the postreview process at Johns Hopkins. I am also grateful for the critiques of the anonymous reviewers and for the careful copyediting of Melanie Mallon.

Even though my family will not let me be as introverted as I want to be, I still love them. Amber, you are my rock and my laughter. Laney, you are my funny, sassy alter ego. David, you are my hockey star and buddy. Alli, you are talented in so many ways—art, creative media, sports—but even if you weren't, I would still love you and your Munchkin face just as much.

The Coming of Democracy

Introduction

On 29 May 1840, approximately 7,500 individuals gathered in Clarksville, Tennessee, to witness a parade celebrating presidential candidate William Henry Harrison. The Whig Party had chosen the War of 1812 hero and former territorial governor, US senator, and diplomat to challenge the incumbent president, Democrat Martin Van Buren. The Clarksville audience watched as 250 Harrison supporters disembarked from the steamboat *Gallatin* and began marching from the dock to the square, then on to the area prepared for the festivities. As bands played, parade members carried banners announcing their devotion to the Whig cause. One banner proclaimed, "Harrison and Tyler—Vox populi, vox dei." This Latin phrase, translated "the voice of the people is the voice of God," indicated their belief that the people's choice of Harrison and his running mate, Virginian John Tyler, reflected providential will.[1]

Floats were also part of the parade, and one proved especially memorable. It incorporated the Log Cabin and Hard Cider campaign theme, introduced by Democrats as a way to criticize Harrison but adopted by the Whigs to indicate their candidate's purported common-man lifestyle. The float consisted of a log cabin with "several coon skins nailed about the door, and a live coon . . . playing upon the bark roof." The obligatory barrel of hard cider rested inside the cabin. Banners were tacked on either end of the building. One identified Harrison with another American military hero, George Washington; the other said, in part, "Harrison and Reform." This last inscription gave a nod to both the Whigs' support of various moral reform movements as well as Harrison's desire to bring a different direction to the presidency. A testament to the latter came from the drummer leading the float, a former British prisoner of war captured by Harrison at the Battle of the Thames, the 1813 engagement on which the Whig candidate's military fame primarily rested. The drummer reportedly testified on his former captor's behalf: "General Harrison saved him from one Monarchy [the British] and is about to save him from another [Van Buren]."[2]

The Whigs had formed in 1834 during Jackson's second administration but had been unsuccessful in their efforts to defeat Van Buren in the 1836 election. Four years later, their chances of replacing him with Harrison were good if they could find a way to convince the growing number of voters that their party held the nation's future success in its hands.

Van Buren's fall from grace came quickly once he ascended to the presidency in 1837. He had risen from his home state of New York to become the trusted confidant of Andrew Jackson, the seventh president. When Jackson took office in 1829, Van Buren served first as his secretary of state (1829–31), then as his vice president (1833–37). In 1836, the New Yorker won election as Jackson's successor. His administration suffered, however, from the Panic of 1837, a series of economic downturns across the nation that began almost immediately after he took office and left him precariously perched to win a second term. He and the Democrats nevertheless were positioned to draw on the organized partisanship of the very two-party system that Van Buren had helped to rejuvenate over the past few years.

At stake in the 1840 presidential election was the future of this political party system. Democrats had formed their party identity during the 1828 campaign and early in Jackson's first administration. They possessed a political ideology based on the Jeffersonian principles of limited government and the will of the people. A Van Buren victory in 1840 would further strengthen the Democrats and seemed likely to, if not scatter the Whigs, at least make them a permanent minority party for the near future. The Whigs, on the other hand, had initially organized as an anti-Jackson party, bringing together disparate individuals and factions who agreed on opposing Old Hickory but not necessarily much else. By 1840, the Whigs were the party of social morality and progressivism; that year's presidential campaign offered the first legitimate opportunity for the Whigs to articulate a focused political agenda and to begin building a stable voting base led by their presidential choice. A Harrison victory would force the Democrats to reexamine their own political program and reconsider whether the principles embodied in Jackson's administrations were enough to recapture the presidency in 1844.

Throughout the early republic and Jacksonian periods, both parties attempted to lure voters to their side by using cultural politics, or political activities that took place outside formal party organization and the act of voting. What sounded and looked like entertainment, things such as music, public events, and cartoons, held important political meaning in the first few decades of the United States' existence. These appeals targeted the growing number of eligible voters, which increased dramatically following the 1824 presidential election, and engaged non-voters, particularly women. The extraordinary voter participation rate (over 80 percent) in the 1840 presidential election indicated that both substantive issues and cultural politics involved Americans in the presidential selection process. Drawing parallels between the Jacksonian era and today is problematic because of the enormous changes that the nation and its politics have experienced. Nevertheless, the question of voter engagement is one that remains relevant in the age of round-the-clock news cycles and social media campaigns, and the maturation of cultural politics during the Jacksonian period is an important starting point for considering what drives twenty-first-century Americans' interest in presidential politics.

Note to readers: In this book, I use "early republic" for the entire period between 1789 and 1840 and reserve the terms "Jacksonian era" or "Jacksonian period" for the years following the 1824 election through the 1840 election. I have also retained the original spelling, punctuation, and other idiosyncrasies of the period's writing, in some cases using bracketed editorial insertions when necessary to help readers understand a quotation or when the insertions were included in the original.

CHAPTER 1

Competing Blueprints for Democracy

The 1840 presidential campaign drew on the long-standing American political culture that employed both formal and informal practices. Formal politics, such as political partisanship, elections, and voting, became more democratic during the early republic and Jacksonian periods, clearly affecting the execution and outcome of the 1840 campaign. At the same time, cultural politics played a significant role in generating interest in the contest. Even before the inception of the United States, cultural politics provided Americans unable to exert power through formal means the opportunity to participate in the political sphere. The growing intersection of formal and cultural politics during the decades of the early republic contributed to growing voter engagement in presidential contests and culminated in the Log Cabin and Hard Cider campaign of 1840.

FORMAL POLITICS IN THE EARLY REPUBLIC

The outline of formal politics in the early United States looks familiar to us today: presidential elections sometimes turning on disputed outcomes, members of Congress failing to get along, and American citizens complaining about the national government's overexpansive power. Nevertheless, there are significant differences between the political world of then and now. Then, presidential voting often stretched over weeks and produced chief executives who typically used their constitutional authority cautiously. Congressional members were divided into two main ideological factions, the Federalists and the Republicans, who were also known as Democratic-Republicans or Jeffersonian Republicans. (Neither of today's two major political parties—Democratic or Republican—exactly resembles the Republicans of the early republic.) States sometimes held more political power than the national government; for example, state legislatures, not voters, selected US senators. In many instances, those same legislatures also apportioned electoral votes without popular elections.

Three specific areas of formal politics are central to understanding the evolution of presidential politics during the early republic: political parties, presidential elections, and voter participation.

Political Parties

During George Washington's presidency (1789–97), political factions developed in Congress that produced the first party system, pitting Federalists against Republicans. Led by Alexander Hamilton and John Adams, Federalists wanted a stronger central government, a vigorous national economy based on industry and urbanization, and a loose, or flexible, interpretation of the Constitution. Thomas Jefferson and James Madison headed the Republican opposition. They advocated a more limited national government; an economy and a society grounded in the rural, agricultural perspective; and a strict, or limited, interpretation of the Constitution. In addition to these ideological differences, the two factions generally found support in different geographic regions: the Federalists in New England and the Republicans in the Old South and the emerging West. The mid-Atlantic states proved to be the most contested partisan ground.[1]

During the first eight years of the nation's existence, Federalists and Republicans fought political battles over several issues, including the national government's role in the economy, the French Revolution that was engulfing Europe in warfare, and the United States' relationship with foreign powers, specifically Great Britain and Spain, that held territory on the North American continent. By the time George Washington's second term was drawing to a close, in the mid-1790s, the two sides were clearly defined political factions with different political philosophies about the best direction for the United States.[2]

These battles continued into the early nineteenth century, helping to draw lines of political demarcation between the two parties at all levels of government. Republicans gained the ascendancy in the 1800 presidential and congressional elections, which propelled them into national power for the next two decades. Although the minority national party, Federalists remained competitive at all levels of government and, at the local and state levels, even existed as the majority party in some areas. Following the War of 1812, Federalists began to decline at the national level, due in part to their public denouncement of President James Madison and congressional Republicans' support of the war against Great Britain. The Federalists ran their last presidential candidate in 1816, but they persisted as a significant political power in some states well into the 1820s.[3]

Prior to the 1824 election, then, two parties—the Federalists and the Republicans—existed, but they lacked the coherent national organization and internal discipline that would emerge during the Jacksonian-era presidential elections. Following the 1824 election, the Federalists continued to fade, and the Republicans split into rival factions that offered "competing blueprints for democracy."[4]

Presidential Elections

Selecting presidential candidates in the early republic was very different from the process used today. George Washington ran unopposed in the first two elections, but his decision not to run for a third term highlighted the need for a process to identify presidential candidates. What developed was the congressional caucus nomination. Unlike today, with a caucus/primary system that allows voters to determine presidential nominations, the congressional caucus system limited the decision to the US representatives and senators of the respective parties, who met and chose their preferred nominees.[5]

The congressional caucus may have been used in 1796, but the first conclusive evidence of its existence appeared four years later. In May 1800, Federalist congressmen convened and decided to support President John Adams and South Carolina's Charles C. Pinckney "without giving one a preference to the other." Republicans met that same month and "unanimously agreed to support [Aaron] Burr for Vice-President," with Thomas Jefferson the presumptive presidential candidate. Over the next few elections, caucus nominations continued. By 1820, with the Federalist Party significantly weakened, this system appeared to be on its way out. About an attempted caucus meeting to select a vice-presidential nominee to run with incumbent president James Monroe, one Republican noted, "Only forty six members, out of two hundred and thirty, attended the Caucus . . . the meeting resolved that it was inexpedient to make any nomination, & then adjourned."[6]

Once presidential candidates were chosen, voter involvement in electing them varied. The Constitution gave state legislatures latitude in determining the assignment of electoral votes. In some cases, state legislatures cast votes without any voter input; in other cases, popular votes determined which candidate received a state's electoral votes. The timing of election dates also affected voter participation in the process. In 1792, Congress designated that elections should be held "within thirty-four days preceding the first Wednesday in December" of the election year.

(Not until 1845 would the first Tuesday following the first Monday in November become the standardized presidential election day with which Americans today are familiar.) This variance in election dates allowed some states to vote earlier than others. The results of these earlier states usually appeared in newspapers before the final polling day, undoubtedly influencing the decisions of individuals living in states with later voting dates.[7]

Voter Participation

One measure of formal political engagement during the early republic was the voter participation rate, which was largely influenced by eligibility requirements. In 1790, the year of the first census, ten of the original thirteen states required voters to own property in order to cast their ballots. That number totaled nine in 1820, with the ten new states that had entered the Union after 1790 generally not introducing a property-owning requirement for suffrage. Conversely, between 1790 and 1820, states began adding racial exclusions to restrict voting access for African Americans. In the first census, only three states (Georgia, South Carolina, and Virginia) limited voting to whites; thirty years later, fourteen of the twenty-three states specifically disallowed African American suffrage. Women were disenfranchised to an even greater extent. New Jersey was the only state in the early republic to allow women to vote; its property-owning women held that right from 1776 until the legislature took it away in 1807.[8]

For these reasons, voter participation in presidential elections was limited. In 1796, the first competitive presidential election took place between John Adams and Thomas Jefferson. The existing popular vote totals cast in that election numbered approximately 47,000. Four years later, the same two candidates competed in a hotly contested and acrimonious campaign, but they drew only about 67,000 votes from 2.16 million free white males. The next two elections (1804 and 1808) were less competitive, with Jefferson defeating South Carolina's Charles C. Pinckney by a 162–14 electoral vote in 1804, and James Madison winning over Pinckney 122–47 in 1808. Nevertheless, the popular votes in each election increased: from 143,000 in 1804 to 191,000 in 1808. In 1812, Madison won a second term in a close contest. He defeated New Yorker DeWitt Clinton 128 to 89 in electoral votes, with only 12,000 popular votes separating the two candidates. The 1812 election also saw an increase in total popular votes, with 269,000 cast. In 1816 and 1820, Federalists put forward little opposition to James Monroe, who secured the presidency for Jeffersonian Republicans for eight more years. As a result, the popular vote total dropped to just over 100,000 in each election, while the number of free white males rose to about 4 million by 1820.[9]

While these data are incomplete, they reveal three features of early republic elections. First, American citizens did not look at presidents as the answer to the nation's problems in the same way that they do today. Therefore, choosing a chief executive was not necessarily regarded as a political priority. Second, the number of eligible voters who participated in presidential elections was low throughout the first three decades of the early republic. This anemic voter participation rate proceeded in part from suffrage restrictions, but also from the lack of strong political parties coordinating national campaigns. Third, cultural politics at the national level did not necessarily produce larger voter turnouts during these elections. For example, the 1800 campaign was one of the dirtiest presidential contests in US political history, yet it failed to elicit much enthusiasm at the polls. Subsequent elections also generated little organized turnout. As Thomas Jefferson noted to Albert Gallatin in 1817, "I have been charmed to see that a presidential election now produces scarcely any agitation. On mr Madison's election there was little, on Monroe's all but none."[10]

Despite the low participation rates in presidential elections, early republic voters undeniably were politically engaged at the local and state levels. Prior to 1800, voter participation rates in most states ranged "between 30 and 50 percent of adult white males." Voter engagement began to increase in the late 1790s as transatlantic issues, particularly the British-French rivalry, began directly influencing US domestic politics and driving increasing partisanship at all levels of government. This shift continued in the early nineteenth century. Between 1800 and 1820, peak voter turnout in most states matched or exceeded that of the 1828–40 presidential elections, usually hailed as the period when democratic political engagement began to flourish. In most cases, substantive issues of concern at the local and state levels, not suffrage reform or national politics, led to increasingly heightened partisan organization. This more structured political system spurred eligible voters to turn out at polling places to make their voices heard, a crucial lesson for Jacksonian-era presidential campaigns that was enhanced by the period's cultural politics.[11]

CHAPTER 2

Exercising the Right of Freemen

Outside the formal political process in the late eighteenth and early nineteenth centuries, an informal political culture existed that both gave voice to those possessing less political power and laid the foundation for the energetic presidential contests that took place between 1824 and 1840. Cultural politics included several organizational and popular electioneering characteristics usually associated with the emergence of Jacksonian democracy, including auxiliary organizations; material, print, and visual culture; political music; public correspondence, events, and speeches; and women's activity. In fact, many of these forms and practices existed prior to the Revolutionary War, which speaks to their long-term existence in American politics. Nevertheless, the presidential campaigns of 1824, 1828, 1832, 1836, and 1840 witnessed the increasing importance of these types of cultural politics.[1]

PUBLIC EVENTS AND SPEECHES

Public events and speechmaking took several forms during the revolutionary and early republic periods, providing Americans with opportunities to express their political views. These events and addresses sometimes allowed them to participate in a form of electioneering; at other times, they afforded Americans the chance to convey their discontent. Nevertheless, by bringing citizens directly into contact with political figures and ideas, public events and speeches increased their interest and investment in the nation's political culture.[2]

During the late seventeenth and early eighteenth centuries, public events, usually centered on food and drink, made it possible for candidates and voters to make and hear political statements. Picnics and barbecues provided one such opportu-

nity. For example, an 1803 barbecue in Maryland was advertised as one for "republican citizens," who joined together to eat and drink in honor of the Jeffersonians
and to condemn "Treason and Apostacy—Benedict Arnold and John Adams."
These gatherings could also unite political opponents, as one 1812 barbecue in
Charles Town, Virginia, did. "The greatest harmony prevailed" at this event,
which witnessed toasts made in support of the military effort against Britain and
"an honorable and speedy termination of the war," as well as the hope that "Republican and Federalists always meet in friendship—their interests are the same."
Elite men also used the promise of smoked meat and strong drink to attract men
of a lower rank to these gatherings, hoping to solidify their loyalty for upcoming
elections, and alcohol and gambling often accompanied visits to polling places
on election day.[3]

While local politicians might be able to participate in these public events, presidential candidates in the early republic were supposed to remain "Mute Tri-
bunes," unlike today, when they are expected to be public and accessible to voters.
Once elected, however, presidents saw the benefit of making public appearances
or even undertaking tours to engender support for their agendas and parties. For
example, George Washington made two tours—one in New England in 1789, the
other in the South in 1791—that elicited significant enthusiasm among those who
participated. In Alexandria, Virginia, one newspaper recounted "the happiness of
the Company" at the president's attendance at the town's Fourth of July celebration. Washington's "extraordinary talents and virtues had contributed to the at-
tainment of that blessing which they were now assembled to commemorate.
Him, therefore, they could not but contemplate, in some sort, as the Father of the
Feast."[4]

Almost twenty-five years later, during the "Era of Good Feelings," President
James Monroe undertook his own tour of New England in the summer of 1817
to establish a climate of nonpartisanship. Federalists in the region coordinated
a series of public ceremonies and events "to work out the stain of the Hartford
Convention and their other rebellions," according to Federalist senator Jeremiah
Mason of New Hampshire. While in Massachusetts, Monroe met with former
president John Adams and other Federalists, as well as many Republicans. The
Fourth of July coincided with Monroe's visit, offering a chance for the president
to emphasize partisan unity. In one address, he confidently proclaimed, "Believing that there is not a section of our Union, nor a citizen, who is not interested in
the success of our government, I indulge a strong hope that they will all unite in
future in the measures necessary to secure it." House Speaker Henry Clay was

skeptical about Monroe's bipartisan gestures: "If indeed they [Federalists] are real converts to the true faith, and their convertion is attributable to the tour of Mr. Monroe, he merits the honors of a political Saint."[5]

One of the main functions of public celebrations was to make political statements, which could be incorporated in long speeches or short toasts. In 1778, David Ramsay spoke at length about his belief in the United States' providential political course: "Our sun of political happiness is already risen, and hath lifted his head over the mountain illuminating our hemisphere with liberty, light, and polished life. Our Independence will redeem one quarter of the globe from tyranny and oppression, and consecrate it the chosen Seat of Truth, Justice, Freedom, Learning, and Religion." Following the writing of the Constitution, its opponents used toasts to express their disapproval. Pennsylvanians celebrated the Fourth of July in 1788 by pronouncing, "May America remain forever free from tyranny, anarchy, and consolidation," while in Rhode Island, they proclaimed, "May the sons of freedom in America never submit to a despotic government." A French observer noted that "Americans derive as much satisfaction [from making toasts], as a Frenchman would in recounting the number of his *love intrigues*."[6]

PUBLIC CORRESPONDENCE

Public correspondence between citizens and presidents represented another way in which political expressions occurred outside the constraints of organized campaigning. Some individuals or groups wrote addresses, letters, or petitions to presidents or presidential candidates asking for specific statements on political issues. These politicians often took time to respond, understanding that both the original inquiry and the response might be published, usually in newspapers and sometimes in pamphlets. Presidents also occasionally used public correspondence to reinforce a message that they wanted to convey to the official recipients, as well as anyone else who read it.[7]

During Washington's presidential tours in the early 1790s, he often received letters and addresses from the citizens of towns he visited. These expressions not only conveyed the writers' gratitude at the president's presence, but also often contained other messages. During his southern tour, for example, Washington received an address from a religious society in Liberty County, Georgia, noting its peaceful relations with local Indians and promising that it would "not fail to implore the Divine blessing in your behalf." Washington echoed the religious language of his Liberty County correspondents, noting that "from the gallantry and fortitude of her citizens, under the auspices of Heaven, America has derived her independence." He also wrote encouragingly, "Continue, my fellow-citizens, to cultivate the peace and harmony which now subsist between you and your Indian neighbors—the happy consequence is immediate."[8]

One of the most notable examples of public correspondence was the address sent by the Danbury (Connecticut) Baptist Association to President Thomas Jefferson in 1801. The Danbury Baptists expressed concerns about the Federalist-controlled state government's attitude toward religious freedom. "What religious privileges we enjoy (as a minor part of the State)," they wrote, "we enjoy as favors granted, and not as inalienable rights: and these favors we receive at the expence of such degrading acknowledgements as are inconsistant with the rights of freemen." After consulting with two New England Republican congressmen, Jefferson responded with a letter indicating his agreement with the Baptists' claim that "religion is a matter which lies solely between Man & his God, that he owes account to none other for his faith or his worship, [and] that the legitimate powers of government reach actions only, & not opinions." True to form, Jefferson's letter appeared in New York and New England newspapers. Most people today know the letter because of Jefferson's claim that the First Amendment created "a wall of separation between Church & State," which remains a flashpoint for debates about American religious freedom.[9]

A decade later, citizens in New Haven, Connecticut, who were "either directly engaged in mercantile pursuits, or in the occupations connected with them," sent President James Madison a petition outlining their concerns about the Republican Congress's passage of the Non-Intercourse Act, which placed embargoes on US shipping to British and French ports. The president responded with an explanation, concluding with an endorsement of their act of petitioning: "In the mode which the town of New Haven has employed, I witness with satisfaction, that in exercising the right of freemen, the obligation of Citizens has not been forgotten." Although public correspondence between presidents and citizens was not yet widespread, these exchanges laid the foundation on which future presidents built successful campaigns.[10]

MATERIAL CULTURE

In an era when few Americans had the opportunity to see, much less personally meet, a president, material culture provided them with the chance to tangibly touch and own pieces of the political process. During the nation's early years, objects invested with political meaning distinguished the American colonies from the British Empire and gave the United States a separate identity. Two of the most famous objects from the revolutionary era were liberty poles and liberty trees. The first liberty tree appeared near the Boston Common in August 1765, with an effigy of a stamp distributor and the figure of the devil hanging from its branches. The following year, another one was planted in Newport, Rhode Island, "as a Monument of the Spirited and Noble Opposition made to the Stamp Act." Liberty poles often served as substitutes for liberty trees because they could be placed anywhere, and they could more easily be reinforced with iron or other metal protection to keep them from being toppled or removed.[11]

The use of these objects persisted into the early republic. During the Whiskey Rebellion, which broke out in western Pennsylvania in 1791 and climaxed in 1794, protesters erected liberty poles inscribed with "Liberty and no Excise," "Liberty and Equality," and "Liberty or Death." In the 1790s, Francophile Americans began adding a liberty cap, a symbol adopted by French Jacobins as part of their revolutionary undertaking, to their liberty poles.[12]

Late in that decade, Republicans still displayed liberty poles as an act of defiance against what they perceived as overzealous Federalist power in Congress. In the lead-up to the 1800 election, the Federalist-controlled Congress passed the Sedition Act, which prohibited criticism of the national government and its officers, in order to protect their political power. Republicans broadcasted their displeasure by employing liberty poles. Federalists responded by tearing down these "wooden gods of sedition" and, in some cases, by prosecuting the men they believed were responsible for erecting them. They argued that the poles served as "a rallying point of insurrection and civil war."[13]

While just two examples, liberty trees and liberty poles reflected how Americans used objects as political symbols. Other types of objects, such as buttons, clothing, and dinnerware, appeared as well, bearing patriotic inscriptions or representations. Although the political statements of these latter objects were relatively tame and not necessarily partisan, they were harbingers of the more expansive material culture to come in later presidential campaigns.[14]

AUXILIARY ORGANIZATIONS

Americans also displayed their informal political opinions through auxiliary organizations, groups operating outside traditional political avenues. As the early republic progressed, many auxiliary groups began to coalesce into the form and function of recognizable political parties.

During the revolutionary era, two significant examples of these groups emerged: committees of correspondence and the Sons of Liberty. Committees of correspondence spanned the thirteen colonies and kept one another informed of the progress of colonial opposition. They sometimes assumed extrapolitical power, particularly in New England. Similarly, the Sons of Liberty was an intercolonial-group of men that grew out of the Stamp Act crisis of the mid-1760s. These men, who primarily came from merchant and artisan backgrounds, set aside their differences and united in common cause against British oversight. They often used acts of violence, such as burning effigies or destroying public property, to express their displeasure with British rule. Extrapolitical violence persisted after the Revolution. Several rebellions—Shays' Rebellion (1786), the Whiskey Rebellion (1791–94), and Fries' Rebellion (1799–1800)—pitted average Americans against the ruling elite and centered on violent protests of taxes. In most cases, however, auxiliary organizations channeled political debate in less destructive ways, and they provided places for Americans to absorb and express political views.[15]

In the early republic, both Federalists and Republicans used auxiliary organizations. Federalists, for example, founded debating societies and social libraries, while Republicans formed Democratic-Republican societies. Members of these latter societies resurrected the use of committees of correspondence and the erection of liberty poles to connect their cause with their revolutionary forebearers. According to one historian, "by organizing public or semi-public discussions of political matters, issuing resolutions and addresses to the people, and remonstrating to local and national leaders," Democratic-Republican societies challenged the deferential political model favored by Federalists and helped to further popular interest in more democratic political forms.[16]

One of the most visible auxiliary organizations was the Masonic lodge, a group of Freemasons. In the words of New Yorker DeWitt Clinton, Freemasonry was a substitute for "that tender connection among men, which the infinite diversities of family, tribe and nation, had nearly reduced to nothing." He believed that the "artificial consanguinity" that the secret fraternal order created "operate[d] with as much force and effect, as the natural relationship of blood." In addition to producing close bonds of brotherhood, Freemasonry sought both to protect liberty and to preserve order, goals that were sometimes contradictory in the early republic. As Freemasonry expanded in the 1790s, Republican membership overtook that of the Federalists, enabling Republican men-on-the-make to create networks of influence that offered them the chance to challenge their Federalist opponents.[17]

Federalists struck back by associating Republican Freemasonry with the Bavarian Illuminati, a secret society in Eastern Europe that allegedly sought to assert its nefarious control over the entire world. New England ministers such as Jedidiah

Morse and Joseph Lathrop believed that the Illuminati had infiltrated some of the Republicans' auxiliary associations. One correspondent wrote Morse that the Illuminati in Germany had taken "control of the greater part of the literary journals, and reading clubs, nay, even of printers and booksellers." The irony of their attacks given President Washington's Masonic membership appeared to escape Federalists. Auxiliary organizations later served an important role in organizing political parties during the Jacksonian period; indeed, opposition to Freemasonry was at the heart of one of the era's third parties.[18]

POLITICAL MUSIC

From the appearance of John Dickinson's "Liberty Song" in 1768, music played a significant role in capturing Americans' political sentiments. One song, which appeared in 1776 as the American colonies were declaring their independence, encompassed the attitude of Patriots toward their former British comrades:

> Your dark unfathom'd Councils, our weakest Heads defeat,
> Our Children rout your Armies, our Boats destroy your Fleet;
> And to complete the dire Disgrace, cooped up within a Town,
> You live the scorn of all our Host, the Slaves of WASHINGTON.[19]

As George Washington made his inaugural journey in 1789, a *"white-robed choir"* serenaded him in Trenton, New Jersey, with what likely was "the first music to have been composed for a president of the United States," according to musicologist Vera Brodsky Lawrence. The song sung by the choir extolled Washington's heroism:

> Welcome, mighty Chief once more!
> Welcome to this graceful shore;
> Now no mercenary Foe
> Aims again the fatal blow;
> Aims at thee, the fatal blow.
>
> Virgins fair & Matrons grave,
> These thy conquering arm did save,
> Build for thee, triumphal bowers,
> Strew ye fair his way with flowers,
> Strew your hero's way with Flowers.[20]

Leading up to the 1800 campaign, music reinforced partisan impressions. One song that circulated among newspapers used the patriotic tune of "Yankee

Doodle" to support John Adams in his fight against the pro-French Jeffersonian Republicans:

> Bold ADAMS did in seventy-six,
> Our Independence sign, Sir;
> And he will not, give up a jot,
> Tho' all the world combine, Sir.
>
> *Chorus.*
> Yankee doodle (mind the tune)
> Yankee doodle dandy,
> If Frenchmen come with naked bum,
> We'll *spank* 'em hard and handy.

Jefferson's victory over Adams prompted "A Patriotic Song for the Glorious Fourth of March, 1801," the date of the Virginian's inauguration.

> THE gloomy night before us flies,
> The reign of Terror now is o'er;
> Its Gags, Inquisitors and Spies,
> Its herds of Harpies are no more!
>
> Rejoice! Columbia's Sons, rejoice!
> To tyrants never bend the knee,
> But join with heart and soul and voice,
> For Jefferson and Liberty.[21]

Songs continued to play a role in presidential politics throughout the rest of the early republic. "Monroe is the Man," which appeared in 1816, regaled James Madison's successor:

> The *firm* friend of freedom in every sphere;
> Whose conscience 'mong kings, and 'mong courts, still was clear;
> Whose actions grow brighter the nearer we scan?
> O! say, sov'reign people—which—which is the man?
> . . .
> *He's* the man that we love—for to hate him *who can?*
> Monroe—yes, Monroe—he, indeed, is the man.

A critic "translated" this song into what he considered a more honest reflection of Monroe's popularity:

O! say, sovereign Caucus, whose voice is law,
Whose will is supreme, and keep freedom in awe,

. . .

Among the Virginians, say, who leads the van—
Mid so many demagogues—which is the man!

. . .

IT IS ONE OUT OF THREE WHO FROM BLADENSBURGH RAN,
TAKE THE STUPIDEST FELLOW—AND HE IS THE MAN.[22]

While the lyrics to these songs may not resonate today, they captured the political sentiments of Americans then. By setting them to catchy and familiar tunes, early republic lyricists ensured that listeners heard, and remembered, their partisan message loud and clear. It was a lesson used to good effect between 1824 and 1840.

PRINT CULTURE

Print culture played a critical role in the rhetorical warfare of the early republic. Especially before newspapers grew in quantity and length, pamphlets provided the opportunity for writers to address issues of concern with fewer restrictions. Pamphlet writers usually published under pseudonyms to protect their identity or to ensure that readers considered their views independent of the writers' public and private reputations.[23]

Supporters of independence, most famously Thomas Paine in *Common Sense*, used pamphlets extensively during the revolutionary period. They continued to be employed in the 1780s and 1790s, as Americans wrestled with the ideological underpinnings of their new nation. According to one estimate, between 1789 and 1800, Americans produced approximately one thousand political writings, many of them pamphlets. Throughout these years, pamphlets continued to capture political sentiments and disseminate them to eligible voters. Court clerk Abraham Bishop, in his 1800 pamphlet *Connecticut Republicanism: An Oration on the Extent and Power of Political Delusion,* for example, criticized "well-fed, well-dressed, chariot-rolling, caucus-keeping, levee-revelling federalists" for having "perverted" the Fourth of July "into days for chastising the enemies of [the] administration by the odious characters of illuminatists, disorganizers and atheists." During the War of 1812, John Lowell wrote a pamphlet outlining his belief that "the war is undertaken not for *our* interests, but for those of France." He claimed that he was writing his pamphlet because he had taken a pledge to defend his state of Massachusetts from "all hostile attempts whatsoever," including from "the men whom a majority of our citizens have unfortunately elevated to ill-deserved power."[24]

Along with pamphlets, newspapers were important sources of information during the revolutionary period, but they became even more crucial in the new nation. They were the main form of national communication in the early republic, and they were openly partisan, with both Federalists and Republicans using them to disseminate their principles and to attack their political enemies. The passage of the Post Office Act of 1792, which gave newspapers preferential postage rates, helped the press grow throughout the decade. Approximately 100 papers existed in 1790; by the end of the decade, close to 250 papers were in print.[25]

Throughout the 1790s, partisan newspapers waged war against the opposition. During the debate over the Jay Treaty, an agreement made during George Washington's second term that sought to lessen lingering tensions between the United States and Great Britain, Republicans attacked the manner in which Federalists secured support for the treaty. "Secrecy is the order of the day in our government," one newspaper contributor observed, "to keep the people in ignorance, and to practice a tyranny upon them!" Once Republicans and Federalists identified Thomas Jefferson and John Adams as their respective nominees for 1796, both parties settled on campaign themes that appeared in print. New York Republicans pronounced Jefferson "the firm republican, the steady patriot, and the truly honest man," while Philadelphia supporters credited him for having "first framed the sacred political sentence, that all men are *born* equal." John Adams, meanwhile, was "an avowed MONARCHIST" and "an advocate for hereditary power and distinctions," who thought that the sentiment of the Declaration of Independence was "all a farce and a falsehood." Federalists responded by emphasizing Jefferson's hypocrisy in allowing his supporters to paint him as a man of the people when "under the assumed cloak of humility lurks the most *ambitious spirit*, the most overweening pride and hauteur." Much like politics today, it was the classic American political trope of the battle between good and evil.[26]

As Republicans and Federalists had done in 1796, both parties employed print culture to attack their opponents in the 1800 campaign. Republican newspaper editors took special delight in castigating the Federalist president. *Richmond Enquirer* editor James T. Callender took the lead in attacking Adams. He called the president a "hideous hermaphroditical character, which has neither the force and firmness of a man, nor the gentleness and sensibility of a woman." Other slurs that he directed at Adams described him as "blind, bald, toothless, [and] querulous," labeled him "the blasted tyrant of America," and declared that Adams was "that scourge, that scorn, that outcast of America." These types of attacks were exactly what inspired the Federalists' passage of the Sedition Act of 1798.[27]

While not as personal, Federalists were just as vicious in their public attacks.

One Virginia Federalist wrote that Republicans were complicit in a failed slave rebellion just outside Richmond in August 1800. "This dreadful conspiracy originates with some vile French Jacobins, aided and abetted by some of our own profligate and abandoned democrats," he wrote condemningly. Republican pronouncements about "liberty and equality have brought the evil upon us," and he predicted that it would result in "either a general insurrection, or a general emancipation." The *Connecticut Courant* feared that a Jefferson victory would result in a civil war and accompanying atrocities: "Murder, robbery, rape, adultery, and incest will all be openly taught and practiced, the air will be rent with the cries of distress, the soil will be soaked with blood, and the nation black with crimes." The writer asked, "Where is the heart which can contemplate such a scene, without shivering with horror?" In recent presidential election cycles, only the 2016 campaign compares in the use of such inflammatory rhetoric.[28]

During the 1804 election, one newspaper episode foreshadowed the personal nature of presidential politics that would become commonplace in the Jacksonian era. In 1802, newspaper editor Callender, who had deserted the Republicans because he believed that Jefferson had mistreated him, wrote about the rumors of a sexual relationship between the president and one of his enslaved women at Monticello, Sally Hemings. The editor accused Jefferson of taking as "his concubine, one of his own slaves. Her name is Sally." Interestingly, while some northern Federalist newspapers printed the accusation, Callender's reputation as a drunk and a purveyor in half-truths kept them from launching a concerted media campaign based on his report. Republicans and southerners also gave the issue little attention. They may have decided that whatever Jefferson's personal peccadilloes, he had proved himself a firm supporter of their political principles by pursuing westward expansion and endorsing, through his own practices, the right to treat enslaved people as property, something in which many of them participated.[29]

Despite the lack of political furor over the Jefferson-Hemings relationship, the die had been cast. From this point forward, the most intimate parts of a president's or candidate's life were no longer off-limits if a party chose to attack them, and newspapers became the primary vehicle for launching these assaults.

VISUAL CULTURE

Like the printed word, visual illustrations also emerged as a significant source of political rhetoric. In a similar fashion to songs, political engravings and caricatures provided condensed representations of complex events and themes. Revolutionary-era prints were shockingly explicit, often depicting human excrement, sexuality, violence, and vomiting. For example, *The Able Doctor, or, America Swallowing the*

FIGURE 1. Americans during the revolutionary era understood the power of visual culture to influence politics. The sexualized imagery in *The Able Doctor, or, America Swallowing the Bitter Draught* (1774) reinforced the argument that British members of Parliament were attempting to wield rapacious power over the American colonies in the form of the Intolerable Acts. Prints and Photographs Division, Library of Congress, http://www.loc.gov/pictures/item/97514782/.

Bitter Draught (1774) presents British politicians violating a bare-breasted America, represented by a woman. While looking up her dress, they restrain her arms, forcing her to drink tea, which she regurgitates.[30]

Illustrations often accompanied poems and song lyrics in published material, but they were produced independently and in newspapers as well. By 1800, visual political culture had seeped into presidential campaigns. During that year's contest, "the one true election cartoon of this whole era" appeared, according to historian Jeffrey L. Pasley. Entitled *The Providential Detection*, it shows a fiery "Altar to Gallic Despotism," on which Jefferson is attempting to throw a document labeled "Constitution and Independence U.S.A." An American eagle, however, has saved the document. Satan watches over the altar from below, while the all-seeing eye of Providence observes from above. The insinuations about Jefferson's heretical political and religious views were clear.[31]

Even after becoming president, Jefferson came in for particular visual criticism. Federalist engraver James Akin encapsulated the accusation about the president's relationship with Sally Hemings in his political cartoon A *Philosophic Cock* (1804). He portrays Jefferson as the rooster and Hemings as the hen, with the caption "Tis not a set of features of complexion or tincture of a Skin that I admire." As historian David Dzurec noted, viewers would have understood "the multiple meanings of Jefferson as a 'cock'": the shortened version of "cockerel," a synonym for rooster; the vulgar euphemism for a male sexual organ; and the nickname for the French cockade, a symbol of that nation's recent revolutionary upheaval.[32]

WOMEN'S ACTIVITY

The "little female band" in Trenton, New Jersey, that sang to Washington in 1789 illuminates the political influence that women held in late eighteenth-century United States. Lacking suffrage (except for those few years in New Jersey), most women faced a circumscribed role in formal politics. Informally, however, they were very politically involved.[33]

During the Revolution, women boycotted British goods, supported the war by providing clothing and other supplies for soldiers, and assumed the responsibilities of men who left home to fight. Once the war was over, many took advantage of expanded access to formal education and increasing literacy. Some "female politicians" gave speeches and wrote for print publications. Mercy Otis Warren, for example, pseudonymously penned an anti-Constitution pamphlet in 1788 and criticized the administrations of Washington and his successor, John Adams, in a later three-volume history of the revolutionary and early republic years. Judith Sargent Murray used a pseudonym for her public writings as well, claiming that she "was ambitious of being considered *independent as a writer*," yet she did not want readers to attribute her writings to a man. In other instances, women attended political events, such as Fourth of July celebrations, where speakers frequently acknowledged their contributions to winning the Revolution and helping to perpetuate its ideals in the new nation.[34]

Many women also fulfilled their roles as "republican mothers," which entailed educating and raising their children as virtuous citizens beholden to the American republic, and "republican wives," which allowed them to exert virtuous influence over their husbands and, by proxy, over American politics. The irony, which persisted well beyond the Civil War, was that while women were charged with inculcating virtue within the household, they were not formally entrusted to bring that same virtue directly into the political sphere via the vote.[35]

While women possessed prescribed domestic roles and were restricted from participating in formal political activities such as voting, they influenced the public sphere in other ways. Margaret Bayard Smith provides a compelling example. The wife of Republican newspaper editor Samuel Harrison Smith, Margaret became a longtime fixture in Washington society as a writer and an observer of the capital city's political and social intrigues. In the summer of 1809, she and her husband visited both Jefferson and Madison at their respective homes. In correspondence written to her family during the trip, Margaret described the recently retired president as satisfied with being among his relatives at Monticello and out of the political limelight. This reassurance quieted questions about Jefferson's desire for power now that he was out of office.[36]

Margaret Bayard Smith's descriptions of her Montpelier visit focused most significantly not on James Madison but on his wife, Dolley. As historian Catherine Allgor noted, while Margaret wanted to evaluate James's reputation as "stiff and quiet in large companies," she also sought to ascertain the character of the new first lady, who would preside over official social functions. She came away satisfied that the new administration was in good hands, both politically and socially, and communicated that assessment to her social network in Washington. Margaret's approval was not the sole determinant of the Madisons' acceptance, of course, but as a leading lady in the nation's capital, she helped ease concerns about the new administration.[37]

The War of 1812 offered another opportunity for women to play a political role. Dolley Madison fulfilled Margaret Bayard Smith's expectations, particularly in rallying support for the war with Great Britain. She hosted parties that allowed congressional members to discuss and resolve their differences over whether to declare war. During the conflict, she personally met with war heroes such as General (and future president) William Henry Harrison to congratulate them on their victories, and she participated in celebrating American triumphs as well. "To the American audience, and especially to Washingtonians," Allgor observed, "Dolley was the public personification of the war effort." As in the Revolution, Republican women organized events to raise money and produced various types of clothing for American soldiers. They also encouraged their fathers, husbands, and sons to join the cause and take to the battlefield. Federalist women, on the other hand, refused to participate in supporting the war. As Harriet Livermore, daughter of Federalist congressman Edward St. Loe Livermore, later remarked, "As my political views were equally aristocratical with my religious, I abhorred the measures adopted by our rulers to secure sailors' rights, and avenge maritime affronts and injuries."[38]

The several forms of cultural politics were in various stages of maturation by the 1824 presidential election. Though all had been part of the early nation's political discourse, only some, such as political music and visual culture, had been used to any great extent in presidential campaigns. Over the next sixteen years, however, from the five-candidate campaign of 1824 to the Log Cabin and Hard Cider campaign of 1840, presidential elections would witness the flourishing of cultural politics and their integration into the formal political structure.

CHAPTER 3

A New Mode of Electioneering

Compared with previous administrations, which were wracked by vindictive partisanship and intense presidential contests, James Monroe's two terms as president (1817–25) were relatively sedate. But while his presidency lacked the fierce national partisanship of earlier administrations, it was hardly the "Era of Good Feelings" that Federalist editor Benjamin Russell called it in 1817. The nation experienced economic turmoil as a result of the Panic of 1819, and the Missouri Crisis of 1819–21 foreshadowed future northern-southern conflict over slavery's existence and the institution's expansion westward. The lack of true national party competition also led Republicans to begin splintering along factional lines as the 1824 election approached, setting the stage for the reenergized partisan activity and growing cultural politics that would mark the presidential contests leading up to 1840.[1]

Assuming that Monroe would follow Washington's lead and step aside after two terms as chief executive, candidates aspiring to succeed him quickly emerged. Three of them served in Monroe's cabinet. One was Secretary of State John Quincy Adams of Massachusetts. In his midfifties, the son of former Federalist president John Adams was an experienced diplomat who had helped negotiate the Treaty of Ghent, which ended the War of 1812. Secretary of War John C. Calhoun of South Carolina was another contender. He had entered Congress at the age of twenty-nine, becoming a member of the congressional War Hawks, who pushed for war with Britain in 1812. Now in his early forties, Calhoun represented the new Republican politicians who embraced the Federalist principle of a more active national government.[2]

Secretary of the Treasury William H. Crawford of Georgia epitomized the traditional Jeffersonian Republican ideology, with its focus on states' rights and a weak national government. The Georgian held a unique position during the 1824 campaign. The Republican caucus that met in February 1824 endorsed him as the party's official candidate. With the Federalists' irrelevancy as a national party, Crawford could have counted on the caucus nomination as the certain path to becoming president in any other election year, but not in 1824. Only 66 out of 240 congressional Republicans participated in the caucus, reflecting the intraparty dissension within their ranks. The fifty-one-year-old Georgian also suffered from a near-fatal illness and stroke in late 1823, which confined him to his home and made it difficult for his supporters to campaign effectively, even with the caucus endorsement.[3]

Two other candidates also joined the presidential race. Speaker of the US House Henry Clay of Kentucky had entered Congress at the same time as Calhoun and, like his South Carolina colleague, became a War Hawk in 1812. Clay was the main proponent of the American System, which called for the federal government to support a protective tariff, internal improvements, and a national bank to help strengthen the nation in the global economy. He also helped broker the compromise that ended the Missouri Crisis during Monroe's presidency. In his midforties during the 1824 campaign, Clay appeared poised to move into the presidential office.[4]

Lastly, retired general Andrew Jackson of Tennessee, who was the same age as Adams, was a proven military leader. Garnering from his troops the nickname Old Hickory for his toughness, Jackson and his men routed a numerically superior and better-trained British force at New Orleans on 8 January 1815. They also defeated Native American groups in the South both during and after the War of 1812, opening up native land for white settlement. During the 1824 election, Jackson faced an uphill battle in securing support for his campaign within the traditional political establishment. His appointment as one of Tennessee's two US senators in October 1823 did little to change his outsider status for the following year's election. Jackson's one advantage over all the other candidates was his spectacular military career. Americans celebrated his troops' victory over the British every January 8, with that date only less important than July 4 on the nation's patriotic calendar.[5]

Several issues drew the attention of candidates and voters in the 1824 election. The consequences of the Panic of 1819 continued to resonate across the nation, and the sectional wounds reopened by the Missouri Crisis remained fresh. While the implementation of the American System, with its platform of internal improvements, tariffs, and a national bank, produced a more well-connected economy, it also caused anxiety among Americans concerned about its harmful effects on the republican virtue of Jefferson's "yeoman republic." Still, the election's outcome "never became a simple referendum on future policy." In this election, more so than in any other since George Washington's two electoral landslides, personalities mattered.[6]

CULTURAL POLITICS IN THE 1824 ELECTION
Print Culture

Central to the 1824 campaign was the construction of candidates' public images, which became a prominent feature of Jacksonian-era politics. Supporters of three of the five candidates seized the opportunity to craft a palatable image of their candidates by using print culture. Calhoun's backers issued the first formal campaign biography in a series of newspaper articles in 1822. It depicted Calhoun as a statesman who put the nation above himself, his region, and his political preferences. While the South Carolinian adhered to the tradition of not campaigning publicly, he privately worked to build a national network of supporters who would promote his cause. Calhoun's expectation that voters would recognize his service to the nation turned out to be overly optimistic. By early 1824, when the key state of Pennsylvania failed to nominate him, it was clear that he would not become the next president. Instead, Calhoun positioned himself to win the vice presidency.[7]

Much like Calhoun, Adams expected voters to reward him for performing his duties. His extensive diplomatic résumé spoke for itself, but supporters dusted off an old biographical sketch to use in the campaign as well. Although not originally written as a campaign piece, its emphasis on his education, genteel background, and diplomatic experience served their purpose. Adams even provided written campaign material to newspapers. When Jonathan Russell, a member of the US delegation that had formulated the Treaty of Ghent, published a falsified document intended to embarrass Adams, the secretary of state seized the opportunity to publish newspaper essays defending himself. He also published a pamphlet of documents related to the Ghent mission. "In the collection of these papers," Adams claimed, "the defence and justification of myself and my colleagues of the majority, forms but a secondary purpose." Clearly, though, he was concerned not only about his diplomatic reputation but also about the effect of the Russell accusations on his election chances.[8]

Because of Jackson's military hero status, attention given to him exceeded that given to his opponents. Opposition to his candidacy centered on fears that he would become an American Napoleon. Jackson's supporters combated this apprehension by ensuring that printed campaign material emphasized his "warmth and affection" to offset fears about tyranny.[9]

Vital to this effort were Jackson's updated military biography and the pseudonymous "Wyoming" letters, both written by Jackson's biographer, unofficial campaign manager, and close Tennessee friend, Senator John H. Eaton. Eaton completed Jackson's military biography in the years immediately following the War of 1812, and the General probably vetted it prior to publication. For the 1824 election, however, Eaton revised the biography to minimize Jackson's negative traits, such as his temper and quarrels with his men, and inserted long soliloquys praising him. Yet even the original 1817 edition provided assessments of Jackson that proved useful in 1824. Eaton described the Hero of New Orleans as someone who in his political career in the 1790s had supported "the rights of man, espousing and advocating the principles of tolerance and free will." Though he admitted, "General Jackson possesses ambition," he also asserted that "it rests on virtue."[10]

The Wyoming letters also proved useful in acquainting voters with Jackson's strengths as a candidate. Originally published in a Philadelphia newspaper in 1823, they were republished as a campaign pamphlet in the heat of the election the following year. As historian Robert P. Hay observed, the Wyoming letters "suggest that early advocates of the General had their eyes set far more firmly upon the Revolutionary past than upon the democratic future." Eaton wrote, "The patriots of the Revolution, and with them those elevated sentiments of the rights of man which characterized that period, have nearly passed away, and intrigue is fast becoming the passport to office and preferment, which in former times was yielded to virtue and to faithful service." The letters posited that "the real menace to the republic was not Jackson but the civilian establishment." In particular, they criticized the "ministerial patronage" of Monroe's cabinet officers who were running to replace him.[11]

By comparison, Eaton argued, Jackson was a link to the virtue of the revolutionary generation. As a Washington outsider, he could drain the corrupt political swamp in the nation's capital. "He is the last of that high-minded and proud corps, who stood upon the tossed battlements of their country, and fearlessly rocked the cradle of the Revolution," Eaton proclaimed. "In the hour of trial," he continued, Jackson would "stand by her [the United States], 'to shield her, and serve her, or perish there too.'" The appeals made in the Wyoming letters and in other printed campaign material reveal that voters, not politicians, were the primary audience for Jackson's supporters. While still new in 1824, appealing directly to voters in this way became a hallmark of the era's presidential campaigns.[12]

Each of the five candidates also had access to a newspaper or, in some cases, several newspapers that supported his cause. Adams (*Daily National Journal*), Calhoun (*Washington Republican and Congressional Examiner*), and Crawford (*Washington Gazette*) all had Washington newspapers advocating for them. In return for trumpeting their nomination, the newspapers received government printing contracts, a form of patronage that became more prevalent and controversial over the next few years. Additionally, Adams and Crawford had a national network of papers. Adams's network included Baltimore's *Niles' Weekly Register*, while Crawford's included Thomas Ritchie's Virginia-based *Richmond Enquirer*.[13]

Clay and Jackson lacked Washington newspapers, so they looked elsewhere for media support. Unsurprisingly, Clay's strength was in Kentucky and in the neighboring state of Ohio. Amos Kendall's *Argus of Western America* in Frankfort, Kentucky, was a critical pro-Clay journal, as was Charles H. Hammond's *Liberty Hall and Cincinnati Gazette* in Ohio. Jackson relied on Stephen Simpson's *Columbian Observer* in Philadelphia and Elijah Hayward's *National Republican* in Cincinnati.[14]

None of the newspapers supporting the five candidates engaged at the time in the confrontational, partisan style indicative of the Jacksonian period. Instead, they served as mostly conservative mouthpieces for the various campaigns, outlining their candidates' strengths more than the opponents' weaknesses. In the next campaign, the story would be very different.[15]

Public Correspondence

Print culture was one of the main forms of campaigning in 1824, but other types of politicking took place as well. As an administration outsider, Clay was not considered a "natural heir-apparent" as some of Monroe's cabinet officers were, so during the campaign, he worked to remind voters of his support for the American System, specifically the protective tariff. Clay understood that his congressional speeches, which communicated his views publicly, were an advantage that Adams, Calhoun, and Crawford did not possess. He pinned his hopes on none of the candidates winning a majority of the electoral votes. This result would send the decision to the House of Representatives, which would select the new president from among the three with the most votes. With Crawford's failing health presumably eliminating him from serious contention, Clay expected that he would be one of the choices that representatives would be able to consider, and as Speaker, he believed that he possessed enough clout to make himself president.[16]

As a US senator, Jackson possessed the same advantage—congressional speech-making—as Clay, but he failed to use it. Instead, he introduced an innovation to presidential campaigning: responding publicly to a correspondent's direct query about a specific campaign issue. In April 1824, Littleton H. Coleman, a North Carolina physician who supported Jackson, sent him a letter asking for his opinion on a tariff bill pending before the US Senate. Jackson replied that he intended to support the bill. More importantly, however, he noted that since his "name has been brought before the nation for the first office in the gift of the people, it is incumbent on me, when asked, frankly to declare my opinion upon any political national question, pending before, and about which the country feels an interest." By doing so, Jackson became "the first presidential candidate to acknowledge that the people had a right to question him on his views, in effect to concede that there could be a dialogue between the electors and the candidate." Pointing out that he had responded to several similar inquiries with "the same answer" also placed pressure on other candidates to express their views. As one New York editor argued in lauding Jackson's letter to Coleman, "The people ought to know the opinion of the several candidates for the Presidency on all great national subjects, in order that they may act understandingly in the important election which is now close at hand." This call went unheeded.[17]

Auxiliary Organizations

Another major development in the use of cultural politics was the establishment of auxiliary organizations to support the candidates. The most prominent of these groups was the Hickory Club, which Jacksonians formed in cities such as Baltimore, New York City, and Philadelphia. According to one report, at a March 1824 meeting of Philadelphia's Hickory Club No. 1, celebrating Jackson's birthday, members gave toasts that "designate[d] as Radicals all who are opposed to the General as President . . . sneer[ed] at Mr. Calhoun . . . proclaim[ed] Gen. Jackson the next President . . . threaten[ed] his enemies with a 'hickory club,' and tender[ed] to his friends the laurelled shelter of a 'hickory tree.'" Following in the footsteps of the Patriots of the Revolutionary War, Jacksonians formed committees of correspondence as well. These committees drafted resolutions and circulated news reflecting positively on their candidate and denigrating the opposition. Helping them in this regard was the Nashville Junto, a group of Jackson's closest friends and advisers. These men, including Eaton and William B. Lewis, served as the Tennessean's unofficial campaign committee, coordinating his election strategy.[18]

Jacksonians also used existing organizations, such as militias, to rally voters to their side. Jackson's military background made militia musters obvious places to poll the white men who were likely to vote. In September 1824, the *Washington (DC) Daily National Journal* reported the results of three militia polls in North Carolina. Jackson won two of the three polls, and cumulatively, he outpolled Adams and Crawford 174 to 45 and 23, respectively. Jackson did not always come out the victor in these polls, however. Rhode Island's *Providence Gazette* reported the results of two Ohio militia muster polls that Clay won by wide margins. In Preble County, Clay outpolled Jackson 400 to 25, with Adams winning only 12 votes. In Miami County, Clay outpaced his Tennessee opponent 321 to 171, with Adams securing 98. The validity of these militia polls was dubious, though. North Carolinian Robert Williamson observed that the militia officers would get their men drunk "and then raise the war whoop for General Jackson. Then the poor, staggering, drunken, and deluded creatures would sally forth for the place pointed for them to vote." Afterward, some of the men told Williamson that "they did not intend to vote that way at the proper election, they voted so just to please their officers."[19]

Even with these questions about Jackson's political support among the various militias, supporters of the other candidates clearly were not as prepared as the Jacksonians when it came to auxiliary organizations. They held meetings, passed resolutions, and disseminated news about their respective candidate and his opponents, but these efforts often produced disappointing results. For example, some Adams committees of correspondence failed to identify Jackson as one of their candidate's main rivals, passing pro-Adams resolutions that often included an endorsement of the Tennessean as vice president based on his "distinguished military services" and his "acknowledged talents, integrity and republican principles." Some meetings were reportedly ill attended at times. One pro-Adams gathering in Rockingham County, Virginia, was "meagre in point of numbers," with no more than twenty-five in attendance, but Adams men accused their opponents of purposely underreporting attendance. Meetings of Clay's supporters sometimes turned out differently than they expected. One Cincinnati event that they organized resulted in only 127 of the 400 in attendance endorsing the Kentuckian's candidacy. A few Crawford events generated a similar lack of enthusiasm; one pro-Crawford Boston meeting was described as "at best but a *slim affair.*"[20]

Visual and Material Culture

Because political cartoons were expensive to produce at this time, they played only a small role in the campaign. Nonetheless, two examples captured popular depictions of the informal political dialogue taking place. One pro-Jackson car-

FIGURE 2. James Akin's *Caucus Curs in Full Yell, or a War Whoop, to Saddle on the People, a Pappoose President* (1824) was one of two political cartoons used during the 1824 campaign. It criticized two election elements: anti-Jackson newspapers and the congressional caucus. Prints and Photographs Division, Library of Congress, http://www.loc.gov/pictures/item/2002708979/.

toon, *Caucus Curs in Full Yell, or a War Whoop, to Saddle on the People, a Pappoose President* (1824), depicts the Tennessean in full military regalia being set upon by a pack of dogs, named for anti-Jackson newspapers. It characterizes Crawford as dispensing favors from the Treasury; a young African American boy also refers to him in dialect as a "ghose," a nod either to Crawford's poor health or to the erroneous reports of his death that periodically circulated. Another political cartoon, *A Foot-Race* (1824), shows Adams, Crawford, and Jackson racing toward the presidential chair at the finish line. Clay, having quit, stands on the sideline, as various observers offer their assessments of the candidates. Both cartoons appeared late in the election and likely reflected rather than influenced the course of the election in any meaningful way. Illustrations in the next few presidential campaigns, however, would be more numerous and prove more complex and vicious in their messages.[21]

Like visual culture, material culture made up only a minor part of the campaigning effort. One enterprising Philadelphia clothier created "a new pattern of black silk, intended for gentlemen's vests." It bore "the portrait and name of *Jackson* stamped upon it" and reportedly was "*all the go* among the members of the Hickory Clubs." A newspaper contributor sarcastically suggested that a more appropriate design would have been "a fashionable stock, to be drawn tight around the neck, and called the JACKSON NECKCLOTH. This would have been all the *swing* among the opponents of the gallant General," an obvious reference to Jackson's execution of British prisoners during his illegal invasion of Florida in 1818. Other objects, such as buttons, also appeared in 1824, but they may not have been intended explicitly for election purposes.[22]

Of all the forms of cultural politics in 1824, material culture was the least used. By 1840, however, one could argue that it had become the most important or, at least, the most recognizable form.

Women's Activity

Women's prescribed roles as republican wives and mothers limited their direct involvement in the 1824 campaign, but they were not absent from the political sphere. In Washington, elite women followed in their predecessors' footsteps by organizing social events that held political importance. For example, Louisa Catherine Adams, wife of John Quincy Adams, held a ball in Jackson's honor on 8 January 1824 that she and her husband hoped would help the secretary of state's image as Monroe's natural successor; instead, it boosted Old Hickory's reputation. In describing the relationships within her social network, Margaret Bayard Smith told one friend, "Some have been estranged by differing and conflicting politics. You have no idea, neither can I in a letter give you an idea of the embittered and violent spirit engendered by this Presidential question." The social events that women planned played no small part in those strained political feelings.[23]

When opportunities to express themselves appeared, women made their opinions known. As one North Carolina newspaper writer argued, the presidential election was "the all-absorbing topic of every circle," and everyone, including "the silver-headed matron, and the blooming maiden—the wrinkled beldame, and the ruddy Miss—all, all must have much to *say*, and much to do, in making a President." In some cases, women followed this advice by participating in informal polls. At a March 1824 gathering in Orange County, North Carolina, men and women discussed the upcoming election. Someone suggested that "an election be held exclusively for the Ladies." When the women cast their votes, Jackson defeated Adams 38 to 2. A Philadelphia newspaper noted that "whenever there have been assemblages of females, and their sense taken on the pretensions of the different candidates, Jackson has been their unanimous choice." Later that year, passengers on the boat *Erie*, consisting of "gentlemen and ladies" and representing five states, held a mock election. Adams won with 17 votes; Jackson garnered only 6, and Crawford, 2.[24]

Newspapers also noted women's influence in the electioneering process. Before Secretary of War Calhoun dropped out of the race, one newspaper accused Jackson of being "the very devil among the women; he has more ladies electioneering for him than the young Hercules of the War Department." Nevertheless, the paper's editor concluded, "We must have a President even if the ladies assist in making one." Another newspaper echoed this sentiment, attributing Jackson's late-summer lead in Maryland to "a new mode of electioneering, which is to enlist the *ladies*." The editor went on to observe that women were trying to elect a "*Presidentess*," with their preference being Louisa Adams over Rachel Jackson. "We are voting for a man, not a woman, as President," he concluded, "and as General Jackson is not under petticoat government, his chance in Maryland, is certainly better than Mr. Adams." A North Carolina newspaper contributor's account of a trip he had made encapsulated male voters' views of political women. When the writer stopped at inns to spend the night, he was careful to guard his thoughts on the election in case they "differ[ed] from that of the Lady of the House." He told readers, "A difference of opinion" with the woman in charge "might have led to a loss of my breakfast."[25]

Jackson men also used female virtue to bolster their candidate's cause. They reminded Americans that the Tennessee general had protected not only the city of New Orleans from British invasion in 1814–15 but also the women living there. Jackson had warned Crescent City's residents in December 1814 to look after "the chastity of your wives and daughters" as the British had stood poised to invade New Orleans. After the battle, reports spread that the British soldiers had used the call sign "Beauty and Booty," an indication of their alleged intent to rape the city's women and plunder its wealth. Nine years later, a Baltimore meeting of Jacksonians resolved to support the Hero of New Orleans, "who preserved a large section of our beloved country from the horrible reward offered to a ruthless soldiery, if they should succeed in taking New Orleans, of 'Beauty and Booty.'" A group of Georgians asked, "Who defended the sanctity of our homes, and the domestic quiet of our fire-sides? Who preserved our daughters from the licentious embraces of the British soldiery, whose watch-word was, 'Beauty and Booty,' and whose ever-lustful propensities were impatient for banqueting on the spoils of injured innocence and virtue?" The group's conclusion: "Gen. Andrew Jackson was the great instrument, in the hands of Heaven." While the situation was not as dire as during the War of 1812, Jacksonians in 1824 wanted voters to view their candidate as the defender of female virtue and, much as is expected of presidents today, the protector of family values.[26]

Political Music

Political music in the 1824 campaign built on the extensive examples of its use since the nation's founding. Newspapers published many poems about the election, with some specifically noting that they were songs. One song ridiculed Virginia's connection to the caucus process:

> This one talks, and that sits still —
> One shrinks, another swaggers;
> But all the Caucus' foes would kill
> With words — if not with daggers.
>
> OLD Virginia, never tire —
> Never tire of Caucus!
> Old Virginia, never tire
> Of forming plans to baulk us.[27]

Other songs focused on specific candidates. Even though Crawford's chances of winning the election were slim because of his serious health problems, critics still attacked how Martin Van Buren (Matty) orchestrated the Republican caucus's nomination of the Treasury secretary (Billy):

> Let us toast Billy Crawford each soul of us,
> Aye, on our souls — if we've *any at all!*
>
> Dear creature! we can't live without him!
> He is all that is sweet and seducing to man,
> Working, and twisting, and turning about him,
> He's found out our price and we'll *do all we can!*
>
> Here's to Matty — whose innocent bosom,
> Is always agog with some foreign desires:
> To day he's no longer in danger to lose 'em,
> Since we've cheated the people as Matty requires.

Another song, "most humbly dedicated to Lord John," took Adams to task for his alleged aristocratic background and political duplicity:

> Oh! Johnny Q—my Joe John,
> When your old Pa' began
> To rule this happy land, John,
> He took a woful plan:
> He sent you off to Courts, John,
> When you were young an' sma',
> That ye might learn o' Kings, John,
>
> Their customs and their law.
> Oh! Johnny Q—my Joe John,
> Your worth how can I paint,
> For once you were a Fed. John,
> An' thought yourself a saint;
> But now your coat is turn'd, John,
> A Democratic ye'd be.

Not every song criticized a candidate. Moses Eaton's "Gen. ANDREW JACKSON" lauded Old Hickory as the only logical choice:

> Come, FREEMEN; pause, before you say,
> Which *candidate* shall win the day,
> There's only *one* who can;
> If *worth* and *skill* have any claim,
> To dignify a mortal's name,
> Brave JACKSON is the *man!*[28]

A lengthy song reprinted in a Connecticut newspaper evaluated all the candidates. Adams was "cold and proud, And somewhat stiff and crusty." Clay was "so cute and funny," but the lyricist was "some afraid, he'll learn the trade, *Of Playing with* OUR *money.*" Calhoun was deemed "too young," and if Jackson became "chief, 'tis my belief, You'll have *tarnation* trouble." Crawford was the best choice, in this writer's mind:

> When friends retired, and rogues conspired,
> And dire disease assail'd him,
> His mighty soul, above control,
> Was firm, and never fail'd him.[29]

A CONTESTED RESULT

Clay's prediction that the election would be resolved in the House turned out to be correct. Jackson won the most electoral and popular votes and the highest number of regions and states, but he was not able to secure the necessary 131 electoral votes to become president. He won only 99 votes, with Adams placing second with 84. Crawford was next with 41, and Clay came in last with 37. Therefore, the three candidates who scored the most electoral votes—Jackson, Adams, and Crawford—had their names submitted to the House for its members to decide the election. With Crawford's health still in question, the contest came down to the only two viable remaining candidates: Adams and Jackson.[30]

Even though the general election results thwarted Clay's plan to use his influence as Speaker to win the election for himself, he still played a prominent role in settling the contest by working to ensure that Adams won the election. Rumors circulated that Adams and Clay met in person and struck an agreement: if Clay helped Adams defeat Jackson, then he would appoint the Kentuckian secretary of state. Adams helped his own cause, in the words of a recent biographer, as he "campaigned vigorously among the presidential electors, soothed ruffled feathers, made generous if ambiguous statements, and promised all things to all people."[31]

In early February, the House elected Adams, and a few days later, the president-elect named Clay to head the State Department. No smoking gun exists to prove an accusation of collusion, but Jacksonians certainly believed it happened. The fact that such an agreement broke no laws made little difference to them. The appearance of a "corrupt bargain" between Adams and Clay "confirm[ed] long-standing prejudices" about the corruptibility of elections, which was one of the Jacksonians' campaign themes. Indeed, the Wyoming letters "had all but predicted" it, making the "corrupt bargain" appear to be "the fulfilment of a prophesy [sic]."[32]

The 1824 election marked the beginning of a change in American presidential politics. Suffrage reform produced a larger electorate than in previous elections, resulting in 356,405 votes being cast. This number exceeded the previous highest election total, in 1812, by almost 90,000 votes and represented a 29 percent participation rate among eligible voters. Although the 1824 election inaugurated the rapid growth of the American voting population, suffrage reform was not the only factor in that increase. The nation's cultural politics, especially its focus on bridging the gap between candidates and voters, also played a role, one that would only grow in the coming years. The next campaign cycle, which witnessed Jackson seeking revenge against Adams and Clay, demonstrated even more dramatically the intersection between formal and cultural politics.[33]

CHAPTER 4

We Must Always Have Party Distinctions

The disputed election of 1824 was the death knell of the caucus nominating system. From this point forward, presidential candidates and voters interacted more directly. It was no coincidence that Jacksonians began adopting the label "Democrats" in reference to themselves; this rhetorical shift indicated their belief that they were beholden to, and represented, the people.[1]

At the same time, the "corrupt bargain" that Jacksonians alleged had stolen the election from their candidate produced a presidential campaign unlike any the American people had witnessed since 1800. In the 1828 campaign, partisan newspaper editors spilled enormous pools of ink berating the opposition, examining their sexual purity, and questioning their loyalty to the Union. Supporters also used cultural politics widely for the first time, in the form of broadsides, lithographs, and other campaign material. It was an ugly election that helped create the Democratic Party and planted the seeds for later campaign histrionics.

ORGANIZING THE JACKSONIAN OPPOSITION

Andrew Jackson did not immediately decide to run again in 1828. By the fall of 1825, however, he resolved that he needed to right the perceived wrong that had taken place in the House election. He resigned his Senate seat on October 12, and two days later, the Tennessee state legislature nominated him as a presidential candidate. He accepted the endorsement, and his supporters launched their campaign against John Quincy Adams and Henry Clay. Jackson intended to convince American voters that the two men had stolen the 1824 election not only from him but, more importantly, from the people.[2]

For the rest of 1825 and much of 1826, Jackson confined himself to corresponding with supporters and making appearances at Middle Tennessee events. Defeating Adams and Clay required more than just Jackson's stubborn determination, and criticizing the Adams administration from his writing desk at the Hermitage would not secure him victory. The General's supporters understood that just as he needed a coordinated strategy to defeat his military foes on the battlefield, political success required an aggressive plan of attack as well.[3]

Much of the vision for building the Jacksonian coalition came not from Jackson but from US senator Martin Van Buren. The New Yorker headed the Albany Regency, a New York political machine that provided many of the ideas for Jackson's 1828 campaign. Van Buren had supported Crawford in 1824, but the Georgian's illness and poor future political prospects left the New York senator looking for an alternative candidate to back. He questioned Jackson's fidelity to Jeffersonian principles, but the Tennessean's ability to attract voters convinced Van Buren, who often chose pragmatism over principle, to throw his support behind Old Hickory.[4]

Van Buren entered the Jackson camp in 1826 during the Senate's debate over the Panama Congress, a meeting of Latin American nations, convened by Gran Colombia president Simón Bolívar, that was to take place in the summer of 1826. Adams asked the US Senate to confirm US minister to Colombia Richard C. Anderson Jr. of Kentucky and former US representative John Sergeant of Pennsylvania as ministers plenipotentiary to the congress. Led by Van Buren, those opposed to the administration made several arguments. They contended that sending US representatives to Panama would entangle the nation in foreign alliances that would lead to war. They also observed that discussing slavery and the slave trade, a topic at the center of the Panama Congress, would exacerbate the sectional fissures left over from the Missouri Crisis of 1819–21. Instead of spreading American values to Latin America, as Adams argued, Van Buren and his allies predicted that the United States would find itself corrupted and destroyed if it allowed itself to be bound by the decisions made in Panama. Anti-administration forces were unable to defeat the ministers' nominations, but in the end, fate intervened on their behalf. Anderson died shortly after confirmation, and Sergeant arrived too late to participate in the congress. More than any other event, the Panama Congress debate produced "the inevitable coalition between the Calhoun, Jackson, and Crawford forces" that Adams had predicted in February 1825, even before the House elected him.[5]

During the summer of 1826, Van Buren met with various politicians at a Saratoga, New York, resort as he attempted to create a coalition to challenge Adams. The men who visited with Van Buren there represented several constituencies:

Levi Woodbury for the Concord Regency, an anti-Adams group located in New Hampshire's capital city; South Carolinian Robert Y. Hayne for the Calhounites; New York's Churchill C. Cambreleng and Delaware's Louis McLane for the Crawfordites; and New Yorker DeWitt Clinton for Jackson.[6]

Van Buren waited to make a final decision about his support for Jackson until he was assured of his own reelection to the US Senate in the fall. Over the 1826 Christmas holiday, Van Buren and Calhoun vacationed together in Virginia and reached an agreement to unite behind Jackson's candidacy. In a January 1827 letter to Thomas Ritchie, Van Buren outlined his desire to reinvigorate the partisan division of the republic's early years. Such a move would focus attention on political principles instead of personalities. "We must always have party distinctions," he suggested, "and the old ones are the best" on which to operate. He proceeded to argue that since partisanship was "unavoidable," the best solution for the Jacksonians was to form a national party uniting "the planters of the South and the plain Republicans of the north." Creating such a party would provide "a complete antidote for sectional prejudices" provoked by slavery. Instead of calling a congressional caucus to nominate Jackson, Van Buren envisioned a meeting of like-minded delegates in a national convention to endorse the Hero of New Orleans. While the idea of a national convention did not come to fruition in 1828, Van Buren's plan to unite Jacksonians, North and South, into the national party that would become the Democrats shaped the 1828 campaign.[7]

THE JACKSONIAN CAMPAIGN AGAINST ADAMS

The campaign against Adams began even before he took office in March 1825, with Jacksonians trumpeting the unfairness of the "corrupt bargain." Jackson, of course, took the lead in levying the charge in his private correspondence, focusing much of his ire on Clay, whom he viewed as a traitor for helping Adams in the 1825 House election. While still uncertain about challenging Adams's reelection at that point, Jackson understood the importance of exposing Clay's disingenuousness for political gain. His supporters agreed, hammering Adams and Clay at every turn.[8]

Jacksonians expressed concern not only about the "corrupt bargain" specifically but also about the general corruption of the Adams administration. Fellow Tennessean Hugh Lawson White told Jackson, "It is a fearful and unequal contest — *money office*, the hope of office and every thing which can be included under the term patronage on the one side, confronted by nothing but intelligence and virtue of the people on the other." One example of corruption that Jackson and his Tennessee supporters pointed out was the influence "that arch juggler, Henry

Clay" had in producing a change in the Nashville postmaster position. The sec-
retary of state, they claimed, swayed the replacement of Robert B. Curry with
John Patton Erwin. It was a blatant display of nepotism, in Jacksonians' minds, for
John Erwin's brother James had married Clay's daughter Anne.[9]

Adams also inflicted harm on himself in his first annual message, delivered to
Congress in December 1825. In it, he made a serious misstep when he suggested
that the United States might fall behind Europe in development if he and members of Congress allowed themselves to be "palsied by the will of our constitu-
ents." Jackson seized on the insinuation. He accused the president of elitism and
warned the American people that Adams was positioning himself to become a
despot. Along with the "corrupt bargain" and patronage charges, this theme of
Adams's elitism became a mainstay among Jacksonians. Jacksonian editor Duff
Green, for example, accused the president of learning his *admiration of monarchy and aristocracy*" and his "*contempt of republics and democracy*" from his formal education, his father, and his time in Europe as a diplomat. In this editor's
estimation, Adams was obviously a Federalist who cloaked himself in Jeffersonian
clothing.[10]

Adams's seemingly innocuous purchase of a billiards table gave political am-
munition to the Jacksonian editors as well. They labeled it a sign of "either his
taste for gentility, or for gambling" and reproached the president for purchasing
the table with money "taken from the pockets of the people," an erroneous assump-
tion. One editorial published late in the campaign summarized Adams's faults: he
was "devoid of sincerity, regardless of means by which his object may be obtained,
an aristocratic, and a moral traitor to his country." In other words, the president
was clearly out of touch with voters.[11]

BREAKING OLD HICKORY

In opposition, Adams and his supporters possessed plenty of material to use
against Jackson. One of the easiest avenues of condemnation was also one of the
Tennessean's campaign strengths: his military career. Much of Jackson's appeal
as a presidential candidate was his leadership in battle, particularly his victory at
New Orleans. During the 1824 election, supporters compared him to George
Washington, and they continued to emphasize this theme in the current campaign. Pro-administration forces, however, chose to focus on the negative aspects
of Jackson's military career. They pointed to his order to court-martial and execute six militiamen during the War of 1812, allegedly for minor offenses. Adams
men also recounted that on two occasions, the General had invaded Spanish
Florida without authorization. They further noted that during one of those inva-

sions, in 1818, Jackson had ordered the execution of two British nationalists, Robert Ambrister and Alexander Arbuthnot, for assisting the Seminole Indians, whom the US Army was fighting.[12]

The theme of Jackson's alleged propensity for military dictatorship served the administration well. Henry Clay highlighted the argument in a speech given in Baltimore in mid-May 1828. Noting that "liberty and the predominence of the military principles were utterly incompatible," the Kentuckian offered this entreaty for divine intervention: "If indeed, we have incurred the divine displeasure, and it be necessary to chastise this people with the rod of his vengeance, I would humbly prostrate myself before HIM, and implore his mercy, to visit our favored land with war, with pestilence, with famine, with any scourge other than military rule or a blind and heedless enthusiasm for mere military renown." Duff Green called Clay "deranged" for his speech. "If Gen. Jackson is elected President," he wrote, "he will be indebted to the votes of freemen, and not to an armed force." Green wrote in another periodical, "The objection to Gen. Jackson, is not that he is a 'Military Chieftain,' but that he is not a Military Chieftain on *their* side."[13]

Another incident that Adams supporters emphasized was Jackson's duel with Charles Dickinson in 1806. The affair of honor originated from an aborted horse race. Joseph Erwin owned a horse that was forced to withdraw from racing against Jackson's. Erwin paid the required forfeit money, but rumors circulated in Nashville that Jackson was dissatisfied with the method of payment. Jackson denied the gossip, but then Dickinson, Erwin's son-in-law, inserted himself into the dispute. The name calling went public, and the two men agreed to meet and duel in Kentucky on May 30. (The practice was illegal in Tennessee.) Jackson allowed Dickinson, an expert marksman, to fire first. Dickinson's bullet struck his opponent in the chest, but Jackson remained standing and fired his shot. His bullet entered Dickinson's stomach, causing him to bleed to death later that day.[14]

In the 1828 campaign, this duel became just one more example of Jackson's bloodthirsty, violent temper and dishonorable conduct. Pro-Adams newspapers accused the Tennessean of murdering Dickinson by contravening the rules of dueling. According to the *Richmond Whig*'s account, in the 1806 encounter, Dickinson fired into the air, but Jackson put his pistol to his opponent's head and "bid him make concessions, or die!" After Dickinson refused several times, Jackson "finally shot the man dead on the spot." The *Alexandria Gazette*, meanwhile, questioned Jackson's allegedly "extraordinary piety," which saw him "recock his pistol, wink at the seconds, . . . and deliberately shoot Dickinson after the latter had fired and stood unarmed."[15]

Other supporters emphasized Jackson's slave ownership as a reason to disqualify him as a presidential candidate. Two particular issues repeatedly appeared in anti-Jacksonian newspapers. The first allegation centered on Jackson's alleged slave trading. In 1810, he and two other men formed a business partnership that primarily focused on shipping cash crops from Nashville to New Orleans. The following year, one of the shipments was a coffle of enslaved people. When one of the partners abandoned this group in Natchez, Jackson made a trip there to try to sell them. When that failed, he brought them back to Nashville. In the course of the trip, he came into conflict with a federal Indian agent, Silas Dinsmoor, in present-day Mississippi. Jackson interpreted Dinsmoor's practice of demanding passports and proof of ownership of slave property as an overextension of federal power and complained to Tennessee governor Willie Blount. Those complaints eventually reached Congress, where they lay dormant until the 1828 campaign made them valuable political fodder. Adams supporter and Nashvillian Andrew Erwin used a pamphlet to accuse Jackson of "being guilty of the odious practice of '*negro trading*,' and '*trafficking in human flesh*.'" This sin, in their estimation, left him unfit for the presidency.[16]

The Adams press also proposed that the death of Gilbert, one of Jackson's enslaved men, in 1827 was the General's fault. Gilbert ran away in June 1827; when he was recaptured two months later, Jackson ordered his overseer to whip Gilbert as an example to the enslaved community on his Hermitage plantation. Gilbert fought with Jackson's overseer, dying in the struggle. According to the Adams campaign, Jackson ordered Gilbert to be whipped one thousand times, making the presidential candidate directly responsible for the man's death. The slave's murder left Jackson to "[wash] the blood of this human being from the escutcheons of the Hermitage," one pro-Adams Nashvillian wrote.[17]

One final charge levied against Jackson was that he was a disunionist. This indictment originated from Aaron Burr's conspiracy to separate part of the southwestern territory of the United States, including Tennessee and Louisiana, from the rest of the nation in 1805–6. He visited Jackson in 1805, warning him that Spain posed a serious threat to the United States. The next year, Burr asked him to help him repel the imminent Spanish threat. Jackson began organizing men and supplies, but his efforts were public knowledge, an indication that he was unaware of Burr's true intentions. He even wrote President Jefferson to report on his preparations. When news of Burr's plot and arrest for treason reached Jackson, he quickly distanced himself from the former vice president.[18]

Adams supporters revived the Burr conspiracy to undermine Jackson's patriotic image as the Hero of New Orleans. His involvement in Burr's intrigue, they argued, was an indication that Jackson's loyalty was not to the Union but to his section. This proof was all they needed to accuse Jackson of planning his own secessionist movement. "What better agent could be found to dissolve the Union," the *Washington (DC) Daily National Journal* asked, than the presidential candidate "disposed and accustomed to arbitrary rule?" Rumors spread that Jackson was going to lead a military coup, with fifty thousand bayonets "pointed at the bosoms of these sovereign people to force them to obey a President selected by a few ambitious, restless, covetous partisans." The Washington newspaper argued, "It is our duty to spread the alarm, . . . and put the people on their guard."[19]

Fueling the gossip was southern discontent with a new tariff bill, passed in May 1828. South Carolinians were especially vocal about their belief that the tariff unfairly targeted them. When James Hamilton Jr., one of the prime agitators, stated his public support of Jackson, "a Southern man, with Southern interests and Southern feelings," it appeared clear to Adams supporters that Jackson intended to unite with his home state in dismembering the Union. Charles H. Hammond accused northern Jacksonians of failing to comprehend that they were supporting a candidate "bound neck and heels to the slave interest of the union."[20]

The Coalition, as Jacksonians called the Adams-Clay combination, did not solely focus its criticism on Old Hickory. The *Washington (DC) Daily National Intelligencer* also recognized the role that Van Buren was playing in the opposition. According to the administration journal, he positioned himself as "the spokesman of the party of which we shall take the freedom to consider him the head and representative, if he be not both its parent and guardian." In an attempt to cause fissures within the Jacksonian ranks, the *Washington (DC) Daily National Journal* also leveled attacks against Duff Green and his friend Vice President John C. Calhoun. The *United States Telegraph* editor's "attachments exclusively centre in Mr. Calhoun," the editorial read. "He has no view, no feeling, no eye, nor heart, but for Mr. Calhoun's advancement. That portion of the Jackson party which embraces the friends of Mr. Crawford, really hate and despise both him and his patron."[21]

The animosity between Jackson and Clay over the "corrupt bargain" and the lies (and truths) spread about Old Hickory would have made the 1828 campaign a tense affair even without the increased use of cultural politics. The injection of a significant media presence, the precipitous growth of informal campaign organizations, and the increased role of women in the political discourse, however, turned the 1828 campaign into one of the nastiest in US presidential politics.

CHAPTER 5

Drums and Fifes and Hickory Clubs

Building on the precedents of the past few decades and energized by the animosity generated by the 1824 election, cultural politics began to emerge as an influential force in presidential politics during the 1828 campaign. Print culture was a particularly potent weapon used by both sides, and auxiliary organizations began to resemble the political parties that were emerging. Women's activity became an important part of the campaign dialogue as well, far more than in any previous presidential election, while political music continued to play a prominent role. The other forms of cultural politics appeared with lesser visibility but still served an important purpose.

PRINT CULTURE

One of the first steps that Jackson supporters took in organizing their opposition to President Adams was founding a newspaper in the nation's capital. Shortly after the 1825 House election, Jacksonians convinced the pro-Crawford *Washington Gazette* to support Jackson. In early 1826, the *Gazette*'s editor, Jonathan Elliot, sold the paper to a group of investors, including John Branch, John Eaton, James Hamilton Jr., Samuel D. Ingham, George Kremer, and James K. Polk. This group founded the *United States Telegraph*, edited for a brief period by John S. Meehan, who was quickly replaced by Missourian Duff Green.[1]

Green's appointment proved extremely important to Jackson's campaign. Operating under the motto "Power is Always Stealing From the Many to the Few," the former editor of the *St. Louis Enquirer* was relentless in assailing the Adams administration and defending Old Hickory. By 1828, he had twenty thousand subscribers and was printing double that number of copies, making it the largest circulating paper in the nation. He also published a *Telegraph Extra* for nineteen months in 1827 and 1828 that served as an unofficial "party handbook for the year." In 1831, satirical writer William J. Snelling paid Duff Green a backhanded compliment. The editor "had, in his capacity of editor of the Telegraph, furthered the election of president Jackson more than any other individual in the United States," Snelling wrote. "He was peculiarly fitted to do the dirty work of a party, and secure the votes of the rabble. To a considerable share of rough talent, he added great boldness, energy, perseverance, and utter recklessness of decency and morals."[2]

Increasing a newspaper's influence required a national media network. The Jacksonians relied on several loyal newspapers to do this: the *Albany Argus* in New York, edited by a group headed by Edwin Crosswell; the *Argus of Western America*, a Frankfort, Kentucky, organ edited by Amos Kendall; the *New-Hampshire Patriot*, edited by Isaac Hill; and the *Richmond Enquirer*, edited by former Crawford supporter Thomas Ritchie. The *Nashville Gazette*, edited by George Wilson, and the *Nashville Republican*, edited by Abram P. Maury, carried the Jackson standard in his home state. The editors of these papers exchanged articles and helped to create a coherent campaign narrative for Jackson.[3]

Many of Adams's supporters were not as reticent to engage in the new political landscape as he was. They had at their disposal two pro-administration papers in Washington: the *Daily National Intelligencer*, published by Joseph Gales Jr. and William W. Seaton, and the *Daily National Journal*, published by Peter Force. The *Daily National Journal* was more partisan than the *Daily National Intelligencer*, which depended on government printing contracts. A third Washington paper, *We the People*, was published in 1828; it focused primarily on mudslinging. For example, it called the *United States Telegraph* the "'Tell-lie-graph'" and accused Jackson of duplicity: "Joseph's coat was of a consistent complexion compared to the patchwork of his political robe." Adams supporters possessed other important pieces of a national press, specifically Virginia's *Richmond Whig*, edited by John H. Pleasants, and Philadelphia's *Democratic Press*, edited by John Binns.[4]

Green's *United States Telegraph* alleged that Adams was using patronage to influence the press. "The money of the people, by passing through the hands of the Executive, is made to operate as a bribe against liberty," the editor argued. "If liberty shall ever expire in our country, it will die of the poisonous draught of corrupt patronage." From his perspective, the administration newspapers were one more example of why a change was necessary.[5]

Prior to the widespread expansion of the American telegraph in the antebellum period, this national communication network of newspapers was the most effective way of spreading political news. In 1828, 859 newspapers covered the nation. Nearly 80 percent were located outside the southern states and territories, which suggests that the Adams campaign possessed a decisive media advantage. In terms of campaign-specific newspapers, more were actually pro-Jackson (11) than pro-Adams (10).[6]

The national government's support of the postal system expanded the geographic reach of newspapers. Between 1790 and 1820, the number of post offices increased from 75 to 4,500. This change created a national communications infrastructure of which newspaper editors and their partisan financiers took advantage. Not only was it cheaper to send a newspaper than a letter by mail (1¢–1.5¢ for newspapers compared with 6¢–25¢ for letters), editors could exchange one copy of their newspaper with other editors at no charge. In practical terms, this meant that one of the Washington newspapers could print an issue, send it without cost to sympathetic editors nationally, who then could choose to print the editorials or speeches most pertinent to the local political situation. In the same way, local editors could send news of national interest to the Washington papers for free. By December 1826, for example, the *United States Telegraph* exchanged material with more than 160 newspapers across the nation. Additionally, US congressional members possessed the "franking" privilege, which allowed them to distribute through the mail, free of charge, any material on which they signed their name. Congressmen (or their designees) franked all manner of printed material, including speeches, books, and, of course, newspapers.[7]

As one historian noted, "It is difficult to see in the 1828 election an obvious and direct relationship between the volume of the press on the one hand and popular political participation on the other." While the campaigns' newspaper coverage may not have been as important in turning out voters as contemporary observers thought, members of both campaigns believed that it was influential and acted on that impression, embracing the print medium as an effective way to rally their political supporters.[8]

AUXILIARY ORGANIZATIONS

Coordinating the information that went out in the national media was not solely the responsibility of newspaper editors. Political committees proved important as well. The primary Jackson committee was the Nashville Junto. This unofficial campaign committee increased its work from the 1824 campaign. John Eaton was the unofficial campaign manager, with William B. Lewis undertaking many tasks that needed to be completed in the background. The Junto helped determine Jackson's campaign strategy, with his longtime friend John Overton serving as a liaison to the Nashville Central Committee, a group of nineteen prominent Nashvillians.[9]

The two Nashville groups coordinated with the central Jacksonian committee in Washington, headed by banker John P. Van Ness; its twenty-four members included prominent local Jacksonians, as well as loyal congressmen such as Thomas Hart Benton, John Eaton, Sam Houston, and Martin Van Buren. The Washington committee orchestrated congressional opposition to President Adams's agenda, helped Duff Green communicate Jacksonian rhetoric to supportive newspapers, and corresponded with several statewide groups to ensure fidelity to Jackson's principles. The most prominent of these statewide political machines included the Albany Regency in New York; the Concord Regency in New Hampshire; and the Richmond Junto in Virginia.[10]

Jacksonian political organization on the local and county levels was crucial in transforming American political culture. Local Jackson committees (or Hickory Clubs) formed in electoral districts and organized the entertainment and social functions, such as barbecues, parades, and rallies, necessary to attract voters. They often coordinated these events with preplanned public gatherings, such as court days, militia musters, and holidays, to ensure an audience. For example, January 8 and July 4 celebrations offered an opportunity to highlight Jackson's military heroism and patriotic support of the Union.[11]

At the county level, committees supervised local organizations, issued public statements of support for Jackson, and nominated loyal candidates for state office. County committees also called for statewide conventions, which allowed delegates to meet and select a statewide central committee, to endorse Jackson and other preferred candidates for office, and to correspond with other states' central committees. Often, central committee members overlapped with the statewide political machines, the Nashville Junto and Nashville Central Committee being a good example. This nascent campaign organization provided the framework for the Democratic Party's organization.[12]

A visible candidate, comprehensive newspaper coverage, and extensive committee coordination were all important, but none of these elements would have been possible without money. Private individuals donated money, of course, but the pomp and circumstance of this election required more monetary investment. County committees often established fund-raising subcommittees to pay for printing and public events and even required fees of delegates. Public dinners, such as those commemorating the Battle of New Orleans, entailed individual payment, sometimes as much as five dollars per plate. Elected officials also shifted some costs to Congress and state legislatures. Franking and postal privileges for newspaper editors, for example, saved hundreds of thousands of dollars in printing and postal costs. When all else failed, party officials solicited sympathetic individuals for whatever contributions they could make. Historian Robert V. Remini estimated that electing Jackson in 1828 cost one million dollars, a paltry sum in today's billion-dollar elections, but a significant amount in the early nineteenth century.[13]

Pro-administration forces organized themselves more slowly than their opponents, and Adams was partly to blame. He refused to heed the advice of allies who encouraged him to replace Jacksonians who held appointive government positions and were actively opposing him. Adams declared that unless government appointees committed some illegal or immoral act, they would be retained in office. Despite the president's reluctance to act in a partisan manner, Adams men used mass meetings and committees of correspondence during the campaign. Some committees tried to gin up support for the president by emphasizing local circumstances. In Nansemond County, Virginia, for example, the county committee solicited local men's support of Adams, pointing out that Jackson was "one of the ignoble few who refused to give to the illustrious Washington a vote of thanks, acknowledging the wisdom and purity of his measures" as the first president. Attendees at many pro-Adams mass meetings passed resolutions. The sentiment of the ones at a Rahway, New Jersey, gathering were typical in their call for Adams's reelection because of their "full confidence in the wisdom, patriotism and integrity of the chief magistrate; that the course which has been pursued by him tended to the best interests of the U. States."[14]

Jacksonians accused Adams organizations of falsely inflating their candidate's support. One editor claimed that administration backers knowingly put prominent Jacksonians on their "list[s] of Adamsmen." In North Carolina, for example, one "General Hatch was, without his approbation, placed on the Adams Committee, at the late Administration meeting in this town." In another case, three Jackson men whom the president's supporters identified as part of an Adams committee publicly denied their membership and chastised their opponents for their embarrassing error: "Had we been previously consulted upon [the] subject, it would have prevented that reg[ret]." Green wrote, "The Adams party must be prodigiously strong where they cannot fill their spy lists and committees" without resorting to this tactic.[15]

The Adams campaign took pleasure in identifying its opponent's weaknesses as well. In 1828, a Maine newspaper pointed out that Jacksonians "make a prodigious bluster, and magnify their own numbers far beyond the reality . . . giv[ing] themselves very imposing names, such as 'genuine republicans' 'democratic republicans,' &c. and applying such terms as 'federalists, 'amalgamators,' and 'twaddlers,' to those who prefer to re-elect Mr. Adams." In analyzing a recent meeting of New Hampshire Jacksonians, however, an Adams editor found that thirty-three delegates were actually Federalists not long ago, with some holding offices in Federalist political organizations. Another seven "were engaged during the late war [of 1812] in *smuggling* and *concealing smuggled goods ! !* . . . And this is the party which is continually ranting and bawling against *federalism, amalgamation, twaddlers ! &c. &c.*" Indiana governor James B. Ray reportedly made a speech in which he accused a Jackson central committee located in his state of publishing some of his private correspondence without his permission. The committee was, in his estimation, "more damnable in their designs than the Spanish Inquisition."[16]

WOMEN'S ACTIVITY

In 1828, women played their most critical role yet in a presidential campaign, although primarily as weapons used by men, not as active political agents of their own. Most significantly, administration supporters showed little restraint in using women's private lives as part of their strategy to attack Jackson, which infuriated the Tennessean.

Jackson's critics made his marriage to his wife, Rachel, one of the most sordid lines of their political assault. Andrew had met Rachel when he had moved to Nashville in 1788 and rented a room from her mother, Rachel Stockley Donelson, widow of Nashville's cofounder John Donelson. At that time, Rachel was married to Lewis Robards. As Jackson and Rachel grew friendly, Lewis became jealous, eventually abandoning his wife. In 1790, Andrew and Rachel traveled together to Spanish Natchez (located in present-day Mississippi); when they came back, they claimed to be married. Robards, however, was not granted a divorce until 1793. (The state legislature had to grant the divorce, a detail that a lawyer such as Jackson should not have overlooked.) Andrew and Rachel married legally in January 1794. The origins of their marriage occasionally caused the Jacksons problems in Middle Tennessee society, but for the most part, they were able to ignore the situation.[17]

That all changed in 1826. Private rumblings about the Jackson marriage took place during the 1824 election, but in November 1826, they became public when Charles H. Hammond, the pro-administration editor of the *Liberty Hall and Cincinnati Gazette,* used his paper's columns to defend himself for soliciting information about the marriage. In March 1827, Hammond published documentary evidence suggesting that the Jacksons' version of their marriage was wrong. The Ohio editor accused Andrew of luring Rachel away from her husband to live in an illicit relationship.[18]

Andrew Jackson became incensed and instructed John Eaton to ask Clay if he was behind the investigation. The secretary of state denied the charge, but the Nashville Central Committee was already in damage control. Its members asked several prominent Tennessee women who had known Rachel when she was married to Robards to give depositions attesting to her good character. Elizabeth Craighead, wife of the deceased minister Thomas B. Craighead, swore in her deposition that "no lady ever conducted herself in a more becoming manner" than Rachel Jackson. Sally Smith, widow of former US senator Daniel Smith (and a Donelson relative), testified that she had "never been acquainted with a lady more exemplary in her deportment" than Rachel. Mary H. Bowen, mother of a former US representative, attested to Rachel's character as well, placing the full blame on Lewis Robards and his "weak and childish disposition." In all three cases, the women were connected to men who gave them social standing to defend the Jacksons, but the Nashville Central Committee placed their testimony at the center of the campaign, an example of the political power that women could exercise even without the vote.[19]

Hammond expanded his attacks on the Jackson marriage in a limited-run publication, *Truth's Advocate and Monthly Anti-Jackson Expositor*, in which he refuted in detail the Jacksons' defense that they were unaware that the Robards' marriage had not been dissolved. He proclaimed the argument absurd and suggested that if Jackson were "a true patriot, who esteemed the honor, the fame, and the interest of his country as deserving all consideration, he would feel that his matrimonial relation ought to exclude him from the office of President." Jackson fumed at "the base & cowardly" men who attacked his wife, but he heeded his advisers and kept publicly silent on the issue.[20]

Duff Green did not remain quiet, however. Calling Hammond a "scavenger of the filth," a "hired assassin," and a "poor reptile," he attacked the editor and his slanderous accusations. "From the fangs of such monsters we have done little else than to rescue Mrs. Jackson," Green wrote.

> Desperate, indeed, must be the fortunes of that faction, which, having exhausted every stratagem which cunning or malice could supply, against a Soldier of two wars and a cherished Patriot, defeated, convicted, and punished as it has been, now turns upon an inoffensive and unoffending woman, the partner of his bosom,

the venerable companion of his declining years—her whose influence is felt, in the circle where she lives, by the practice of every virtue which belongs to the tenderness, the dignity, the sensibility of her sex.[21]

Adams men also linked gender and race in ways unseen since 1804, when Thomas Jefferson's relationship with Sally Hemings, one of the women he had enslaved, became campaign fodder. Pro-Adams newspapers labeled Rachel Jackson a *"dirty, black wench!"* Hammond also privately circulated an affidavit that purportedly proved that Jackson's mother, Elizabeth, had been a prostitute—not just a prostitute, but one who "married a MULATTO MAN, with whom she had several children, of which number GENERAL JACKSON IS ONE! ! !" When Jackson learned what Hammond was doing, he understood the editor's true intention: to spread the gossip without risking the backlash that might come by publishing words from his own pen. In an attempt to turn the tables on the Adams campaign, Jacksonian newspapers published the affidavit as an example of the administration's willingness to vilify female character in order to win reelection. It was just one more piece of evidence to support the Jacksonian argument that Adams, Clay, and company were corrupt.[22]

PUBLIC EVENTS

The Adams campaign experienced mixed results with using public events to bolster the president. One the one hand, Adams supporters were able to utilize them to highlight their differences from the Jacksonians. At a Fourth of July event in Philadelphia, for example, Adams men made sure to offer toasts that "displayed the same sort of republican spirit, and Christian meekness," a contrast to the Jacksonian toasts that included "every species of opprobrium" levied at the Adams administration. On the other hand, participating in public events also proved detrimental to the president and those associated with his administration. One Cincinnati newspaper derided Clay for assuming "the garb of a sick man" to embark "on an electioneering peregrination." With the blessing of doctors, according to the editor, Clay had traveled across the country to "display at sundry barbecues, drop the tone of menace and violence which he used last year, invoke the compassion of the country for himself, adjure them to avoid Jacksonism as worse, than 'war, pestilence and famine, or any other scourge,' and conclude by appealing to the state of his health."[23]

Jacksonians took glee in pointing out how members of the Adams administration were abusing their offices in the service of the president's reelection bid. The president "has permitted, if not encouraged, his Secretaries to quit their official posts, and neglect the business of the nation," one New York editor wrote, "for the purpose of making electioneering journies, attending barbacues, and addressing inflammatory harangues to the people, with a view to the perpetuation of his power." Duff Green called Adams's advisers "the traveling cabinet." The president "has gone to set his own dear New England to right," he informed readers, while Secretary of War Peter B. Porter "is to go west on a wooing trip." Secretary of State Henry Clay, meanwhile, "is to have a barbecue in a few days, at Higbees, and a Ball at Nobles." Green smirked, "We will be much indebted to some one who will calculate, how much Uncle Sam will pay by the day, for *electioneering extraordinary*."[24]

President Adams himself expressed reluctance to participate in any public events that smacked of campaigning. "A stranger would think that the people of the United States have no other occupation than electioneering," he confided to his diary. When he did become involved, though, he found ways to convey his political beliefs. At a 4 July 1828 ceremony celebrating the building of the Chesapeake and Ohio Canal, for example, the president spoke at length about the historical and spiritual nature of the nation and its workers. Near the end of his speech, Adams invoked "the spirit of Internal Improvement" and expressed his hope that "its practical advantages will be extended to every individual in our Union." His speech was ponderous and dry, but Adams energized the crowd when he attempted turn over the ceremonial first spade of dirt for the canal. According to Adams's diary, when his shovel hit a root, "I threw off my coat, and, resuming the spade, raised a shovelful of the earth, at which a general shout burst forth from the surrounding multitude." This theatrical appeal to the crowd was the rare exception for Adams, however, not the rule.[25]

Instead, Adams tended to reinforce Jacksonians' arguments about his elitist attitude. A December 1827 event provided a clear example of this tendency. That month, Adams visited Baltimore to commemorate the American victory over the British invaders in 1814. At a celebratory meal that afternoon, attendees, including veterans of the city's defense, made a round of toasts. When it came time for Adams's contribution, he said, "*Ebony and Topaz*—Gen. Ross's Posthumous Coat of Arms, and the Republican militia-man who gave it." It was an obscure reference to one of the literary works of the European philosopher Voltaire that undoubtedly left listeners puzzled. What made the president's situation worse was that he immediately acknowledged that "the allusions upon which this sentiment is founded, may not be familiar to every one of you at this table; and that it will therefore need a short explanation," a lecture that he promptly delivered.[26]

For a man accused of aristocratic arrogance, this toast was ill advised, to say the least. Not only did it smack of elitism, but invoking the name of the British general who had invaded Baltimore appeared disrespectful. Jacksonians enjoyed ridiculing Adams for his tone-deaf speech. "If any one can wade through his rigmarole of an explanation, and make common sense of it, he will deserve to be placed high on the pension list," remarked a Boston newspaper. "The toast and the speech are so totally beyond our comprehension," one New Hampshire editor pronounced, "that we are waiting with anxious expectation, for some of our kind administration cousins to enlighten us upon the subject." A Lancaster, Pennsylvania, newspaper reported that the toast's reception was so bad, "one of the most intelligent of Mr. Adams' supporters in this city, had the candour to say, that he at first believed it to be a hoax or quiz of some of the Jackson editors."[27]

On the other hand, Jacksonians employed public events to great effect in the 1828 election, using them to reinforce their campaign themes. In 1826, a Pennsylvania meeting commemorating the American victory at New Orleans produced toasts that indicated voter discontent with the Adams administration and the alleged "corrupt bargain." One toast declared, "I feel sorry for all those real Americans who were so egregiously deceived by Congress, on the 9th of February 1825." A series of July Fourth toasts in Philadelphia, according to a pro-Adams newspaper, resulted in "the most fulsome and sickening adulation of General Jackson" and "the most viperish, and disgraceful calumnies against the Administration." Attendees of pro-Jackson meetings also used the events to defend their candidate. Residents of Troy, New York, crowded the courthouse "to meet and express their opinion on the baseness of the efforts" to attack Jackson "on the worn out subject of the six militiamen." One newspaper editorial observed, "One opinion prevails upon this subject . . . Public indignation is justly awakened and will not slumber until such infamous methods of electioneering are suspended."[28]

More so than their opponents, Jacksonians understood how entertainment could draw crowds of potential voters. A prime example was a "grand barbecue" scheduled to be held in Baltimore in September 1827. Minister John Robb informed Jackson that "three Bullocks are to be roasted, and each man is to wear a Hickory leaf in his hat by way of designation." According to another supporter, M. C. Jenkins, this "Jackson barbecue" would include "700 marshals on horseback" and "all the respectable portion of the resident Jacksonians," including former Revolutionary War veteran and US representative Alexander McKim and Maryland attorney general Roger B. Taney. The organizers planned to have the crowd give three cheers for Jackson and "quaff their bumpers to his health." This fusion of food, alcohol, material culture, and patriotism illustrated the future direction of presidential politics.[29]

PUBLIC CORRESPONDENCE

Writing directly to the public remained a new and little-used campaigning approach in 1828. One example appeared in February 1825, when Jackson, shortly before leaving Washington, wrote a highly critical letter about Clay to New Yorker Samuel Swartwout. In the letter, Jackson defended his public career against Clay's charge that he was "a 'Military chieftain'" who would destroy the Union. (In the weeks prior to the House election, this was one of the reasons that Clay gave for supporting Adams.) Without seeking Jackson's approval, Swartwout published his letter in one of his state's anti-Adams newspapers. The published letter gave Jackson the opportunity to attack Clay publicly without appearing to openly electioneer, which was still frowned on at this point.[30]

This strategy of using public correspondence as a political tool played an important role in shaping the Jackson campaign's narrative. In the spring of 1827, Virginian Carter Beverly wrote a letter describing a visit to Jackson at the Hermitage, during which the General told him that prior to the February 1825 House election, Clay's friends had promised they "would, in *one hour*, make *him* (Jackson) the President" if he pledged to exclude Adams from his cabinet. The letter, published in April, set off a public exchange of opinions about the alleged "corrupt bargain" between Adams and Clay. In a private interview published in a Philadelphia newspaper, Clay called the charge "*utterly* destitute of foundation" and questioned whether Jackson had actually made the accusation. Jackson answered the Kentuckian by writing Beverly, noting that he had spoken "freely & frankly" to him during his visit "without any calculation that they [i.e., his opinions] were to be thrown into the public journals." Upon learning of Jackson's confirmation of the exchange with Beverly, Clay declared his "intention to address a note to the public denying the charges and demanding the proof." This he did in late June, in an address "to the public" that issued "a direct, unqualified and indignant denial" of the "corrupt bargain" charge. These public engagements in the newspapers did not resolve the question of whether Adams and Clay had stolen the presidency from Jackson; however, they did demonstrate the growing usefulness of public correspondence in presidential campaigns.[31]

Jackson also dictated and wrote newspaper editorials as retorts to campaign attacks. In September 1827, a pseudonymous editorial appeared in the *Nashville Republican*. Written either by Jackson or at his direction, it defended his use of the "corrupt bargain" charge against the Adams administration. "No secret springs, nor 'midnight tapers,' nor closed doors, nor back stairs arrangements, are the movements at the hermitage," "A Republican" wrote. "Frankness and candor are the predominant features of republicanism; so it is with Andrew Jackson; he is a man who never conceals." A few months later, Jackson used the pseudonym "A Subscriber" to defend himself from the accusation that Thomas Jefferson opposed his presidential candidacy. When one of Jackson's former officers from the War of 1812, William Martin, denounced his wartime conduct in a national newspaper, Jackson wrote a newspaper editorial under the pseudonym "A Volunteer." "It may then be proper for me, to take a general view, of all the slanders that have been propagated against me," he argued to his friend William B. Lewis.[32]

Couching Jackson's idea as a plan under consideration by "some of Genl. Jacksons ablest and most efficient friends," Lewis asked several people, including Van Buren, about the advisability of this proposed scheme of public letter writing, which he thought was a bad idea. "They think a publication in his own name in refutation of those charges, judiciously drawn up and addressed to the good sense and feelings of the people, would have a most salutary and beneficial effect," Lewis wrote. "The project had been abandoned . . . as injudicious and hazardous," he later informed Van Buren, who had expressed his own doubts about the undertaking. Future candidates were not so cautious.[33]

POLITICAL MUSIC

In the 1828 campaign, Jacksonians went to great lengths to employ music in bolstering their cause. At a September 1827 celebration in Boston, for example, they enlisted "a stout, brazen-lunged Stentorian journeyman" to sing a song entitled "Hickory Wood." Other songs appeared in print. One such song, "Huzza! For General Jackson," encouraged Old Hickory's supporters to stand firm against the Adams campaign's attempts to dissuade their fidelity:

> Our opposition party say,
> If Jackson should but gain the day,
> There will be war without delay,
> And proselytes they gain this way,
> To build their fed'ral faction.
> But all who are for liberty,
> Their deepest plans can sometimes see,
> But always let our motto be,
> "We're determin'd to be free,"
> Huzza! for Gen'ral Jackson.

"The Hickory Tree" proclaimed "Old Hickory's the Hero for me," accentuating the differences in his background with that of Adams:

> While Jonny was gorging the fat of the land
> And bartering for Cod d'ye see—
> Brave Jackson was feeding his patriot band,
> On nuts of the Hickory Tree, . . .
>
> When Jonny had bought his commission of Clay,
> And mounted the throne dy'e see,
> Brave Jackson disgusted at rogues turn'd away
> And again sought his Hickory Tree.

Yet another song, "The Jackson Toast," promised success in 1828:

> Though Adams now misrules the land,
> And strives t' oppress the free
> He must soon yield his high command
> "Unto OLD HICKORY."[34]

The most popular pro-Jackson song to come out of the 1828 campaign was "The Hunters of Kentucky." In 1822, theatrical pioneer Noah M. Ludlow took Samuel Woodworth's poem and set it to music. The song was first used in a Kentucky gubernatorial race, but Jacksonians associated it with their candidate in 1828. The original version focused on the contributions of Kentuckians to the victory at New Orleans in 1815:

> I s'pose you've read it in the prints,
> How Packenham attempted
> To make old Hickory Jackson wince,
> But soon his scheme repeated;
> For we, with rifles ready cock'd,
> Thought such occasion lucky,
> And soon around the gen'ral flock'd
> The hunters of Kentucky.

Other versions gave a specific campaign context to the lyrics:

> I spose you've heard how Johnny Q
> And Harry were detected
> In the bargain, 'tween them two,
> Which Johnny Q elected;

Now Harry he has made his boast,
Should he again be lucky,
For four years more he'll keep his post,
And laugh at Old Kentucky!

O Kentucky! the Voters of Kentucky!
O Kentucky! the Voters of Kentucky![35]

Adams's supporters redeemed themselves a bit with their song "Little Know Ye Who's Comin'," which predicted, in words recalling Clay's recent speech about "war, pestilence, and famine," the dire consequences of a Jackson victory:

Little know ye who's comin'
If John Quincy not be comin'
Fire's comin', swords are comin'
Pistols, guns and knives are comin'
Famine's comin', famine's comin'
Slavery's coming, knavery's comin'
Fears are coming, tears are comin'
Plague and Pestilence's comin'
Satan's comin', Satan's comin'.

Another version, "Little Wat Ye Wha's A Comin'," compared Jackson to the Roman emperor Nero and direly predicted that after all the atrocities that it listed took place under Jackson, "Calhoun's a comin'." Not to be outdone, Jacksonians used the same song to lampoon Clay:

HENRY CLAY himself is coming,
He'll gloom, he'll glower, he'll look sae big,
He'll strut and snuff, and swear and swig,
He'll roar sublime for Johnny Q,
And curse Old Hickory black and blue—
And then another prayer is coming![36]

MATERIAL CULTURE

One new strategy that the Jackson camp employed in this campaign was the extensive use of material culture objects to identify political loyalty. In previous elections, very few objects, such as buttons, decorative plates and pitchers, medalets, and ribbons, existed to deliver intentional partisan campaign messages. All that changed in 1828.

Most of the 1828 campaign objects were pro-Jackson, with only a few produced by or for the Adams campaign. Of the pro-Jackson objects, many referenced his military background. For example, one type of chintz (a cotton fabric) depicted Jackson in the center, with "Magnanimous in Peace, Victorious in War" underneath his likeness. The previous six presidents surrounded the Jackson image. Other objects, such as flasks, medalets, and snuff boxes, made direct reference to the Battle of New Orleans. Still others, such as a tortoise-shell comb that presented Jackson in the center, with George Washington on his left and the Marquis de Lafayette on his right, linked the Tennessean to the nation's revolutionary roots. One anomalous object that directly referenced a campaign issue was a thread box with the inscription "Jackson and no Corruption."[37]

In addition to these manufactured objects, Jacksonians also expressed their support by wearing hickory sprigs, "plant[ing] hickory saplings, or rais[ing] hickory poles." As James Parton, Jackson's first posthumous biographer recounted, "In every village, as well as upon the corners of many city streets, was erected a Hickory Pole. Many of these poles were standing as late as 1845, rotten momentoes of the delirium of 1828." Pro-Adams newspapers roundly criticized the practice. "Planting hickory trees! odds nuts and drumsticks! what have hickory trees to do with republicanism and 'the great contest'?"[38]

Adams supporters found other reasons to criticize Jacksonian campaign objects. In Winchester, Tennessee, Jacksonian congressman Jacob C. Isacks reportedly "paraded a MOB" of two or three hundred men in front of the residence of Judge Williams on July 4. The mob was "armed with hickory clubs 'taunting him in the lowest style of opprobrium, vulgarity and blackguardism.'" One newspaper noted, "This infamous proceeding reminds one of the first dawnings of the French Revolution, . . . and should force conviction upon the minds of the sober and reflecting, that it would be a dangerous experiment to confer the first office in our country upon a headstrong, impetuous, and ignorant Military Chieftain, whose followers thus early manifest so savage and ferocious a disposition." A Pennsylvania newspaper humorously noted that in Jackson's dictionary, reasons to vote for him were defined as "Drums and fifes and hickory clubs."[39]

The Adams campaign lagged far behind the Jacksonians in its use of material culture; what little campaign paraphernalia the president's supporters created was uninspiring or undercut their candidate's message. Objects containing slogans such as "Victory for Adams" and "Be Firm for Adams" failed to match the eye-catching military allusions of the pro-Jackson material. Other slogans, such as "Adams Forever" and "His Excellency John Quincy Adams," only reinforced Jacksonians' accusations that the president possessed aristocratic tendencies that put him out of touch with the "common man" to whom Old Hickory was appealing. Not until 1840 would anti-Jacksonians (by that time called the Whigs) find objects that united their supporters as the hickory symbol unified the Jacksonians in 1828.[40]

VISUAL CULTURE

Since the conclusion of the 1824 election, lithography had grown in use with the establishment of firms that specialized in the process. Creating a lithograph required drawing an image on limestone using "grease-based crayons or inks applied by pen or brush." Lithographers then sealed the drawing and applied water to it to make it "even more receptive to the printing ink." When ink was applied to the stone, it stuck to the grease, allowing the drawing to be transferred to paper. More importantly, the limestone provided a permanent surface to use, allowing for multiple printings and making the images cheaper to produce than through etching or engraving.[41]

While lithography remained largely outside the 1828 campaign, one noted example hinted at its potential combustibility as a political medium. Russell Jarvis, whom Green brought in to assist with the *United States Telegraph*'s editorial duties, took offense at one lithograph, *The Crack'd Joke: A Late Student*, that depicted Green instructing Satan on lying, telling the devil, *"If I cannot teach you alone, I have lately engaged an assistant* [Jarvis], *and both of us will surely succeed."* Jarvis confronted the engraver, David Claypoole Johnston, and the lithographers, John and William Pendleton. When the Pendleton brothers printed the cartoon over his objection, Jarvis took to the *United States Telegraph*'s pages to condemn Daniel Webster, who had been asked to find an engraver for the controversial cartoon. Jarvis accused Webster of abetting "the publication of a base and scurrilous libel" and for associating himself "with the scum of Piccadilly, the refuse, the outcast from the vermin of Grub-street, to fabricate obscene and scurril jests upon a fellow citizen." Jarvis's episode and Green's assault of another critic led one Adams editor to conclude, "We expect soon to hear of the senators themselves dirking, biting and gouging each other."[42]

One of the most effective uses of visual culture was not a lithograph but Philadelphia editor John Binns's "coffin handbill." This broadside, so named for the coffins that lined the top, captured the Adams camp's accusations about Jackson's temper and violent confrontations. Binns published the original in his *Democratic Press* newspaper in January 1828, probably aware of previous uses of similar handbills that had lambasted British soldiers during the Revolution and Indian fighters in Louisiana immediately prior to the War of 1812. At least twenty-seven different versions of this broadside appeared in 1828, with the variations using

FIGURE 3. One of the main criticisms of Jackson during the 1828 campaign was his propensity for violence. *Monumental Inscriptions!* (1828) was the first of a series of "coffin handbills" that attacked the Tennessean for allowing the court-martial and execution of men serving under him during the War of 1812. Rare Books and Special Collections, Library of Congress, http://www.loc.gov/pictures/item/2007680069/.

Binns's handbill as a template. The execution of the six militiamen usually serves as the centerpiece, and most versions employ the coffin imagery. Many depict six coffins, but one printing uses 184 coffins, symbolically representing "Sir E. Pakenham and 2500 Officers and Soldiers of His Majesty the King of Britain, Who on the Eighth of January 1815, were condemned without even the benefit of a Drum Head Court Martial, and cruelly shot to death by Andrew Jackson, a Sanguinary Military Chieftan." Other variations illustrate or address Jackson's shortcomings: his 1813 fight with Jesse and Thomas Hart Benton over a perceived slight, his reputation as a slave trader, and a relatively obscure 1807 confrontation that he had with Samuel D. Jackson (no relation). Thousands of Binns's "coffin handbills" were produced and distributed during the campaign.[43]

Jackson supporters countered these attacks with their own creative works. They produced two text-only versions of their own handbill defending his decision to have the six militiamen court-martialed and executed. One pro-Jackson illustrator attempted to turn the tables on the Adams campaign by depicting Binns carrying a load of coffins, as well as Adams and Clay, on his back. Binns's alleged lust for patronage appears in the illustration in his claim that he "must have an extra dose of Treasury-pap, or down go the Coffins Harry, for I feel faint already." Adams's grip on the presidential chair reveals his true motive: "I'll hang on to the Chair Harry, in spite of Coffin hand-bills Harris's letter Panama mission or the wishes of the People." It is unclear whether this print, *The Pedlar and His Pack or the Desperate Effort, an Over Balance*, or the two pro-Jackson handbills diminished the effectiveness of Binns's coffin handbills.[44]

Two other prominent anti-Jackson caricatures also appeared during the campaign. One, *Symptoms of a Locked Jaw*, depicts Clay astride Jackson, sewing his mouth shut. According to historian John Sullivan, the image illustrated Clay's speech of 12 July 1827, in which he defended himself against the accusation of having committed "a political crime" by helping Adams win the 1824 election. Another illustration, David Claypoole Johnston's 1828 political caricature of Jackson as Richard III, references the General's violent past. Johnston portrays Jackson with "a face composed of the bodies of dead Indians, each strand of his hair . . . a sword." The six militia men that he ordered court-martialed and executed "comprised his right epaulet." In case observers missed the point of the illustration, Johnston includes a line from Shakespeare's *King Richard III* to make clear his intended message: "Methought the souls of all that I had murder'd came to my tent."[45]

As Sullivan noted in his analysis of Jacksonian-era caricatures, these types of illustrations were "a short circuit form of argument." They "cut through the complexities of issues and the evidence surrounding them; they are simplified, if distorted, versions of reality more effective in supporting opinion than in changing it." One need only think of the memes that populate today's social media to understand how Jacksonian-era caricatures potentially influenced voters.[46]

ELECTION RESULTS AND THE AFTERMATH

Early in the campaign, the *Washington (DC) Daily National Journal* brushed off the seriousness of the Jacksonian challenge to Adams's reelection bid: "From the

FIGURE 4. During the 1828 campaign, the antagonism between Jackson and Clay drew more attention than Jackson's rivalry with the incumbent president. David Claypoole Johnston's *Symptoms of a Locked Jaw* [1827] was probably intended to illustrate Clay's attempt to keep the Tennessean from talking about the alleged "corrupt bargain" that won John Quincy Adams the 1824 election. Prints and Photographs Division, Library of Congress, http://www.loc.gov/pictures/item /2008661773/.

ridiculous and extravagant conduct of the majority of its members, it has become rather a source of amusement, than of annoyance or apprehension." By 1828, Adams supporters no longer found the Jacksonians amusing. As the campaign wound down, the competing newspapers made their final pleas for their respective candidates. The *Daily National Journal* took the tack of comparing Adams's and Jackson's backgrounds and preparation for serving as chief executive: "Mr. Adams is a scholar. Is he to be superseded by a man of no education? Mr. Adams is a statesman. Is he to give way to a mere soldier? Mr. Adams has been bred in the Cabinet or in the school where national laws and interests are the objects of study. Is he to make room for a man bred in the camp, experienced only in civil broils, and who has resigned every civil appointment on account of his admitted incompetency to fill it?"[47]

Duff Green's *United States Telegraph* asked its readers to consider "whether this government shall be a Republic, or degenerate into a Monarchy . . . It therefore behooves all who love liberty and prefer a republican to a monarchical government, to rally to the polls and vote for the People's ticket—Andrew Jackson, and John C. Calhoun." The *Telegraph* compared the Adams-Jackson campaign to the presidential fights between John Adams and Thomas Jefferson. "The contest, then, is now as in 1798 [*sic*] and 1800, between the PEOPLE on one side and the power and patronage of Government on the other," Green argued. "The press is the fountain whence the people drink the living waters of political truth. The administration of the elder Adams attempted to dry up this fountain by *sedition laws*; that of the younger attempts to poison it by *bribery*. The reign of the one was *the reign of terror*; that of the other is *the reign of corruption*." Like Jefferson, the editor concluded, Andrew Jackson was "the Candidate of the People."[48]

The election results confirmed for Jacksonians their belief in the righteousness of their cause. Jackson defeated Adams 178–83 in the electoral vote. (In a move that seems improbable in today's political climate, Calhoun, who was serving as Adams's vice president, won election as Jackson's vice president.) The victorious Tennessean won over 55 percent of the popular vote and secured majorities in every region of the country except New England. Outside New England, Jackson won a majority of popular votes in every state except two: Maryland and New Jersey. The number of voters who went to the polls totaled more than 1.15 million, an increase of almost 750,000 votes from the previous election. The voter participation rate nearly doubled from 1824, reaching 58 percent.[49]

In the absence of opinion polls, it is difficult to say with certainty exactly what role cultural politics played in increasing voter participation in the 1828 election. Suffrage reform expanded the potential voting pool, but those changes did not necessarily guarantee a substantial increase in voters in 1828. It certainly seems plausible, if not likely, that just as voters today have become enamored of modern manifestations of cultural politics, voters then were energized by the connections both campaigns made between issues of concern and cultural politics. Whatever the case, a new era in presidential politics had clearly arrived.

CHAPTER 6

A Disastrous, Perhaps a Fatal Revolution

Shortly after Jackson took office in March 1829, the Adams-Clay faction in Massachusetts and Kentucky organized its members under the National Republican label, which had been used sporadically by both sides during the recent campaign. One sympathetic newspaper embraced the term, calling it "an excellent designation for a national party in our republican Union." The name represented, to this newspaper at least, those "who would uphold the Federal Constitution; secure the independence and continuance of the Supreme Court; preserve a sound currency; possess a substantive and enlightened President of the United States; prevent offices from becoming the booty of mere partisans and parasites; and obtain a truly responsible and visible government." Predictably, Duff Green called the National Republicans "an unholy coalition," comparing them to the Federalists. "The opposition party is the *old* federal party, maintaining, in the spirit of the Hartford Convention, the principles of the reign of terror," he wrote in the *United States Telegraph*. "It consists of ultra federalists, *amalgamated* with recreant republicans, who have renounced the Republican [i.e., Democratic] party, and whom that party have in turn renounced."[1]

The disagreement over the National Republican name indicated the struggle at the heart of Jackson's presidency. On the one side, Adams and Clay supporters criticized the president's agenda for hewing too closely to his Jeffersonian beliefs, but they stumbled in identifying what gave them cohesiveness other than their hatred of Jackson. On the other side, Democrats believed that they knew who the president's opponents truly were: they were Federalists in disguise, intent on expanding the government's power beyond its constitutional authority. In many ways, their arguments resemble modern-day political rhetoric, which uses presidents to encapsulate all the ills of a party and demonizes all politicians as duplicitous agents of evil.

During Jackson's time as chief executive, and particularly during the 1832 presidential campaign, Democrats and their opponents both used cultural politics to influence the formal political structure. The 1832 election also gave cultural politics a more prominent place on the political landscape.

THE FORMAL POLITICS OF JACKSON'S FIRST TERM
Political Patronage

Contrary to the observations of some Washingtonians, many of the people who came to the nation's capital in 1829 to attend Jackson's inauguration were not "rabble" looking to witness one of their own ascend to the presidency. Rather, they were job seekers who came hoping, sometimes expecting, that Jackson would find a place for them in his government. Most were disappointed, of course. The new president took office determined to appoint honest, competent men who were loyal supporters. He made substantive changes, particularly in the Treasury Department, the Post Office, and the General Land Office, but they were not as widespread as many expected.[2]

Historians generally agree that the percentage of Jackson's patronage replacements was comparable to that of his predecessors, but the National Republicans were not so generous in their assessment. Jackson's opponents criticized his patronage policy as an attempt to install himself as a monarch. They especially hated the government appointments of newspaper editors such as Isaac Hill and Amos Kendall, whom they believed were opportunistic men seeking to make money at the people's expense. Jackson's contention that he acted out of principle and the desire for reform fell on deaf ears.[3]

The Eaton Affair

Even before he took office, Jackson's political opponents found another means to discredit him. In early 1829, as Jackson was preparing to move to Washington, John H. Eaton, the president's close friend and secretary of war, married a notorious Washington widow, Margaret O'Neale Timberlake. Washington socialites had long gossiped about Margaret, first for being a flirt prior to marrying navy purser John Timberlake, then for allegedly having an affair with Eaton, one of her husband's best friends. When her husband committed suicide while away at sea, rumors spread that the alleged affair prompted his fateful decision. The Eaton wedding took place less than nine months after Timberlake's death, which only confirmed the suspicions of some of Washington's most prominent women: the new Mrs. Eaton really was a whore.[4]

This scandal might have dissipated had Jackson not appointed John Eaton as his secretary of war. It also might have faded away if the president had not insisted that his official and unofficial advisers socialize with the newly married couple. But he did, and what resulted was more than two years of political animosity and personal venom that threatened to destroy both Jackson's presidency and the Democratic Party.[5]

Jackson, who was still grieving the death of his wife, Rachel, in December 1828, appeared to see parallels between the controversy over his own marriage and that of the Eatons. He spent a considerable amount of time trying to identify the culprit behind his friends' troubles. Jackson's intransigence on the Eaton marriage eventually alienated every member of his cabinet except two: Secretary of State Martin Van Buren and Postmaster General William T. Barry.[6]

Throughout 1830 and into 1831, Jackson's advisers divided over whether they accepted the Eatons as part of their social circle. On one side were Jackson, Eaton, and Van Buren; on the other were Vice President John C. Calhoun and the rest of the cabinet secretaries except for Barry, who stayed above the fray. In April 1831, Van Buren proposed a way out of the imbroglio: he and Eaton would resign their cabinet positions, thus allowing the president to request the other officers' resignations as well, providing him with the opportunity to reformulate his cabinet. Jackson reluctantly agreed to the proposal. The other cabinet officers initially balked at the request but eventually agreed to comply. (Barry, who remained a dispassionate observer of the entire "Petticoat War," as it became known, was the only cabinet member to survive with his job.)[7]

While female society drove the treatment of the Eatons, the contretemps held great importance for political party development. Jackson decided to reward Van Buren's loyalty by endorsing him as his successor. This choice exacerbated the friction between the president and Calhoun, leading to a permanent break between the two Democratic leaders. The Eaton affair also left many Democrats close to Jackson dissatisfied. Hugh Lawson White, for example, refused to replace John Eaton in the War Department because he had felt slighted during Jackson's original cabinet appointments. Eaton himself became disgruntled with the president's reluctance to support him openly for a US Senate seat. Both men eventually broke with the president and joined the opposition. All these political consequences reinforce the sly double entendre made by nineteenth-century historian James Parton: "The political history of the United states, for the last thirty years, dates from the moment when the soft hand of Mr. Van Buren touched Mrs. Eaton's knocker."[8]

The Nullification Crisis

The Eaton affair also marked the beginning of the end for Vice President Calhoun's role in the Jackson administration. The seed of Calhoun's rift with the president had been planted years earlier. In 1818, Jackson had invaded Spanish Florida to quell incursions made by the Seminole and their free black allies against white Americans. The invasion, as well as the execution of Ambrister and Arbuthnot, brought condemnation from congressional members, especially House Speaker Henry Clay, and prompted discussion among President James Monroe's cabinet members of disciplining Jackson. Ironically, only John Quincy Adams defended the General; the others, including Secretary of War Calhoun, criticized him. Hints of Calhoun's duplicity reached Jackson during the 1828 campaign, but he and members of the Nashville Junto chose to disregard them for the sake of the election. Adding to Jackson's displeasure was the knowledge that, in response to the passage of the 1828 tariff, the South Carolinian had penned an anonymous essay advocating a state's right to nullify unconstitutional federal laws.[9]

All three issues—the Eaton affair, the Seminole controversy, and nullification—finally drove a wedge between Jackson and Calhoun in 1830. At the April 13 Jefferson Day dinner, several southern politicians made pro-nullification toasts. Jackson responded with his own toast, "Our Union—*It must be preserved.*" The following month, Jackson asked his vice president to explain his lack of support during the Seminole affair. Calhoun responded with a defensive letter. Then, inexplicably, he brought their dispute into the public eye by publishing his private correspondence with the president in February 1831. Later that year, Calhoun also publicly admitted his support of nullification, marking a final, permanent break with Jackson.[10]

The interpersonal conflict between Jackson and Calhoun took on greater significance when Congress passed a new tariff bill in 1832. South Carolina nullifiers met in November and passed an ordinance nullifying both the 1828 and 1832 tariffs. They also began planning to defend the port city of Charleston in case the federal government attempted to collect the import tax. Jackson responded in early December with his Nullification Proclamation, which pronounced the nullifiers traitors. He also began to make his own military preparations. If needed, Tennessean James W. Wyly confidently predicted, "the old chief could rally force enough to Stand on the Saluda Mountain [in northwest South Carolina] and piss enough . . . to float the whole nullifying crew of South Carolina into the Atlantic Ocean."[11]

Jackson did not operate independently, however. He asked Congress for autho-rization to use force against South Carolina if necessary. Congressional members considered Jackson's request, but some of its leaders also began looking for ways to produce a compromise that would avoid civil war. The two men most respon-sible for working out a compromise were, surprisingly, Calhoun and Clay. Cal-houn resigned the vice presidency in December 1832 and was immediately ap-pointed to the Senate. While he supported nullification, he was more moderate than many of the radicals pushing secession in his home state. Both he and Clay likely saw an opportunity to undermine Jackson's stature among the American people by claiming that they, not the president, provided a solution that kept the nation from falling apart. The two senators helped forge a compromise tariff that slowly lowered rates over the next decade, and the legislation sated many nullifi-ers. Congress's simultaneous passage of the so-called Force Bill, authorizing Jack-son to use the military to collect tariff revenue, proved inconsequential.[12]

Much like the Eaton affair, the Nullification Crisis influenced American pol-itics beyond Jackson's presidency. Nullification sympathizers in South Carolina and other southern states believed that Jackson was a traitor to his region, and their unsubstantiated suspicions about Van Buren's role in opposing the nullifiers caused future problems for the Democrats. But to many Americans, Old Hickory had once again saved the Union. Calhoun, meanwhile, was able to claim credit for both supporting his principles and producing a resolution to the crisis. Finally, the compromise solidified Clay's reputation as a statesman and seemed to position him favorably for a future run at the presidency.

Indian Removal

In addition to the Eaton affair, another issue that prompted discussion about the intersection of morality and politics was Indian removal. As a military leader during and after the War of 1812, Jackson followed a policy of removing Indian tribes—by force, treaty, or a combination of the two—for several reasons, in-cluding racism, personal aggrandizement, and national security. As president, he continued to pursue this strategy, also adopting his predecessors' argument that Native Americans needed to be civilized, just as long as it happened west of the Mississippi River.[13]

Implementation of Indian removal under Jackson's watch came in the form of the Indian Removal Act of 1830. This legislation authorized funding to remove Native Americans from the East to land in the West, which would be given to the tribes permanently. Individual Indians who chose to remain behind were allo-cated a small parcel of land on which to live; they also had to agree to conform to the laws of the state in which they resided. The vote on the Indian Removal Act indicated how divisive the issue was, with Democrats and southerners generally favoring the legislation, and National Republicans and northerners usually opposing it. The Senate passed the bill first in April, but the 28 to 19 vote in favor was along purely partisan lines. The House proceeded to vote in late May, and the bill barely passed, 102 to 97. The debate in both chambers was emotionally charged. Senator Theodore Frelinghuysen of New Jersey denounced the bill as racist, while Georgia representative Wilson Lumpkin called his opponents "canting fanatics."[14]

Attempts by politicians, religious groups, and female societies to stop removal ultimately failed. Jackson's policy, supported by congressional Democrats, led to the displacement of tens of thousands of Native Americans. Most prominent among the Indians removed were five tribes in the Southeast: the Cherokee, Chickasaw, Choctaw, Creek, and Seminole. Often referred to as "civilized" because of their acceptance of predominant white culture, such as Christianity and slavery, these tribes were nevertheless required to give up their land. For many Americans then and now, the most prominent example of removal became the Trail of Tears, the relocation of the Cherokees that led to the death of approximately 25 percent of those moved from Georgia, North Carolina, and Tennessee to present-day Oklahoma. (Although Cherokee removal began under Jackson, the Trail of Tears actually took place after he left office.) While the Cherokees' plight drew a lot of attention, the Seminoles in Florida were the only one of the five tribes to fight removal with sustained violence, resulting in the Second Seminole War (1835–42).[15]

Internal Improvements

The question of internal improvements was closely tied to both Indian removal and the nullification controversy. Jackson's inconsistent approach to federal funding of projects understandably confused some of his allies and, along with his support of states' rights regarding Native Americans, may have contributed to the belief that he sided with southerners who wanted a more limited central government.

During the winter 1829–30 session of the Twenty-First Congress, debate over the sale of public lands in the West intersected with a number of other issues related to internal improvements. Westerners accused eastern politicians of wanting to stop the sale of new public lands to keep industrial workers from migrating west; southerners used the opportunity to emphasize how the 1828 "Tariff of Abominations" unfairly penalized the South. In a Senate debate with Daniel Webster over the land issue, South Carolina's Robert Y. Hayne argued that revenue from land sales and tariffs gave the national government too much power. The Massachusetts senator responded by proclaiming the sanctity of the Union, "Liberty and Union, now and forever, one and inseparable!" Several months later, this debate over which political theory should prevail—states' rights or nationalism—provided the context for the April 1830 Jefferson Day confrontation between Jackson and Calhoun.[16]

The great test of Jackson's approach to internal improvements came just over a month later. Congress passed a bill that provided funding for the Maysville Road, which would connect Maysville, Kentucky, to nearby Lexington. Many Democrats supported the bill, but their backing proved ineffective in convincing Jackson. After consulting with Van Buren, an opponent of federally funded internal improvements, the president decided to veto the bill. Jackson waited until Congress passed the Indian Removal Act on May 26 before presenting his Maysville Road veto the next day. The message accompanying the veto reiterated the president's suggestion that states should fund internal improvements by using the surplus revenue produced by the national debt's extinguishment. An attempt to override Jackson's veto failed, with anti-administration forces able to muster only a majority vote of 96 to 90 against the veto, not the two-thirds needed to overturn his decision.[17]

Over the rest of his presidency, Jackson continued to display inconsistency when it came to internal improvements. By the time he left office, federal expenditures for internal improvements totaled over 16 million dollars, surpassing the expenses of the John Quincy Adams administration by nearly 10 million dollars. Expenditures during the last two years of Jackson's presidency, in fact, nearly totaled that of Adams's four years.[18]

The Bank Veto

The issue that framed much of the election-year debate was Jackson's refusal to extend the charter of the Second Bank of the United States (BUS). His decision to attack the BUS stemmed from several sources. Early in his adult life, he had almost suffered financial ruin because of a debt, and he, like many other southerners, had experienced hard economic times because of the Panic of 1819. He thus developed a distrust of banks. What galvanized Jackson's thinking regarding the BUS, however, was his belief that it had used its funds, which were a mixture of private and government deposits, against him during the 1828 election. BUS president Nicholas Biddle's personal investigation into some of the accusations produced no evidence of wrongdoing, but Jackson remained suspicious of the financial institution and expressed his distrust of the BUS in his first three annual messages.[19]

Biddle and BUS supporters in Congress failed to heed the president's warnings. In early 1832, they decided to push for a new charter, four years prior to the current charter's expiration. If Jackson "means to wage war upon the Bank," Biddle said, "he may perhaps awaken a spirit which has hitherto been checked & reined in." The president saw the recharter effort as an attempt by "The Coalition" to make the BUS an election-year issue. After both congressional chambers passed the recharter bill in early July 1832, Jackson vetoed it. In his message explaining the veto to Congress, he accused "rich men" of "attempting to gratify their desires" by passing legislation pitting "section against section, interest against interest, and man against man, in a fearful commotion which threatens to shake the foundations of our Union." Jackson called on Americans to oppose "any prostitution of our Government to the advancement of the few at the expense of the many." This recharter battle set the tone for the 1832 presidential election, and its consequences reverberated throughout the politics of the rest of the decade.[20]

THE 1832 ELECTION

The many issues that caused Jackson problems during his first term presented his opponents with the opportunity to unseat him in 1832. Often overlooked because of the attention paid to the 1828 and 1840 campaigns, the 1832 contest furthered the use of cultural politics and reshaped presidential politics in significant ways.

The formal presidential campaign proceeded from the introduction of the national nominating convention in 1831. While common at the state level, nominating conventions had never before been used in a presidential contest. The first national nominating convention actually originated with a third party, the Anti-Masons. Recalling the debates about Freemasonry that had taken place during the partisan fervor of the 1790s, this party denounced the Masonic influence of men such as Jackson on US politics. Delegates representing twelve states met in Philadelphia on 26 September 1831 to select Anti-Masonic presidential and vice-presidential candidates. After considering six possible candidates, including Adams, Calhoun, Clay, Webster, former secretary of the Treasury Richard Rush, and Supreme Court justice John McLean, the delegates selected former US attorney general William Wirt as their nominee, an ironic choice given his Masonic ties. The fifty-eight-year-old Wirt reluctantly accepted. The Anti-Masons then chose forty-four-year-old Amos Ellmaker, from the swing state of Pennsylvania, as their vice-presidential candidate. The convention's address emphasized "the evils of freemasonry" and argued that "the application of the right of suffrage against it is just, peaceable, effective, and may be as comprehensive as the evils which alarm us."[21]

Three months later, 155 National Republican delegates from seventeen states convened in Baltimore. Now fifty-four years old, Henry Clay was the convention's presumptive candidate. In mid-June 1830, a Fayette County, Kentucky, meeting had endorsed him for the presidency. Just over two months later, a statewide meeting of Delaware National Republicans had nominated him as well. Now, in December 1831, the national convention officially formalized Clay's selection as the nominee. Mimicking the Anti-Masons' recognition of the Keystone State's importance, National Republicans chose fifty-two-year-old John Sergeant of Pennsylvania for the vice-presidential slot. The convention address lamented the nation's present course under a president so opposite from the character of George Washington. To continue along this path, it warned, would lead to "a disastrous, perhaps a fatal revolution." The address criticized the Democratic press's use of "reckless and persevering calumny" against "the best and purest men in the nation" and listed Jackson's many failures, emphasizing his dissolved cabinet, his patronage appointments, and his opposition to the BUS. By contrast, Clay was "an ardent, fearless, and consistent friend of liberty and republican institutions," and National Republicans assured voters that "he will, on all occasions, assert the supremacy of the laws, and that executive power in his hands, will be their faithful auxiliary."[22]

The Democrats' choice for president in 1832 was never in question, although Jackson's decision to make himself available for a second term had not been inevitable. His first annual message, in fact, proposed the adoption of a constitutional amendment limiting presidents to one term. In February 1830, he indicated that "it is too early yet for me to judge whether I can permit my name to be voted for again by the people. My own inclinations ever lead to retirement." In December 1830, the Washington *Globe*'s prospectus noted that Jackson was the only Democratic candidate capable "of producing unanimity in the support of their principles." In early 1831, Jackson informed the American public of his decision to stand for a second term. "Considering . . . the numerous declarations which I have received from large portions of my countrymen, in various quarters," the president wrote in a letter to Pennsylvania state legislators, he was choosing "to yield my personal wishes to their solicitations" and run for reelection.[23]

Jackson's candidacy may have been a foregone conclusion, but the vice-presidential question presented the Democratic Party with problems. Calhoun's falling-out with Jackson ensured that the South Carolinian would leave office, but the party divided on who should replace him. Jackson and several close advisers wanted Van Buren, the president's loyal ally during the Eaton affair. Jackson had privately endorsed his former secretary of state in a December 1829 letter to his Nashville friend and adviser John Overton. "I have found him every thing that I could desire him to be, and believe him not only deserving *my* confidence, but the *confidence of the nation*," Jackson wrote. "He, my dear friend, is not only well qualified, but deserves to fill the highest office in the gift of the people who, in him, will find a true friend and safe depository of their rights and liberty." Van Buren's sacrifice of his cabinet post during the Eaton affair only confirmed to Jackson that he was the right choice to succeed him.[24]

In December 1831, the *Globe* called for a Democratic national convention, not to nominate Jackson but to "produce concert in relation to the Vice-Presidency." Democrats responded by meeting in Baltimore on 21 May 1832. The 320 delegates, representing every state but Missouri, framed the convention as a chance to unite voters behind the president and his principles. They never formally voted on Jackson's nomination, instead concurring in the several state nominations for his candidacy. The vice-presidential nomination was less clear cut. As the *Richmond Enquirer* observed, "We hear from no quarter where the voice of the People has not openly declared against" Van Buren. In the months preceding the convention, some Democrats, particularly in the South, pushed for federal judge Philip P. Barbour of Virginia to be the nominee. They considered him more reliable on states' rights than the New Yorker. Despite this intraparty dissension, Van Buren successfully fended off the challenges posed by Barbour and Colonel Richard M. Johnson of Kentucky, the candidates respectively receiving 208, 49, and 26 votes.[25]

As the 1832 presidential campaign began, political prognosticators might have expected the election to sink to the same depths of mudslinging as seen four years prior. The 1832 campaign proved relatively tame compared to the previous contest, but the maturation of cultural politics continued, exerting a growing influence on how American politicians and voters interacted.

CHAPTER 7

Freemen, Cheer the Hickory Tree

Some of the most vulgar forms of campaigning had marked the 1828 election, including attacks on women's morality, violent images, and unsubstantiated personal slurs. Those expecting a similar tone in 1832 were likely disappointed in the relative tameness of the Jackson and Clay campaigns. Cultural politics remained important, however, suggesting that presidential candidates were beginning to understand its significance for the growing number of American voters.

PUBLIC EVENTS

In 1832, presidential candidates were still expected to refrain from openly soliciting votes at public events. Undertaking an official campaign tour was a development that would not realize its potential for another eight years. Even with these limitations, however, public events still served an important political purpose.

Wirt and Clay particularly showed restraint in attending public events that could be construed as campaigning. Wirt was apathetic about being placed on the Anti-Masonic ticket, telling one confidant that it was the Anti-Masons' "duty" to select someone else if doing so would defeat Jackson. They ignored his advice, and he appeared to ignore his nomination. Clay, meanwhile, told a group of supporters that from the time the Fayette County meeting had presented his name as a presidential candidate in 1830, he had "not accepted, nor, whilst it remains thus before the public, shall I accept, any public entertainment tendered on my own account." His place in the Senate, however, allowed him to give speeches, which Democrats took note of, accusing Clay of using his congressional seat for electioneering purposes. They also observed that while the Kentucky senator appeared to have abandoned "the occupation of eating dinners and making electioneering speeches, laudatory of himself and abusive of the President" outside of Washington, he had recruited someone else as his proxy: Cherokee leader Major Ridge. According to the *Globe*, Ridge was touring New England, "beging — not dinner — but money, making speeches and abusing Georgia and the President in the most approved style," all to bolster Clay's cause.[1]

The Democratic ticket was not as resolute in refraining from hints of electioneering. Jackson took advantage of a trip to his Hermitage plantation during the summer of 1832 to participate in some events to which he was invited. In Nashville, he turned down opportunities to attend public dinners given in his honor, but he agreed "to meet the citizens and shake them by the hand." On his way back to Washington, Jackson attended a barbecue in Lexington, Kentucky. He conveyed to one of his nephews his impression of the crowds who gathered to meet with or cheer him on as he traveled through the Bluegrass State. "Never have I seen such a gathering as met us in advance of Lexington three miles," Jackson wrote Andrew J. Donelson. He calculated that five thousand people assembled "without any concert, or notification." Jackson concluded that "the political horizon is bright as far as we have seen or heard." Like Clay, however, he did not make campaign speeches.[2]

Martin Van Buren did not escape criticism of his involvement in public events. One National Republican editor in New York condemned him for "flying about with his aid-de-camps, detached to electioneer in Pennsylvania and this state." A New York Anti-Masonic newspaper accused Van Buren, a "modern Machieval," of "peregrinating the state . . . electioneering for himself and the Grand Master of masonry." The accusation of electioneering bore some resemblance to the truth: Van Buren was politicking in his home state but primarily to help his friends in the Albany Regency. Or so he said. A strong Regency would only help him and Jackson carry New York in the national election, of course, a benefit of which Van Buren was well aware.[3]

The political parties organized other public events intended to rally voters, even if they did not include the candidates themselves. French observer Michel Chevalier spoke admiringly of the Democrats' political processions in 1832, which he considered "the most brilliant and animated" that he had ever seen. He described one such procession, which had "gigantic hickory-poles" on carts, accompanied by "fifes and drums" and Democrats wearing hickory twigs on their hats. One pole "was drawn by eight horses, decorated with ribbands and mottoes," Chevalier wrote. "Astride on the tree itself," he continued, "were a dozen Jackson men of the first water, waving flags with an air of anticipated triumph, and shouting, *Hurrah for Jackson!*" The Frenchman was less impressed with a public dinner given by the Philadelphia anti-Jacksonians. "I have never seen a more miserable affair," he commented.[4]

This "new mode of electioneering" by the Democrats came under fire. The pro-Clay *Washington (DC) Daily National Intelligencer* commented derisively, "We do not recollect before to have heard of a President of the United States descending in person into the political arena." Another anti-Jackson newspaper wrote, "Accounts of the President's electioneering visit in Kentucky are daily received. This is the patriot! this is the man who asked for but one term! This is the personage that never attended dinners, parades nor barbecues!" National Republicans criticized the Democrats' appeals to voters' appetites as well. Whatever their political setbacks, one newspaper opined, they responded *"by swallowing a pig . . . , devouring a turkey . . . , [or] pouring off a pint of whiskey or apple-toddy."*[5]

Former president John Quincy Adams criticized both Democrats and National Republicans for their electioneering practices. After the election, he recalled his complaints about "this fashion of peddling for popularity by travelling round the country gathering crowds together, hawking for public dinners, and spouting empty speeches . . . President Jackson made an awkward figure of it last summer," he remarked, and "Mr. Clay has mounted that hobby horse, and rides him very hard."[6]

AUXILIARY ORGANIZATIONS

The auxiliary organizations that had planned the many public events in previous election years continued to do so during the 1832 campaign. For the Democrats, Hickory Clubs continued to play an important role in defending the president and his policies and attacking his opponents. "The objects of the Hickory Club," according to members of one branch in Ithaca, New York, "are—to discuss political subjects—to interchange views and opinions—to collect, imbody, and impart, information and to be prepared to meet and refute the many [fal]sehoods which a heartless and unprincipled oppo[sit]ion is continually inventing and promulgating." Hickory Clubs did just that. The Philadelphia Hickory Club, for example, resolved that "the Veto upon the Bank leaves our highest confidence unimpaired in the wisdom and patriotism of the President." A meeting in the town of Lebanon, Pennsylvania, drew a reported two thousand attendees, who passed a sarcastic resolution condemning Clay for asking Jackson to issue a call to fast and pray for an end to a cholera outbreak when the Kentuckian was the one "who invoked the pestilence on our country" in his 1828 Baltimore speech. In addition to Pennsylvania and New York, Hickory Clubs appeared in Maine, Maryland, New Jersey, Ohio, and Washington, DC.[7]

Though not on par with the Democrats, National Republicans mustered more of an effort at organization than the Adams campaign had four years earlier. Having learned from the 1828 campaign, delegates to the National Republican convention endorsed a plan to establish town, county, and state corresponding committees to coordinate their campaign and called for a meeting of "the young men of the national republican party" in Washington in May. A group of Bostonians sympathetic to Clay endorsed the idea. "The convention, if it be successful, will rouse the young men, and through them the whole country to action," they noted.[8]

From 7 to 12 May 1832, 314 delegates from seventeen states met in Washington, DC, at the Young Men's National Republican Convention. They passed resolutions nominating Henry Clay and John Sergeant as the party's presidential and vice-presidential candidates; honoring Charles Carroll, the last living signer of the Declaration of Independence; and proposing a visit to George Washington's home, Mount Vernon. The delegates also spent significant time criticizing Van Buren. They approved a resolution endorsing the Senate's "wisdom and firmness" in rejecting the New Yorker's appointment as minister to Great Britain following his resignation from Jackson's cabinet. Delegate Erastus C. Benedict of the Empire State denied that Van Buren "was a distinguished son" of their state. New York "acknowledged no man to be such, who would lick the dust from the foot of a monarch's throne," he argued. The convention closed with an address that asked the nation's young men to join the fight against the Jackson administration: "You must not only think, but you must also act with us."[9]

The National Republicans' better organization helped bring out larger numbers than in 1828; one New York gathering reported "at least 2000 persons present." The tone of the organizations' meetings went as expected. At a Cayuga, New York, event, Clay supporters "annihilated Gen. Jackson . . . as a misruling dotard" and called Jacksonians "dolts and servile tools." A Connecticut meeting resolved that while Jackson was a military hero, his presidential term had not changed their minds about him. They were convinced, however, that Clay would "administer the government on sound constitutional principles, with an eye to the best good of the Union."[10]

All three parties criticized their opponents' organizations. National Republicans argued that the Washington, DC, Hickory Club "appears to be the rickety bantling of the Kitchen Cabinet," the disparaging term used for Jackson's group of unofficial advisers, men such as Francis P. Blair, Amos Kendall, and William B. Lewis. "The object of the Club is to circulate Extra Globes," they noted, "and do other such *interesting* business in furtherance of General Jackson's election." An

Anti-Masonic notice about a meeting warned party members that Clay's supporters were "using all honorable and dishonorable means, to draw the Anti-masons off from their principles and their candidates, and the partizans of Jackson know that if a union is effected their hopes in this state are prostrated." A Democratic editor in Maine noted that a Clay meeting of "federalists assembled to the number of *four!*" After solving the nation's problems, they adjourned; "after the most laborious exertions," at their next meeting, the group grew to "twelve or fifteen present."[11]

PUBLIC CORRESPONDENCE

Neither Jackson nor Clay engaged substantively with voters through public correspondence. The president responded with letters of regret when some groups of Americans invited him to attend public dinners. When a group of New Jersey hatters sent him one of their products, accompanied by resolutions commending Jackson for supporting "a Judicious Tariff," he thanked them for the hat and commented on the tariff issue, which was heating up with the election season. "Nothing can be more gratifying to me than the evidence it affords of the wisdom of that policy under which this and many other branches of our domestic manufacture have grown up," Jackson wrote.[12]

Clay's public letters also consisted of turning down invitations to attend public dinners. Although he did not express explicit political views, the Kentuckian used these invitations to drive home his desire to remain above the partisan fray by not electioneering. His 1832 letter to the citizens of Vincennes, Indiana, made sure to point out that he would be justified in attending public dinners to "[vindicate] my character there, which has been unjustly reproached," yet he was refraining because of the "considerations connected with the existing relation to the community in which I have been placed." Voters could not help but notice his self-sacrifice, or so Clay hoped. In an 1832 letter to the citizens of Hanover County, Virginia, he reiterated his reasons for declining their invitation to attend a public dinner "at the place of my nativity." At the same time, he expounded on his fond childhood memories of the area. It would not be giving Clay too much credit, political animal that he was, to think that he used emotional manipulation to endear himself to potential voters in the area where he was raised.[13]

The notable exception to active engagement through public correspondence was Van Buren. Standing on shaky ground with some Democrats, the New Yorker attempted to bolster his cause, as Jackson had in 1824, by embracing direct contact with voters. The Senate's rejection of Van Buren's appointment as minister to England in January 1832 not only solidified Jackson's decision to push for the New

Yorker's nomination at the national convention, but it also prompted several resolutions from state legislatures and citizens' groups. The president's support might
have been enough to win his friend the vice presidency, but Van Buren decided
to take his message to the people. He replied to notifications of the resolutions,
thanking the groups for their support and noting that while "the courtesy due to
the highest of our Legislative bodies" required acknowledgment that those senators who opposed him had their reasons, he believed that "public sentiment of
which I have an [sic] earnest before me, is likely to determine the futility of those
reasons, and the injustice of that decision."[14]

After Van Buren received the vice-presidential nomination, he outlined specific policy positions in public correspondence. Replying to a letter from a group
of New Yorkers expressing their support for him against "unjust attacks," Van
Buren praised Americans' "redeeming spirit" in ignoring these "worthless" assaults
and encouraged them to continue supporting "civil authority" against "the insid-
ious approaches of wealth, ambition, and arbitrary power." A group of North Carolinians requested his views on the tariff, internal improvements, the Second
Bank's recharter, and nullification. In his response, Van Buren acknowledged that
"the right of those you represent, to be informed of my opinions upon these interesting subjects, as derived from the position in which the favor of my fellow citizens
has placed me, is undoubted." Although he believed that his reply was "a brief but
explicit avowal of my opinions," Van Buren later said of his letter, "I have never
prepared a paper of that character with which I have been better satisfied."[15]

POLITICAL MUSIC

In person and in print, the campaigns employed music to make political points.
The president's opponents used one song, "King Log and the Frogs," to satirize
what they perceived as Jackson's monarchical tendencies (King Log) and his advisers' foolishness (the Frogs). In the lyrics, the frogs compare Jackson to a donkey
who tried on a lion's skin, but his "bray for a roar prov'd him never a lion." "King
Log," meanwhile, chastised his advisers for croaking too loudly: "I took you my
lieges, for men of more breeding."[16]

National Republicans also lauded their own candidate in song:

Here's a health to the workingman's friend,
Here's good luck to the PLOUGH and the LOOM,
And who will not join in support of our cause,
May light-dinners and ill luck attend.
It's good from *true faith* ne'er to swerve,

It's good from the Right ne'er to stray,
It's good to maintain AMERICA'S Cause
And stick by our own HARRY CLAY.

Another pro-Clay song encouraged "fence-men" (i.e., undecided voters) to "jump down in good season on solid Clay land." It warned, "Take care of yourselves, lest you soon rue the day, you rallied not with us for great HARRY CLAY."[17]

Not to be outdone, Democrats drummed up support for Jackson by reminding voters,

Now every freeman again should pay
On the ensuing Election day,
Their united suffrages to the Chief,
Without the least reluctancy.

"The Hickory Tree" was another Democratic favorite:

Hurra for the Hickory Tree!
Hurra for the Hickory Tree!
Its branches will wave o'er tyranny's grave.
And bloom for the brave and the free.

Democrats also challenged Clay in a song entitled "Ho! Why Dost Thou Shiver and Shake, Harry Clay?" The song went, in part,

Are not the *high tariff* men thine,
Harry Clay,
And will they not help thee along?—
My American System
Was framed to enlist 'em,
But trick cannot make the weak strong,
Well-a-day!
The *Anties* [Anti-Masons] will sure take thee up,
Harry Clay;
And their principles drop, with their Wirt?
The Anties are frantic,
And in some mad antic,
Will spill me again in the dirt—
Well-a-day!
The *Feds*, who live high on the Bank,
Harry Clay,

Hate Jackson, and money adore:—
The folks term them tories,
And scorn their Bank stories,
And love the *Old Hero* the More—[18]

MATERIAL CULTURE

The Democratic and National Republican campaigns both used political paraphernalia to support their candidates and attack the opposition. Two objects specifically addressed campaign issues. New York Democrats created a token inscribed
with a motto incorporating Jackson's words: "The Bank Must Perish/the Union
Must and Shall Be Preserved." In Philadelphia, home of the BUS, Democrats
manufactured an anti-Bank silk ribbon. The National Republicans were more
successful in creating relevant campaign objects in 1832 than Adams's supporters
had been in 1828. They produced a button calling Clay "The Champion of Internal Improv[ement]s" and a token hailing him as "The Champion of Republicanism and the American System." He also appeared on tokens in the classical
Roman toga, an allusion to his oratorical skills and statesmanship.[19]

Just as in 1828, hickory was the main Democratic symbol. Pennsylvania Jacksonians produced a silk ribbon celebrating the president's strength with a slogan
adapted from the 1824 campaign: "Freemen, Cheer the Hickory Tree; In Storms
Its Boughs Have Sheltered Thee." Jackson gave New York merchant Silas E. Bur-
rows a hickory cane made of wood taken from the Hermitage, while some of the
president's supporters, such as John R. Burke, sent Jackson hickory canes. Democrats also placed hickory poles in prominent places, such as the one erected "in
front of the hotel kept by Mrs. Moose, in South Front street" in Philadelphia.
(Taking a page from the Jacksonians' playbook, Clay supporters used ash poles to
celebrate "the Sage of Ashland," the name of their candidate's Kentucky estate.)[20]

Just as in 1828, however, National Republicans criticized the Democrats' main
symbol. One set of satirical poems included in its choruses an homage to the
hickory pole:

Round about the Hickory Pole
Let us tumble, kneel and roll.
Let us swear by all the Gods,
To bow the neck when Andrew nods.

The president's critics also pointed out the violence associated with the hickory
club. When Jackson's close Tennessee friend Sam Houston attacked Ohio representative William Stanbery for intemperate remarks made about Houston's in-

volvement in contracts for Indian removal, National Republicans claimed that Houston had wielded a hickory cane in the assault. "General Jackson has surrounded himself with a set of bullies, bravos, brawlers, ruffians, ragamuffins and stabbers," one anonymous letter writer observed. "Whenever one of your grim-looking hard fighters from Tennessee, Kentucky, Alabama, North Carolina, or elsewhere, comes to Washington, . . . the Chief Magistrate delivers to him one of these hickory clubs, cut from his own farm, and at the same time tells him to signalize himself by knocking somebody down." The result was a roving "regiment of bravos . . . called the 'Jackson Pets,' and Houston is the commander." According to this individual, "The assault on Stanberry was by order of General Jackson." The image of the president sending armed thugs to wreak havoc on the streets of the nation's capital made for great theater, even if it failed to match reality.[21]

VISUAL CULTURE

Much as the Adams campaign had in 1828, National Republicans produced a handful of lithographs. The lack of numerous lithographs, however, points to its slow emergence as a new media technology and highlights how political parties were still working to understand its effectiveness as a campaign tool.

One of the most prolific lithographers of the antebellum era, Edward W. Clay (no relation to the National Republican nominee), placed his stamp on the 1832 campaign when two of his creations appeared in early 1831. Both lithographs addressed Jackson's cabinet breakup resulting from the Eaton affair. In *.00001 the Value of a Unit with Four Cyphers Going Before It*, Jackson sits in a collapsing chair while his cabinet members, in the form of rats, scatter. One of the most memorable set of images from the lithograph depicted the rivalry between the secretary of state and the vice president. Van Buren tries to climb the "Ladder of Political Preferment," while Calhoun, in the form of a terrier, stands nearby, saying, "You don't get up if I can help it." Clay and Webster peer through a window at the chaotic scene, with the Kentuckian proclaiming, in words recalling an 1828 speech, "Famine! War! Pestilence!" Edward Clay employed similar imagery in *The Rats Leaving a Falling House*. John Quincy Adams noted the popularity of one of the two lithographs (it is unclear which) by remarking, "Two thousand copies of this print have been sold in Philadelphia this day. Ten thousand copies have been struck off, and will all be disposed of within a fortnight."[22]

Another anti-Jackson lithograph, *Uncle Sam in Danger*, portrayed Jackson giving medical help to Uncle Sam, who is ill and wrapped in the American flag. The president has lanced Uncle Sam's arm in an attempt to "bleed" him, a common

The Rats leaving a Falling House

FIGURE 5. *The Rats Leaving a Falling House* (1831) depicts cabinet members, in the form of rats, attempting to flee a collapsing edifice. The cartoon references the chaos of Jackson's administration in the wake of the Eaton affair. Prints and Photographs Division, Library of Congress, http://www.loc.gov/pictures/item /2008661748/.

medical practice. Fictional character Major Jack Downing stands to Jackson's right, commenting, "Twixt the Giniril (since He's taken to Doctring) & the little Dutch Potercary 'Uncle Sam' stands no more chance than a stump tailed Bull in fly time." To the side, an observer rests his arm on a ballot box, saying, "They are ruining your constitution these Pills alone can restore your strength."[23]

PRINT CULTURE

Likely because the two major candidates were so well known, very few campaign biographies appeared in the 1832 election. New England transplant George D. Prentice intended his *Biography of Henry Clay* (1831) "to influence an approaching political election." He suggested that if the Kentuckian lost in 1832, his fate would resemble that of "the Titan, who, for his divine gift to the human race, was doomed to undying agonies." Prentice defended Clay at every turn. For example, he called the "corrupt bargain" charge against the Kentuckian "utterly preposterous" and attributed it to "a mind [i.e., Jackson's] enfeebled by age and perverted by long-cherished passion."[24]

William J. Snelling, a writer noted at the time for his work on Native American life, produced a negative campaign biography of Jackson under the pseudonym "A Free Man." Snelling disingenuously claimed that he had "no personal interest in the result of the approaching political contest," but he showed Jackson no mercy when it came to the president's many public quarrels. For example, he called Jackson's 1813 brawl with the Benton brothers "one of the grossest and most outrageous violations of law and order ever heard of in a Christian land." According to Snelling, Jackson's victory at New Orleans in January 1815, which helped to propel him into the presidential chair, "was almost inevitable. Never was victory more easily or safely won." As for Jackson's administration, "for nearly two years we have seen Martin Van Buren leading the political bull by the nose," Snelling remarked, "and Duff Green, in the spirit of his original occupation, following in the rear, goad in hand."[25]

Philo A. Goodwin's biography of Jackson, by contrast, was laudatory. In discussing the aftermath at New Orleans, for instance, he recounted Jackson's kind conduct toward British prisoners. He "treated and spoke to them as his children," Goodwin said. He presented the 1828 campaign in the most positive light as well. "Almost every act of his [Jackson's] life, either public or private, was represented as embodying some crime which degrades and dishonors our common nature," he wrote. "But his fame passed every ordeal with a renovated brilliancy." Jackson's removal of pro-Adams government workers upon becoming president, in Goodwin's estimation, was "his solemn duty." While John Eaton did not publish a

new edition of his campaign biography, his work undoubtedly continued to circulate among Democrats in 1832, reinforcing Goodwin's positive portrayal of Old
Hickory.[26]

Newspapers once again proved to be a major partisan tool. The Nullification
Crisis, along with the Eaton affair, had accelerated one of the most significant
patronage decisions that Jackson made. Both incidents also indicated the central
role of cultural politics during his first term. During 1829 and 1830, while the
Petticoat War was raging, and Jackson and Calhoun were sparring about the future of the Union, Duff Green and his *United States Telegraph* fell out of favor
with Old Hickory, and the editor became a frequent and fierce critic of the president and anyone associated with him. Jackson, who valued loyalty, believed that
the editor was guilty of treacherous behavior by not supporting all his policies and
by aligning himself with the vice president. "His idol controles him as much as
the shewman does his puppits," Jackson wrote William B. Lewis. "We must get
another organ to . . . defend the administration,—in his hands, it is more injured
than by all the opposition."[27]

Late in 1830, Jackson moved to establish a new administration newspaper in
Washington named the *Globe*. In the first issue, published on December 7, *Globe*
editor Francis P. Blair declared that to ensure the continuation of Jackson's "principles, which are considered essential to the preservation, peace, and prosperity
of the Union," he would use his media platform to work for the president's reelection. The *Globe*'s motto was "The world is governed too much," a reference to the
Democrats' claim that their party supported limited government. Green was aware
of his isolation, telling Illinois governor Ninian Edwards that William H. Crawford
was working toward "the elevation of Mr. Van Buren to the Presidency." Despite
Green's declaration that he "intend[ed] to sustain the administration, [and] support the re-election of Gen. Jackson," his decision to publish the Jackson-Calhoun
correspondence in February 1831 sealed his, and his newspaper's, fate with the
president and those within his inner circle.[28]

Unsurprisingly, Democratic papers such as the *Globe* lambasted National Republicans for choosing Clay as their candidate. Several newspapers spread an
editorial from the *New-Hampshire Patriot and State Gazette*, which quoted former Massachusetts congressman Timothy Fuller's observation that Clay "spent
his days at the gaming table and his nights in a brothel." That same New England
newspaper also published an exhaustive list of "Twenty-three reasons why Henry
Clay should not be elected President." It included that Clay had "prayed for 'war,
pestilence, and famine,' in preference to the election of General Jackson," and
that he would "reinstate the old federal party in office and adopt their principles."

The list continued, "If [Clay is] elected, there will be a division of the Union before his term expires." Finally, Clay's election would bring corruption back to the federal government, allowing "embezzlers, [s]peculators, [and] defaulters . . . [to] be restored to office, and again live on the plunder of the treasury."[29]

Globe editor Blair was especially vigorous in his attacks. Like other Democratic editors, he reminded readers of Clay's questionable private morals:

> How monstrous it is, that a man who was publicly alluded to in the pulpit of his own State, as one whose immoral but successful course, had tended to injure its rising generation, should now be held up as worthy of the highest honor, and as an example of "PUBLIC AND PRIVATE VIRTUE" . . . The upstart aristocracy of this country have, among other privileges of the great ones of Europe, laid claim to the prerogative of loading every friend of popular rights, with unfounded calumnies, while they assume a perfect license for every vice of their own persons.

He also compared Clay's machinations to the "corrupt bargain" and asked, "Do the people wish to see the scenes of that election repeated, and our Union shaken to its foundations?"[30]

Blair broadened his attacks beyond just Clay. For example, he compared Clay and Calhoun to the coalition of "Octavius and Anthony, which severed the Roman Empire." Clay's election would thrill Calhoun, Blair wrote, because "it would instantly establish the *Southern League*." The *Globe* editor lumped together all Jackson's enemies, labeling them "malcontents who wish the Government pulled down and re-edified on their own principles, or severed and multiplied, to make the chief power accessible to the different aspirants—uniting their strength against one of the fathers of the Republic [i.e., Jackson], whose patriotism and popularity rebukes their ambitious hopes." They were a "conspiracy against this, the best Government on earth," language that echoes modern-day American partisanship.[31]

Debate about Jackson's veto of the BUS recharter bill also infused the campaign, drawing the *Globe* editor's ire. As the campaign was winding down, Blair wrote that the Second Bank "was secretly purchasing up presses and politicians . . . [and] preparing to coerce the people of certain sections of the country into submission to its views." He noted that the presidential and vice-presidential candidates opposing the Democrats were all BUS attorneys. Voters would do well to remember, Blair argued, that the Jackson–Van Buren ticket was "the ticket of UNION AND LIBERTY."[32]

Opposition editors struck at one of the Democrats' weakest points: Van Buren's vice-presidential nomination. Skeptical of the New Yorker's loyalty to their region, some southern Democrats formed Jackson-Barbour tickets, even after the Virginian declared himself uninterested in running. Newspaper editorials accused Democrats of instituting an American monarchy. "In what will our republic differ from a monarchy, if the people relinquish to the president the power of nominating his successor?" asked Duff Green, no longer the loyal Democratic Party editor. "Is Andrew Jackson to be the first of a line of Presidents who are to use the patronage of the government to control the choice of his successor?" Green argued that he was not pro-Clay but anti-Jackson. He accused the president of having "stooped from his station, and become actively enlisted in the electioneering warfare, as a partisan of Mr. Van Buren." Green conveyed his suspicions of Van Buren's ambitions by suggesting that he thought that Jackson was "under the dictation of an irresponsible and corrupt junto, who use his name and popularity to enrich themselves at the expense of the people, and of our institutions." He also feared that the Jacksonian Democrats' lust for power would "destroy our institutions by corrupting the people themselves."[33]

WOMEN'S ACTIVITY

The Democrats received help in the print war from an unexpected quarter: Anne Royall, an outspoken travel writer who founded the newspaper *Paul Pry* in December 1831. She supported many of Jackson's policies, including his BUS veto and Indian removal policy. The newspaper's inaugural issue outlined Royall's intentions: "The welfare and happiness of our country are our politics. We shall expose all and every species of political evil, and religious fraud, without fear or affection," she wrote. "We shall advocate liberty of the press, the liberty of speech, and the liberty of conscience. The enemies of our common safety, as they have shown none, shall receive no mercy at our hands!"[34]

During the campaign, Royall framed the election as a "QUESTION of LIBERTY or SLAVERY, the VETO or the BANK, General Jackson or Henry Clay, DEMOCRACY or ARISTOCRACY." She lauded Jackson's congressional supporters, criticized anti-Jackson newspapers, and "reported on the illegal electioneering techniques of Clay's backers." She was particularly concerned about Britain's involvement in the BUS, in her eyes a foreign conspiracy that threatened the nation's future. The Second Bank's shareholders, Clay's supporters, and those who wanted to unite church and state, Royall wrote, all "speak the same voice from whatever place they hail, and are moved by one and the same machine—the U.S. Bank."[35]

Royall used gendered language to make her arguments more effective. She observed that congressmen, instead of doing their constitutional duty and serving the people, spent most of their time in Washington "divided between temperance meetings, missionary meetings, Jackson meetings, Clay meetings, oyster meetings, champagne meetings, and last, though not least, *lady* meetings." Commenting on Clay supporters' attempts to raise money for a loyal newspaper in Philadelphia, Royall again turned to sexual innuendo: "Mr. Clay would do well to turn MISSIONARY, as he seems to be a great favorite with the women; he would never want cash then." She criticized Clay's American System for its "barbarous" tariff that would harm "tender females and children." While women could not vote, Royall understood their influence. As one newspaper editor observed, "It is true, that the ladies are not called to command in the field, or to figure in the halls of legislation; but their husbands, children and brothers are." Thus, he continued, "it is in the power of every intelligent mother to enstamp upon the mind, such an impression of rectitude and virtue," that it would last a lifetime.[36]

An exceptional woman operating in a male-dominated sphere, Royall struggled to keep her paper afloat financially. She won few admirers from among those whom she criticized with her acidic pen and tongue. One fellow editor commented that *Paul Pry* was a "*strong* Jackson print . . . [that] contains all the scum, billingsgate, and political filth extant." Anti-Royall newspapers, such as the *Prying Eye* and *Anne Royall Jr.*, arose to counteract her paper, a testimony to her perceived influence as well as to the animosity she engendered. Despite her struggles, Royall's paper helped Jackson's campaign by keeping his supporters informed about meetings, bolstering their belief in the president and his party, and reinforcing their negative impressions of the National Republicans and the Anti-Masons.[37]

Jackson supporters also reminded voters that their candidate was the one who defended womanly virtue. They revived the 1824 campaign's focus on Jackson as "the *Hero* who despoiled the invading foe when '*booty and beauty*' was the watchword." The *Albany Argus* asked, "Was not the *watch-word* VETOED by General Jackson? Ye who have wives, daughters and sisters, can you prove ingrates to the man who will pledge his purse and hazard his life for your protection?" Following news of Jackson's triumph over Clay and Wirt, one woman made the following toast at a Washington, DC, celebration:

> Gen. Andrew Jackson: His country women will ever remember his protection
>   to their sisters of Louisiana:—
> He who bares his breast and nerves his arm,
> To shield our tender sex from harm,
> Shall with our prayers to Heaven renewed,
> Receive our thanks of gratitude.[38]

National Republicans utilized women in the campaign as well. One Maine newspaper recounted a July Fourth celebration at which Jackson and Clay supporters appeared. Not only did the Clay supporters outnumber their opponents, but "the ladies were almost all on the Clay side," and reportedly, "no 'respectable' ladies would be seen" on the Jackson side. Female respectability was important to National Republicans, so when women were referenced as part of the presidential campaign, they often mentioned the controversial Margaret Eaton. The National Republican press made much of her social "ban" by "the ladies of Washington." One Portland, Maine, correspondent called it "a splendid triumph of female excellence, purity and virtue." Margaret Eaton appeared frequently in this commentary as "Bellona," the Roman goddess of war, a female counterpart to the bellicose Jackson and a representation of Democratic female impropriety. As controversial as Margaret was, however, she was often depicted as a passive agent in Van Buren's alleged political machinations. A National Republican newspaper described one public event as an opportunity for the former secretary of state to use "various stratagems to keep Bellona afloat" as a way to sway "the prospect of the succession and the whole power of the Executive" in his favor. Margaret Eaton was also used as a yardstick by which to measure Van Buren's own rumored immorality. "It ill becomes the Globe to talk of Martin Van Buren's *private worth*," wrote one National Republican, "when stories are circulating, and facts are known in almost every house in Washington, which would rank him as a *man* with Mrs. Eaton as a *woman*."[39]

Margaret Eaton's treatment reflected the National Republicans' tendency to use women as gendered political props. As the election drew to a close, the *United States Telegraph* published a political cartoon entitled *Granny Jackson's Lullaby to Little Martin*. The accompanying lyrics, to the tune of "Rock-a-bye Baby," promised that "When Granny is gone, You shall sit in her chair." National Republicans continued the theme of depicting Jackson in female terms by referring to him as "Aunty Jackson." Once the election results were known, a Boston National Republican wrote about a dream he had that lamented Jackson's election. "A female of dazzling beauty" dressed in stars, stripes, and "black crape," according to his telling, "held forth a scroll" that predicted a litany of disasters that awaited the nation during Jackson's second term, including race wars, a Jackson monarchy, and "General anarchy." Before the correspondent could finish reading the scroll, "the goddess uttered a bitter groan, shook the dust from her feet, with a gesture of unutterable scorn, and soared toward the empyrean [heaven]."[40]

The opposition that Anne Royall faced and the criticism that Margaret Eaton continued to receive spoke to the expected, though not actual, role of women in the 1830s: the public world of politics was not their sphere. As one Democratic newspaper noted, a woman had written the editor complaining that it was "in danger of depriving our female readers of their portion of reading, by treating so much upon political subjects." Expectations for women's political activism were changing, but overcoming this perspective, even among women, was a slow process.[41]

JACKSON WINS REELECTION

When the votes cast in the 1832 election were tallied, Jackson defeated Clay, 219 electoral votes to 49. The president's popular vote majority decreased only slightly from that of 1828, despite the criticism that he faced on multiple issues. The assignment of the remaining 18 electoral votes testified to some of that disapproval. Seven electoral votes went to the Anti-Mason Party's William Wirt. Virginia's John Floyd received South Carolina's 11 electoral votes as a protest against the president's tariff stance. Despite these minor losses, Jackson won a convincing victory. The 1,309,534 popular votes cast and the voter participation rate of 55 percent indicated the growing interest in presidential elections as a result of substantive issues, cultural politics, and fewer suffrage restrictions.[42]

When it was clear that Jackson had won reelection, the *Globe* observed, "During the contest the line has been clearly drawn between the combined powers of aristocracy, manufacturing monopoly, political priest-craft, and pecuniary corruption on the one side, and the stern republican virtue of the people on the other." James K. Polk crowed at Jackson's victory. "Did you ever know such a complete route?" he asked John Coffee. "The enemy is literally driven from the field." Michel Chevalier witnessed the postelectoral scene in New York: "The procession was nearly a mile long; the democrats marched in good order to the glare of torches; the banners were more numerous than I had ever seen them in any religious festival; all were in transparency, on account of the darkness." He described banners that "bore imprecations" against Biddle and the BUS; portraits of Jackson, Washington, and Jefferson; and even a live eagle "hoisted upon a pole, after the manner of the Roman standards." The procession members stopped and cheered in front of Democratic homes and groaned in front of anti-Jacksonian residences. "These scenes," Chevalier admired, "are the episodes of a wondrous epic which will bequeath a lasting memory to posterity; that of the coming of democracy."[43]

The Democrats' opponents reacted with predictable despondency after their loss. Until the last days of the campaign, Clay had remained optimistic that National Republicans were "assured of a certain victory" and that the election results would "heal the wounds of our bleeding Country, inflicted by the folly & madness of a lawless Military Chieftain!" After Jackson's victory, the defeated Kentuckian switched his tone. "The dark cloud which had been so long suspended over our devoted Country," he wrote to editor Charles H. Hammond, "instead of being dispelled, as we had only hoped it would be, has become more dense, more menacing[,] more alarming. Whether we shall ever see light, and law and liberty again, is very questionable." Wirt wrote a lengthy letter explaining how unrealistic expectations about Jackson's defeat had been. "I never expected Mr. Clay's election or my own, from the moment I saw that the opposition would not unite upon either of us," he told one correspondent. "I see that General Jackson has already been nominated by one of the northern papers for a third term. My opinion is, he may be President for life, if he chooses." The *Niles' Weekly Register* indicated its acceptance of the election results "as 'the will of the people,'" but it lamented that the election affirmed "the objectionable and repulsive power of the veto."[44]

The disappointment that anti-Jacksonians experienced as a result of the 1832 election steeled their will for the next electoral cycle, in 1836, which gave them the opportunity to challenge Democratic control of the executive branch and its patronage appointments. Even as they reconstituted themselves into the new Whig Party, however, they knew that defeating Van Buren, the man designated as Old Hickory's successor, was not going to be an easy task. They needed to marshal all their efforts, through both formal means and the more informal cultural politics, to win the White House.

CHAPTER 8

We Are in the Midst of a Revolution

Jackson's second term focused not just on the immediate political battles but also on the nation's future. Who would lead after Old Hickory? Jackson and many Democrats wanted Vice President Martin Van Buren, but their opponents had other ideas. The anti-Jacksonians' formation of a new political party, the Whigs, in 1834 presented them with an opportunity to break the Democrats' hold on the presidency in 1836.

THE BANK WAR

The issue that transformed the National Republicans into the Whigs was the Bank War. Andrew Jackson's fight with Nicholas Biddle and the Second Bank of the United States, so important to his reelection, exploded in his second term. The Bank War centered on arguments about the constitutionality of the chief executive's power over the national economy, and it provided much of the political context for the 1836 campaign.[1]

In the summer of 1833, Jackson ordered the government's deposits removed from the BUS. He believed that this action would cripple the institution and cause it to die a slow death. Pennsylvanian William J. Duane, who had recently replaced Louis McLane in the Treasury Department, refused to carry out the order, so Jackson fired him and put Roger B. Taney in his place. Taney implemented the president's order, moving the government deposits into a series of state (or "pet") banks that were pro-Democratic. Most of Jackson's cabinet disagreed with this new policy, but informal advisers, such as Amos Kendall and Francis P. Blair, encouraged the president in his course.[2]

The deposits' removal infuriated the president's congressional opponents and galvanized them into an organized opposition in a way that no other issue had been able to do. In the Senate, the "Great Triumvirate" of Calhoun, Clay, and Webster lashed out at what they considered Jackson's dictatorial powers. Clay led the charge to censure Jackson and Taney, a symbolic action that he hoped would weaken the president and his party. "We are in the midst of a revolution, hitherto bloodless, but rapidly tending toward a total change of the pure republican character of the government, and to the concentration of all power in the hands of one man," Clay argued. Failing to stop the president's march toward tyranny would make Americans "base, mean and abject slaves—the scorn and contempt of mankind!"[3]

Clay won the battle but lost the war. In late March 1834, the Senate voted 26–20 to censure Jackson, just as the Kentuckian had hoped. Not one to accept criticism gracefully, the president responded with a "Protest" message in mid-April. Jackson defended his actions regarding Duane and the government deposits and argued that "the President is the direct representative of the American People." Concurrently, House Democrats investigated the BUS for alleged improprieties. The investigation arose from suspicions that Biddle, to protect his bank, had precipitated a short economic contraction by calling in loans. In what Jackson called "a glorious triumph," the lower chamber passed resolutions confirming his call for a nonrenewal of the Second Bank's charter, supporting his "pet bank" policy, and calling for an investigation into the BUS. Although a Senate investigation later that year found Biddle guiltless, the damage had already been done.[4]

The end of the BUS came in 1836. The Second Bank's charter ran out that year, and Biddle reconstituted it into a Pennsylvania state bank. More importantly for Jackson, Democrats successfully expunged the 1834 censure resolution against him from the official Senate journal. Unsurprisingly, the 24–19 vote to do so fell along partisan lines.[5]

The Bank War fortified anti-Jacksonians, who adopted the Whig moniker in April 1834. In a Senate speech on the BUS, Henry Clay used the name to refer to the president's opponents. The Whigs of eighteenth-century Britain, he noted, "were the champions of liberty, the friends of the people, and the defenders of the power of their representatives in the House of Commons." Much like the opposition Whigs in England who fought against King George III's tyranny in the eighteenth century, present-day American Whigs faced a tyrant in the form of "King Andrew I," Clay argued. Whigs found themselves "opposing Executive encroachments, and a most alarming extension of Executive power and prerogative. They are ferreting out the abuses and corruption of an administration, under a

Chief Magistrate who is endeavoring to concentrate in his own person the whole powers of Government. They are contending for the rights of the people, for civil liberty, for free institutions, for the supremacy of the constitution and the laws." Clay and Daniel Webster were the recognized leaders of the new party, with their fellow senator John C. Calhoun a prominent ally out of expediency. Former president John Quincy Adams also lent his aid from his House seat. Joining them, immediately or over the next several years, were former Jackson allies John Bell, John Eaton, Hugh Lawson White, and even David Crockett, known to history as Davy Crockett, one of the heroes of the Alamo.[6]

Democrats were quick to point out the new party's weaknesses. Francis P. Blair, of the Washington *Globe*, argued that the Whigs chose a name that obfuscated their true, nefarious principles. "Whiggism does not pretend to have any principles common to the party," he carped. Instead, they became "members of the same party, without having one single principle in common, except the pledge among them all to support the recharter of the Bank." Another *Globe* editorial, "The Modern Wig—A Cover for Bald Federalism," contended that the Whigs believed that *"the few should govern the many"* and *"the* RICH *minority* should enjoy the whole power now conferred on the mass of the People through the right of suffrage."[7]

Undeterred, the Whigs prepared for the 1836 election. They had identified the central issue that they opposed—Jackson's dictatorial power—and they were going to attempt to use it to build a party and elect a president.

JACKSON'S HEIR APPARENT

The 1836 campaign started early in Jackson's first term. Within months of his 1829 inauguration, interested observers were postulating that Calhoun and Van Buren were positioning themselves to succeed Old Hickory. Calhoun's implosion and the Jackson–Van Buren ticket's victory in 1832 seemed to solidify Van Buren's place as the Democratic candidate in 1836.[8]

Not everyone within the party was thrilled at the idea of supporting the New Yorker, however. Some Democrats believed that Van Buren had ingratiated himself with Jackson to advance his career, while southern party members questioned his slavery bona fides. Both Whigs and former Jacksonians argued that Jackson's attempt to force his vice president on the people was indicative of his approach toward government. "Under the Spoils system," the *Washington (DC) Daily National Intelligencer* wrote, "the sentiment of the body of the office-holders . . . is but the reflection of the will of him, the breath of whose nostrils they are." The *United States Telegraph* warned, "If a stop be not put to the progress of servility and corruption, we shall follow the footsteps of the Romans." Duff Green also noted, "Mr. Van Buren is the direct representative of the patronage of the General Government. It is to it, and to it alone, that he owes his standing in the party."[9]

The Democratic national convention, which met in Baltimore on 20–22 May 1835, reflected the dissension within the party's ranks. Although more than six hundred delegates attended, nearly one-third were from Maryland. Four states (Alabama, Illinois, South Carolina, and Tennessee) were unrepresented. Tennessee's lack of delegates infuriated Jackson. "How is it that there is no man in the Republican ranks to take the stump, and relieve Tennessee from her degraded attitude of abandoning principle to sustain men who have apostatised from the republican fold?" he complained to James K. Polk. "The Baltimore convention will be filled by high talents, . . . how degraded, and humiliated must Tennessee appear." The decision to cajole Edmund Rucker, a Tennessee man who was visiting the city, into attending the convention as the state's representative only annoyed the president more. The states that were present at Baltimore unanimously nominated the fifty-two-year-old Van Buren on the first ballot, but everyone attending recognized that the New Yorker faced a potentially challenging campaign.[10]

The vice-presidential nomination once again proved controversial. Many westerners preferred Colonel Richard M. Johnson, who had served Kentucky in both the US House and the US Senate. Johnson's prominence derived largely from his military fame. He fought under General William Henry Harrison during the War of 1812 and allegedly was the one who shot and killed the Shawnee leader Tecumseh at the Battle of the Thames in October 1813. (Because of the lack of evidence, Johnson's claim was disputed even during his lifetime.) His reputation ascended during Jackson's presidency, in part because of the attention paid to Old Hickory's military career. If military heroism was a predictor of political success, some Democrats argued, then Johnson was a safe bet that would pay dividends for the party.[11]

Although two years older than Van Buren, the Kentucky colonel appeared to be the perfect Democratic candidate to balance his running mate's less-boisterous personality and focus on political details. But there was a problem. Johnson had engaged in a relationship with his enslaved woman, Julia Chinn, for several years, until her death from cholera in 1833. She bore him two daughters, Imogene and Adaline. Johnson orchestrated their marriages to white husbands and gave each couple claims to a portion of his Kentucky estate. Following Chinn's death, he began a relationship with another of his enslaved women, Cornelia Parthene. Johnson's personal life caused trepidation among some Americans. As the *Providence Journal* asked, "How it would look in the eyes of civilized Europe and the world, to see the Vice President, and his yellow children, and his wooly headed African wife, in the city of Washington, mingling in all the giddy mazes of the most fashionable and respectable society in the country?"[12]

Some southerners particularly objected to Johnson's candidacy. Several papers carried Duff Green's sarcastic attack on the Democratic candidate's personal proclivities:

> It may be a matter of no importance to mere political automatons whether Richard M. Johnson is a *White* or a *Black* man—whether he is *free* or a *slave*—or whether he is married to, or has been in connexion with a jet black, thick-lipped, odoriferous negro wench, by whom he has reared a family of children whom he has endeavored to force upon society as every way worthy of being considered the equals and the associates of his free white fellow citizens . . . It matters not, we say, with Mr. Van Buren and his followers, what may be the *color* of either Johnson, his wife, or his children.

One anonymous writer to the *Richmond Whig*, who called himself "A Farmer and a Whig," worried that Johnson's example would lead to white southern daughters being "assailed by the sable hand of a crude depredator, or claimed to deck the chamber of some 'lusty Moor.'" Another contributor to the *Richmond Whig*, writing under the pseudonym "Virginius," worried that Johnson's political elevation would lead to "bevies of mulattoes" in the nation's capital, encouraging enslaved people "to revolt for equality" and corrupting "the purity of our maidens, the chaste dignity of our matrons."[13]

Democratic Party leaders apparently did not share these reservations. The national convention nominated Johnson, choosing him over Virginia's William C. Rives 178 to 87. Questions about Johnson's familial circumstances, however, only heightened attention to one of the major southern Democratic questions about Van Buren: Could the New Yorker be trusted on the slavery issue? As the convention concluded, he clearly had work to do to convince southern Democrats that they could depend on him.[14]

THE WHIG CANDIDATES

The Democrats had found their candidate, but the Whigs were struggling to sort out their own campaign. The presumptive opposition candidate appeared to be Clay, who continued to express his alarm at the general course of the nation under Jackson. "Blackguards, Bankrupts and Scoundrels, Profligacy and Corruption are the order of the day, and no one can see the time when it will be changed," he complained to one friend. But personal circumstances, including the death of his daughter Anne in December 1835, led him to contemplate retirement. More importantly, the Whigs lacked enthusiasm for his candidacy. "Judging from all that I see and hear," Clay told one supporter, "the good opinion which you entertain of me is shar[e]d by too few to make it exp[ed]ient to present my name to the public." He blamed his loss in the 1832 election for causing "respectable portions of the Whigs, in different States, to divert their views to other Candidates than myself." Ultimately, Clay decided not to pursue the presidency in 1836.[15]

Clay's absence left the field wide open for other Whig aspirants to emerge as Van Buren's challenger. The party decided against holding a national convention or issuing an official nomination, thus allowing multiple contenders to come forward. Former US general William Henry Harrison was first mentioned as a possible candidate in the winter of 1834–35. The scion of a prominent and wealthy Virginia family, Harrison had served in the US Army under General Anthony Wayne in the 1790s. He was then selected as territorial delegate for the Northwest Territory and, subsequently, as territorial governor of Indiana. Harrison won fame prior to the War of 1812 by leading his men to victory over Native American forces at the Battle of Tippecanoe in November 1811. He also served in the War of 1812, rising to command the Army of the Northwest and winning a major victory at the Battle of the Thames. The death of Shawnee leader Tecumseh at this battle proved significant in quelling the Native American uprising in the Old Northwest (Illinois, Indiana, Michigan, part of Minnesota, Ohio, and Wisconsin); it also provided Harrison's campaign with the opportunity to portray him as a military hero. Following the war, he served in the Ohio state legislature and in both the US House and the US Senate. John Quincy Adams appointed him minister plenipotentiary to Colombia in 1828; just a few months later, President Jackson recalled him.[16]

When a Pennsylvania newspaper endorsed Harrison in mid-December 1834 as a possible presidential candidate for 1836, the sixty-one-year-old former general was serving as county clerk in North Bend, Ohio. Harrison, whom noted French observer Michel Chevalier described at the time as possessing "the active step and lively air of youth . . . [and] a certain air of command, which appeared through his plain dress," reacted to the newspaper endorsement with surprise. "Some folks are silly enough to have formed a plan to make a President of the United States out of this *Clerk* and Clodhopper!" he wrote his former comrade-in-arms Solomon Van Rensselaer. His friends, Harrison observed, thought he was "the only one at all likely to overthrow the Champion of the Empire State [Van Buren]." His candidacy was unexpected, but the Democrats' own success in running Andrew Jackson, a military hero, gave the Whigs hope that they could replicate their opponents' strategy.[17]

The second candidate to unfurl the Whig banner was Senator Hugh Lawson White. Prior to replacing Jackson in the US Senate in 1825, the East Tennessean had served as a state judge and legislator. White had been a loyal Jacksonian, supporting the president's congressional fight for Indian removal and against the BUS. Friction developed between the two, however, because of Jackson's decision to let White and John Eaton decide between themselves who would take the secretary of war position in his original cabinet. Eaton had convinced his rival that Jackson preferred him, so White had conceded the appointment. He resented Eaton for it, however, and became disenchanted with the president's decision making.[18]

Anti-Jackson Tennessee legislators had first discussed White as a candidate to succeed Old Hickory in late 1833, but they had decided against that course because "such a measure at this early day might be imprudent." The following December, after the Whig Party had formed, members of the state's congressional delegation moved ahead with their plan. White accepted their endorsement, and when the Alabama state legislature nominated him in January 1835, it provided the sixty-one-year-old senator's campaign with even more momentum. Even though he chose to join the Whig Party and challenge the president's endorsed successor, White remained popular with Tennessee Democrats. One pro-Jackson Nashville newspaper said that White was "an efficient, sincere, and independent, though not a sycophantic, supporter of the most important measures of General Jackson's Administration, and no man would, we are convinced, *carry out* those measures with more ability, firmness, and discretion." In some Tennesseans' eyes, the Whig White was the more logical heir to Jackson's legacy than Vice President Van Buren.[19]

White's supporters presented him as a safe alternative for those who liked Jackson but distrusted Van Buren and his "officeholders and demagogues." White himself argued that the Democrats were a party "composed of men belonging to every political sect, having no common bond of union save that of a wish to place one of themselves in the highest office known to the constitution, for the purpose of having all the honors, offices, and emoluments of the government distributed by him among his followers." Jackson, who believed that another former friend-turned-apostate, Representative John Bell, was behind the White candidacy, told James K. Polk that White was being "*used to distract and divide*" southern Democrats until they joined the Whigs in supporting Clay, whom Jackson thought would eventually become the Whigs' one and only candidate.[20]

The final Whig contender was Senator Daniel Webster of Massachusetts. As a leading Whig congressman, Webster seemed a logical choice to challenge Van Buren. He had served in the US House for eight years, then had been sent to the US Senate in 1827. Webster distinguished himself with his oratorical skills and his support of the Union during an 1830 Senate debate with Robert Y. Hayne of South Carolina. A tentative movement toward forming a Union Party that would unite Webster and Jackson even developed during the Nullification Crisis. Webster's support of the BUS, however, prevented that political coalition. In December 1834, shortly before his fifty-third birthday, Webster received the endorsement of the Boston *Atlas*. The Massachusetts legislature also nominated him the next month, putting three Whigs into the contest.[21]

On the surface, Webster appeared to be the strongest Whig challenger, but he floundered from the beginning. When a coalition of Pennsylvania Whigs and Anti-Masons nominated Harrison in December 1835, Webster understood that the loss of the Keystone State likely ended his campaign. Before he had entered the contest, he declared his loyalty to the new party by declaring that "however the Jackson jugglers may conduct their own nomination, the duty of the Whigs is plain . . . They will support a Whig, & none but a Whig." Webster decided to stay in the race to maintain the Whigs' semblance of strategy and to bolster their chances in the 1836 local and congressional elections. (A fourth Whig candidate, Supreme Court justice John McLean, made only a brief foray into the campaign before withdrawing.)[22]

One possible outcome of running multiple Whig candidates was producing a repeat of the 1824 election, which required the House to select a president. Even though Henry Clay was not in the race, he commented extensively on the prospect of a contested House election. He believed that regional differences made it unlikely that the Whigs would unite behind one candidate. Therefore, he told Samuel L. Southard, the party's best chance was to "run two Candidates, one to unite the Southern votes (let him be White, if they please) and the other to embody the votes of the States in favor . . . [of] opposition to Executive power and enmity to Va. Buren." If Whigs could do that, then Clay was confident that "V. Buren would enter the House the lowest Candidate." He thought that the two Whig candidates would likely be White, whom he believed was a Whig of convenience, not principle, and Harrison, whom he called "weak, vain, and far inferior to Webster." Still, Clay said about Harrison, "I believe him to be honest and of good intentions. Objectionable as he is, . . . he is preferable to either V. Buren or White."[23]

With multiple candidates running on the Whig side, a Democratic vice-presidential candidate whose private life challenged contemporary social norms, and a Democratic presidential nominee who was looking to succeed a controversial chief executive, the 1836 campaign was ripe for the increased use of cultural politics. What resulted was only a foreshadowing of what was to come.

CHAPTER 9

A Movement of the People

Some of the cultural politics employed in the early republic, and particularly in the three previous presidential elections, expanded during the 1836 campaign. Most prominent among those practices were public events, lithography, and campaign literature. Other aspects of cultural politics, such as campaign objects and music, were little used or showed no demonstrable increase in frequency. Of course, voters in this campaign had no idea how prominent cultural politics would become four years later.

PUBLIC EVENTS AND PUBLIC SPEECHES

Hugh Lawson White's supporters were especially adept at using public dinners and toasts to highlight his strengths and his opponent's weaknesses. His adherents held events for the US senator across the nation, but they were particularly active in Tennessee. At a Knox County, Tennessee, dinner, for example, toasts connected the Tennessee senator to Washington, Jefferson, and Madison; praised him for his political "consistency, independence and usefulness"; and promised that his home state would "sustain him firmly and fearlessly against the slanders of malice and magic of the most influential name," meaning Andrew Jackson. One toast at the dinner said of the soon-retiring president, "His memory is treacherous; he has forgotten his early friends and supporters, and listens only to the voice of flattery and the siren song of sycophancy. He misdirects his influence when he stoops to canvass for his successor." According to this supporter, White possessed none of these deficiencies.[1]

Harrison undertook the most innovative and vigorous Whig campaign. He did this despite BUS president Nicholas Biddle's observation that the old general should "say not one single word about his principles, or his creed." Harrison's success instead should "rely entirely on the past." If he heard Biddle's advice, Harrison chose to ignore it by taking his message straight to the voters. It was an intentional public campaign that he believed necessary to counteract questions about his political inexperience, age, and health.[2]

Beginning in the summer of 1835, Harrison traveled to the sites of his former military glory. In May, for example, he visited Vincennes, Indiana, where he gave a speech at a public dinner. After a lengthy recounting of his military career and the battle at Vincennes, Harrison spent the second half of his remarks denouncing "the weak, injudicious, presumptuous and unconstitutional efforts" of abolitionists and trumpeting his support of southern states' rights. One toast at the event remarked, "Like Cato, his countrymen are about to call him from the rural pursuits which have occupied his attention in later years, to preside as Chief Magistrate over the destinies of that nation known as *the Land of Washington*." Harrison then took a trip to the Tippecanoe battlefield, visiting several Indiana towns along the way. At various stops, locals feted him with public dinners and toasts, and the old general often made public remarks. At Tippecanoe, Harrison noted that "there would be an evident impropriety in introducing political topics" in his speech, but the tenor of the events and the topics of his speeches indicated that he and the attendees were not simply commemorating past military glory.[3]

Harrison continued this practice of meeting voters face to face, often at his home, throughout the campaign. Questions about his health, however, prompted him to spend the fall of 1836 touring the East Coast. Harrison's stated purpose for the trip—to show that he was not "an old broken down feeble man"—was successful. One observer noted that "the General is in vigorous health, and fine spirits, in fact looks younger than he did when I saw him twenty years ago." Privately, Harrison explained to a friend on reaching White Sulphur Springs, Virginia, "I am here in a way to give cause for no unfavorable remark. I am on a visit to near relatives whom I have not seen for several years. No one can with propriety object to it; particularly as I decline all public dinners, travel rapidly, and mingle as little as I can do without giving offence—with the people."[4]

Harrison did not want to give the opposition reason to accuse him of "traveling for the purpose of Electioneering," but his supporters had other ideas. Once he reached Richmond, Virginia, he began attending a series of public receptions and dinners along the eastern seaboard. In Baltimore, his speech to an "immense assemblage," given on a platform erected for the event, was "ready, fluent, and eloquent." A celebration in Philadelphia reportedly drew thirty thousand spectators, which Harrison capped off with a speech given across from Independence

Hall. After acknowledging his nomination and his father's role in gaining the nation's independence, he made a short political speech, concluding with the promise to "rigidly and to the utmost extent of my power to maintain the honor, glory, and dignity of my native land." Harrison continued on to New York, then turned toward home. All along the way, he met publicly with groups of citizens and made public remarks.[5]

Whig observers responded positively to Harrison's overt campaigning, a first for a presidential candidate. One editor wrote that the Philadelphia rally "was truly and emphatically a movement of the People, who permitted their feelings to have full vent, and poured forth in the true spirit of republicanism their gratitude towards one of the best and bravest of those who bared their bosoms to the bullets of the enemies of their country." Another commended Harrison for his "plain farmer-like appearance" and predicted that if he and Van Buren conducted a public tour together, then Harrison would easily win.[6]

Democrats, however, were appalled at Harrison's blatant stumping for votes, which blurred the line between the traditional political culture and the open campaigning that seemed to grow every election cycle. "For the first time in the history of this country, we find a candidate for the Presidency traversing the land as an openmouthed electioneerer for that high and dignified station," one Kentucky newspaper lamented. "Suppose that Martin Van Buren should take a tour through the western States, making speeches, eating public dinners, and eulogising himself in every way, whether in good or bad taste. — What would the whig editors say? . . . Call ye this consistency?" Another newspaper from that same state noted Harrison's calculated movements. "Several days in advance he notifies" his friends of his anticipated arrival time so that they had "an opportunity to turn out." This was not "electioneering and hunting the Presidency," the newspaper sarcastically sneered, but simply Harrison's chance to meet up with "his dear brother feds [Federalists]." William C. Rives told Van Buren that "the *grand electioneering tour*" appeared to be as much a failure as some of Harrison's military campaigns.[7]

While Harrison was publicly campaigning in 1835 and 1836, Van Buren observed the election from a distance. Following his nomination in May 1835, the New Yorker traveled to his home state to vacation. The vice president returned to New York as the election wound down the following year, splitting his time between Albany and short trips to places such as Oswego and Saratoga Springs. While he paid attention to the campaign and discussed it with supporters and voters alike, Van Buren likely saw no reason to follow in Harrison's footsteps, as his behind-the-scenes politicking, reflected in his Little Magician nickname, had always worked for him.[8]

AUXILIARY ORGANIZATIONS

As in previous campaigns, auxiliary organizations put together many of these public events to publicize their candidates. Democrats saw them as a means to make a smooth transition from Jackson to Van Buren. After Van Buren won the Democratic nomination in May 1835, some Hickory Clubs transformed into Kinderhook Clubs, named for his New York hometown. This change elicited criticism from Whigs, who wondered about the Democrats' willingness to switch allegiance from Jackson to Van Buren "without any compunc[tio]n of conscience." Whether Hickory or Kinderhook Clubs, these organizations made sure to remind Democrats that Jackson was the forefather of the party. At an 8 January 1834 commemoration of the victory over the British at New Orleans, a New Yorker toasted the Eighth Ward Hickory Club: "May they, like our venerable Chief Magistrate, whom they intend to honor, be always [f]ound in the front ranks maintaining the liberties and in[d]ependence of our beloved country."[9]

As had been the case in the previous two presidential campaigns, Democrats out-organized their opponents, but Whigs still saw the value of employing auxiliary organizations. In June 1836, Harrison supporters formed a Tippecanoe Club in Philadelphia's Northern Liberties neighborhood, and they held mass meetings in all regions of the country to generate enthusiasm for their candidate. Resolutions at a New York meeting pronounced that Harrison, like Jackson, was a man of the people, his candidacy "the result of the spontaneously avowed preference of the people." Attendees at that meeting made sure to note, however, that unlike Van Buren, their candidate stood "apart from organized party movements, unstimulated by needy office seekers, by hungry avarice or the accursed lust of power." A Harrisburg, Pennsylvania, newspaper proclaimed, "We had another tremendous Harrison Meeting.—All is excitement, confidence, exultation. His friends here are more enthusiastic than any party I ever saw or heard of. Such feelings must conquer." Supporters of Webster and White did not appear to establish formal clubs on par with the Kinderhook or Tippecanoe Clubs, but they still generated excitement with mass meetings. Reflecting their distinct regional appeals, White meetings took place throughout the South and Midwest, and Webster meetings were held in the New England and mid-Atlantic states.[10]

PUBLIC CORRESPONDENCE

The 1836 campaign witnessed an increased use of public correspondence. In large part, this proliferation proceeded from the growing racial discord taking place in the nation. During Jackson's presidency, questions about slavery once again came to the forefront of national politics, leading to debates that would not end until the Civil War. Nat Turner's short-lived 1831 rebellion in the Virginia countryside created widespread fear of slave insurrections across the South. The establishment of the American Anti-Slavery Society (AAS) in 1833 only heightened southerners' concerns about their right to own slave property. During a period of increasing violence, the number of antiabolition mobs peaked in 1835, the year that the AAS decided to pursue a national antislavery campaign. Depending largely on cultural politics to sway opinions, the AAS sent more than one million pieces of printed material through the postal system; it also distributed objects, such as handkerchiefs and medals, to raise awareness of slavery's evils.[11]

In this climate of fear, Van Buren found himself asked to explain publicly his thoughts about slavery. Southern critics wanted him to defend his actions during the Missouri Crisis of 1819–21, when he avoided declaring himself on the question of slavery's expansion, and at the New York constitutional convention of 1821, when he voted to lower property requirements for suffrage, which would have made it possible for free blacks to vote.[12]

Van Buren regularly responded to the allegations that he supported abolitionism. As he explained in a September 1835 letter to Georgia gubernatorial candidate William Schley, "The allegations which attribute to me views and opinions that are so justly obnoxious to the slave-holding States, are made in the face of the most explicit declarations on my part, denying all authority on the part of the Federal Government to interfere in the matter—against the propriety of agitating the question in the District of Columbia, and in the absence of a single fact, giving the least countenance to the unfounded imputations." Van Buren told Schley that he had "encouraged" the calling of a meeting of Albany citizens to discuss the subject of slavery and abolitionism. The Albany meeting passed resolutions that stated, in part, that according to the Constitution, "the relation of master and slave is a matter belonging exclusively to the people of each state within its own boundary." Van Buren told Schley, "[I] authorise you to say, that I concur fully in the sentiments they advance." In reply to a question about the topic posed by a group of North Carolinians, Van Buren declared that if elected president, he would be "the inflexible and uncompromising opponent of any attempt on the part of congress to abolish slavery in the District of Columbia, against the wishes of the slaveholding states." He also promised "to resist the slightest interference with the subject in the states where it exists" and cautioned both northerners and southerners to respect one another's opinions on slavery.[13]

The Democratic *Globe* applauded Van Buren's support of antiabolitionist resolutions originating from the Albany, New York, meeting. Its editor, Francis P. Blair, praised Van Buren for demonstrating that "he considers it a question of deeper import than one of mere administrative policy or party principle—as one involving the fate of the Confederacy, and the issues of peace or war." The *United States Telegraph* took a different tack. "The truth is that Mr. Van Buren has left the matter just as he found it," Duff Green wrote. "We know *now* just what we knew before. He declares that he is opposed to the *Immediate* Abolitionists. No one ever supposed that he was otherwise. He disclaims the right in Congress to emancipate the Slaves. So do the Abolitionists. He thinks it *impolitic* to abolish Slavery in the District; thus claiming a right in Congress to do so whenever they may deem it expedient."[14]

Whigs, like their opponents, had to address issues publicly as well. Hugh Lawson White answered a Richmond, Virginia, man's question about slavery in the nation's capital by telling him, "I do not believe congress has the power to abolish slavery in the District of Columbia, and if that body did possess the power, I think the exercise of it would be the very worst policy." Given White's base of support among slaveholders, his stance was unsurprising. Supporters also refuted the charge that he "locked arms with a *free negro* and walked with him to the ballot box" in 1825. A question among some Marylanders about Harrison's support of "*selling white men*" held in debtors' prison prompted him to issue a public response. "The charge is a vile calumny," he insisted. Harrison also replied in another public letter to a question about his role in burning a Moravian Indian town and its provisions during the War of 1812. He denied personal responsibility but indicated that he thought the action "perfectly justifiable" in the context of warfare.[15]

Even the Whigs' vice-presidential candidates found themselves drawn into the public fray. A group of Lexington, Kentucky, citizens wrote a public letter to Henry Clay asking if he could confirm whether Representative Francis Granger of New York, who appeared as the vice-presidential candidate on tickets with both Webster and Harrison, was an abolitionist and "one of the organs of that party." Based on his conversations with Granger, Clay replied publicly, "I understood him clearly and distinctly to disapprove of all interference with slavery, as it exists in the states tolerating that institution, either on the part of congress or the northern states." Likewise, Virginia's John Tyler, who appeared on some tickets with Harrison and some with White, found himself defending his senatorial record. He considered it "strange" that some Democrats thought that he supported the idea that Congress, "on an application of *the people* of the District, had a right to abolish slavery within the District." Instead, the Senate committee that Tyler chaired passed resolutions that, in part, stated that the end of slavery in the District of Columbia "would be unjust and despotic, and in violation of the constitution of the United States." In reality, he opposed the slave trade, but not slavery, his seemingly contradictory opinions on the issue mirroring some white southerners' ambivalence at that time.[16]

Surprisingly, given the criticism of Richard M. Johnson's mixed-race relationships, the Democratic vice-presidential contender escaped public questioning, if not criticism, on the issue of slavery. He did, however, encourage two friends, Thomas J. Pew and Rev. Thomas B. Henderson, to write public letters defending his "domestic relations." Henderson's letter was especially poignant, praising his neighbor for admitting that the daughters that Chinn bore him "are his children" instead of having "sent them to a cotton farm." Johnson wrote public letters himself to encourage Kentucky voters to set aside *the principles of party politics* and to support him as someone who had "served them faithfully without respect to persons or politics."[17]

POLITICAL MUSIC

Music played a limited but colorful role in the campaign theatrics of 1836. During Harrison's 1836 tour in the East, public events were replete with songs such as "'See the conquering hero comes'—together with Yankee Doodle and other national and appropriate airs." Other Whig songs took on a more negative tone. "King Andrew" (1834) reinforced Whig impressions that the Kitchen Cabinet controlled the president:

> King Andrew had five trusty Squires,
> Whom he held his bid to do,
> He also had three pilot fish,
> To give the sharks their cue.
> There was Lou, and Ben. And Lev, and Bill;
> And Roger of Tawney hue,
> And Blair the Book and Kendall chief cook,
> And Isaac surnamed the True.
> And Blair push'd Lewis and Ben touch'd Billy
> And Ike jogg'd Levi and *Cass* touch'd Amos
> And Roger of Tawney hue,
> Now was not this a medley crew
> As ever a mortal knew.

Another Whig song about Van Buren emphasized the vice president's alleged lust for power:

> Buren, Buren, luckless Van Buren,
> Your desperate ambition has met with its doom,
> Your Augean stable and vile kitchen vermin,
> Our freemen will sweep with the Harrison broom.

"Johnson's Wife of Old Kentucky," a Whig song that criticized Richard M. Johnson and his influence in a possible Van Buren administration, alluded to the questions about the Kentucky senator's personal life:

> And none amid the courtly throng
> Will lower bow to dusky Sukey,
> Than him, the little chief of all
> Our magic knight, bold Kinderhooky.
> Johnson's wife of old Kentucky,
> Johnson's wife of old Kentucky;
> She'll bask fore'er in fortune's smiles,
> The magic smiles of Kinderhooky. . . .
> Come kneel, ye slaves, on freedom's land,
> And own the sway of Kinderhooky;
> And when he waves his magic wand,
> Be sure to bow to dusky Sukey.[18]

Democrats used music less frequently than the Whigs, but they still took opportunities to mock their opponents. One song pointed out the Whigs' attachment to the BUS:

> A wiggy's life's a life of woe,
> He works now late now early;
> From DAN to NORTH BEND forced to go
> But to be shipwrecked yearly. . . .
> We fib a little, and forge a little,
> And screw a little, and bribe a little,
> And *Biddle* a little, and borrow a little,
>
> And milk our mother Bank—
> And milk our mother Bank.

Another mocked Harrison's status as a military hero:

Our pæans quite lately were raised, it is true,
To Harry the Turncoat [Clay], and Daniel the Blue [Webster],
But, finding the people could not be hoodwinked,
We'll next try a *"Hero whose eye never blinked!"*
Then huzza! for the General—the peerless and bold—
Let his *petticoat flag* to the breeze be unrolled;
Since with *Tories* and *Feds* all his wishes are linked,
They must VOTE *for the "Hero whose eye never blinked!"*[19]

MATERIAL CULTURE

One type of cultural politics that receded during this election was the production and use of campaign objects to attract voters. Roger A. Fischer, the foremost expert on presidential campaign memorabilia, identified only two Van Buren objects (a banner and a token), one each for Harrison (a token) and Webster (a snuff box), and none for White.[20]

That does not mean, however, that material culture disappeared. Between 1834 and 1836, the Whigs produced a plethora of objects not specifically intended for the presidential campaign but that made statements about the nation's partisan political environment. They used their official symbol (a liberty cap on top of a pole) on buttons, often with slogans such as "Whigs of 76 & 34" or "For the Constitution." Along similar lines, Whigs incorporated George Washington's image into paraphernalia, such as ribbons, to connect them to the Revolution. Additionally, they produced satirical tokens that portrayed Jackson as a jackass, mocked his alleged illiteracy by stamping them with "LL.D." (a reference to the honorary degree that Harvard gave him in 1833), and showed him holding a sword and removing bags of money from a vault, a reference to the fear of a despot controlling both sword and purse. This latter trope Whigs later found helpful as a weapon to use against Van Buren during his presidency.[21]

The Democrats continued to rely on tried-and-true material culture, specifically the sturdy hickory tree. Participants in an 1835 Democratic meeting in Wentworth, New Hampshire, erected "a hickory pole of prodigious length," and attendees heard a toast that invoked the hickory symbol: *"The Congress of the United States.*—May its deadly rotten brand [*sic*] (the Senate) be pruned from the main tree, and a pure hickory twig be engrafted therein." Other Democratic meetings used the hickory pole as landmarks for their meeting place. "Democrats! Remember the great meeting in the square, at the Hickory Pole," reminded one Pennsylvania newspaper. In almost every case, the hickory symbol was used to recall Old Hickory himself, Andrew Jackson. John Eaton, who had not yet decided to abandon the Democratic Party, sent Richard M. Johnson "a handsome gold mounted Hickory Cane, cut from the Hermitage," Jackson's Tennessee plantation home. Johnson expressed his thanks for the gift, which was "emblematical of that strength of character for which he [Jackson] has always been distinguished; and, like him, it is a support to the weak—a defence in danger."[22]

The *New York American* called this exchange "the sublime of the ridiculous," and Whigs reveled in arguing that if there was a symbol that best represented Van Buren, the supposed political manipulator, it was "the *slippery elm*." Whigs in Milton, Pennsylvania, even co-opted the hickory tree, putting on one a banner that read, "The People's choice for president, WILLIAM H. HARRISON, the farmer of North Bend, the hero of Tippecanoe and the Thames." When they did not find their own use for hickory objects, Whigs sometimes destroyed them. In Guilford, Connecticut, a Democratic newspaper reported that a hickory pole placed on the public square had been "sawed down." When it came time to vote for president, the editor urged, "We hope the democrats of that town will muster in their full strength . . . and erect the standard of liberty and justice so firmly that it cannot be sawed off, cut down, or rooted up."[23]

PRINT CULTURE

Print material from both parties expanded significantly during the 1836 campaign. Francis P. Blair's *Globe* continued to carry the Democratic banner in Washington, and several of the president's associates established the *Nashville Union* in his home state of Tennessee. (This latter effort was hampered by editor Samuel H. Laughlin's frequent bouts with alcoholism.) The *United States Telegraph* and the *Washington (DC) Daily National Intelligencer* proclaimed the Whig cause. The *Telegraph* first put forward Calhoun as a potential Whig presidential contender. When that suggestion fizzled, Duff Green supported White, then threw his weight behind Harrison. The *Intelligencer* wanted Webster; when he ostensibly withdrew as an active candidate, editors Joseph Gales Jr. and William W. Seaton, like Green, chose to back Harrison.[24]

Throughout the campaign, the Whigs continued to receive help in critiquing Van Buren from Green's *United States Telegraph*, the former Democratic mouthpiece. "All the Humbugites are rallying around Mr. Van Buren," the editor warned. "Van Burenism is the common sewer for all the filth of the country. Agrarianism, Fanny Wrightism, Abolitionism, Amalgamationism, all melt their distinguishing characteristics in Van Burenism." Green even lumped Van Buren with the emerging Church of Jesus Christ of Latter-day Saints (more commonly known as the Mormons). "We see by the Ohio State Journal that the Mormons have established a paper in which they raise the tri-coloured flag. Mormon, Van Buren, and Johnson—Yellow, blue, and black! Three great humbugs," Green wrote. "The New York magician is to be the Grand Interpreter of the Mormon Bible, *vice* Joe Smith, who will *resign* after the election of his old friend from New York!"[25]

The *United States Telegraph* also condemned the vice president for his allegedly ostentatious lifestyle. "It is certainly a matter of little consequence whether Mr. Van Buren rides in an English coach that cost $2,400, in a Yankee wagon worth $150, walks, rides on horseback, or gets along in any other way. He certainly has a right to do as he pleases," Green sniffed. "But we wish to see Mr. Van Buren presented to the people in his proper character. We do not like to see a proud, rich nabob, who dashes through our streets in a fine coach, with all the pomp and parade of an heir apparent, and who is attended by English waiters, *dressed in livery*, after the fashion of a British lord, attempt to pass himself off as a true workingman's democrat." Although Van Buren came from a modest economic background, this criticism was a constant refrain for the next four years and would be an important theme in the 1840 campaign.[26]

In addition to the continued influence of newspapers, campaign biographies appeared in greater numbers than in the previous election. William Emmons wrote a biography of Richard M. Johnson in 1833, with a new edition following the next year. In the 1834 edition, Emmons accused William Henry Harrison of downplaying Johnson's killing of Tecumseh, and he promised that "truth is mighty, and will prevail." Emmons also produced a Van Buren biography in 1835. It portrayed the vice president as the victim of "unnatural coalitions" who would "ultimately receive, at the hands of a free and intelligent community, a full and triumphant vindication."[27]

Whigs countered with their own works. They capitalized on the fame of David Crockett to issue a scurrilous biography of Van Buren under the Tennessee congressman's name. This biography was likely ghostwritten by Georgia Whig Augustin S. Clayton, but it captured the frontier persona that Crockett cultivated. "Many persons will take up this book with an expectation that they will be very much amused at my odd expressions, and hope to find a number of droll stories to laugh at," "Crockett" observed, "but they ought to recollect that the life of a man that is about to clothe his country in sackcloth and ashes is no laughing matter." Democrats "know that Van ain't the choice of the people, no how, nor of his *whole* party." A novel by Nathaniel Beverly Tucker, a leading southern intellectual, conceived of a future world in which Van Buren was elected "to the presidential throne" term after term until 1848, leading the southern states, but not Tucker's Virginia, to secede.[28]

Other Whig publications focused on lauding Harrison. Henry K. Strong, editor of the *Pennsylvania Intelligencer*, wrote A *Brief History of the Public Services of Gen. William Henry Harrison*. Strong proclaimed that Harrison "possesses the true bravery of the school of [George] Washington . . . His services have been many, his sufferings great, and verily he deserves the gratitude of his countrymen." James Hall's A *Memoir of the Public Services of William Henry Harrison* highlighted Harrison's military heroism and rural connection. "The politicians may hesitate, because he owes them nothing," Hall wrote. "The leaders of parties may stand aloof, because he is not enlisted under any of their banners.—He is the candidate of the people, chosen by themselves from their own ranks, and indebted to none but them for their support."[29]

The character of Major Jack Downing, who first appeared in 1830, produced some of the most interesting literary observations used during the presidential campaign. Maine writer Seba Smith created Downing to make light-hearted, satirical jabs at national politicians, particularly Jackson. For example, Downing's cousin, Ephraim, wrote him about a situation in their hometown of Downingville that readers who followed the Eaton affair would have recognized. Ephraim said that General Combs fired one of their cousins, Joshua, because some of their female relatives "wouldn't invite poor Mrs. No-tea to their husking and quilting parties." (Astute readers could see that "Mrs. No-tea" was supposed to represent Margaret Eaton.) Ephraim described the general as "hopping mad" and determined that "he would turn out every man and woman off of his farm and out of his mills rather than that good woman should be treated in the manner she had been."[30]

Other writers, Charles Augustus Davis being the most prominent, co-opted the Jack Downing character for more stridently partisan purposes. A BUS supporter, Davis's satire proved more biting than Smith's. In one episode, his Downing character addressed Van Buren's chances in 1836. The fictional major related his opinion that "Mr. Van Buren would stand a good chance in a race, when a good many are runnin, and if the ground is muddy and slippery; for he is a master hand at trippin folks." If Clay was the vice president's only opponent, however, Downing believed "he'd stand a slim chance." If that happened, then he agreed with Jackson's decision to "hold on for a third heat," or a third term, a prospect that some Whigs still thought that the "American Caesar" might pursue.[31]

VISUAL CULTURE

Lithography emerged as a major part of cultural politics in the 1836 presidential campaign, with Whigs producing the most examples. One of the most prominent lithographs was a cartoon entitled *King Andrew the First* (1833). It presents Jackson as a despotic monarch trampling on a torn Constitution. He holds a veto in his hand, symbolic of his veto of the 1832 Second Bank recharter bill. An 1834 version attributed to lithographer Edward Clay includes text outlining the president's abrogation of constitutional power. It describes him as "A KING who has placed himself above the laws, . . . who would destroy our currency, . . . [who] was feeding his favourites out of the public money, . . . [and] whose *Prime Minister* and *Heir Apparent*, was thought unfit for the office of ambassador by the people." It ends with the question, "Shall he reign over us, Or shall the PEOPLE RULE?"[32]

Other Whig examples of visual criticism centered on gaming or sporting themes. *All Fours—Important State of the Game—The Knave about to Be Lost* (1836) depicted Van Buren and Harrison playing cards. Jackson peers over Harrison's shoulder, signaling which cards he holds and exclaiming, "What a h——l of a hand old Harrison's got." Richard M. Johnson stands behind the New Yorker, telling him that Harrison's cards mean that "the jig's up! You'd better beg." Another lithograph, *Grand Match Between the Kinderhook Poney and the Ohio Ploughman* (1836), used a billiards game between Harrison and Van Buren as the setting. In intentional placement, Harrison stands under a portrait of George Washington, while Jackson appears under a portrait of Napoleon Bonaparte. A third pro-Harrison lithograph, *Set-to between the Champion Old Tip & the Swell Dutcheman of Kinderhook* (1836), portrayed a boxing match between Harrison and Van Buren. Different figures representing true Americanism stand in the crowd adding commentary. A frontiersman expresses great confidence in Harrison's ultimate success. "Whoop! wake snakes!" the "Western lad" cries. Harrison "puts it into him as fast as a streak of greased lightning through a gooseberry bush. That 'Cold blooded' Kinderhooker will be row'd up Salt River or I'm a nigger!" A Revolutionary War veteran ("Old Seventy-six") expresses the Whigs' hope for Harrison: "Thank Heaven the People have a Champion at last who will support the Constitution and laws that we fought and bled to obtain." Harrison, meanwhile, tells Van Buren, "Look out for your bread-basket Matty, I'll remove the deposits for you," a reference to one of the major issues of the Bank War. In Van Buren's corner, Jackson calls for Amos Kendall, who holds a bottle of alcohol, to give the New Yorker some liquid courage. Van Buren demonstrates his dependency on the president by pleading, "Stand by me Old Hickory or I'm a gone Chicken!"[33]

The Whigs directed some of their most creative ire against Richard M. Johnson. *An Affecting Scene in Kentucky* (likely 1836) depicts Johnson in dismay at a Whig newspaper attack on his "domestic situation." He cries, "When I read the scurrilous attacks in the Newspapers on the Mother of my Children, pardon me, my friends if I give way to feelings!!!" He then asks his "dear Girls to bring me

FIGURE 6. Edward Williams Clay's *Set-to between the Champion Old Tip & the Swell Dutcheman of Kinderhook* (1836) shows that despite the presence of three Whig candidates, contemporaries understood that the real contest in 1836 was between Van Buren and Harrison. The boxing-ring setting and the comments of onlookers underscore Jacksonian expectations about masculinity. Prints and Photographs Division, Library of Congress, http://www.loc.gov/pictures/item/2008661284/.

your Mother's picture, that I may show it to my friends here," which one of them does. A male observer comments, "Pickle! Pop!! and Ginger!!! Can the slayer of Tecumseh be thus overcome like a summer cloud!" An abolitionist and an African American man offer Johnson their support, while the postmaster hints at the Democrats' allegedly corrupt patronage by saying, "Your Excellency, I am sure all of us Postmasters and deputies will stick to you; if you promise to keep us in office."[34]

What these and several other examples of lithography demonstrate is the growing awareness of visual imagery's place in US politics. In an era when few Americans ever met or interacted with presidential candidates, colorful illustrations that captured political messages potentially carried significant weight with eligible voters. The Whigs latched on to this type of cultural politics and used it to good effect in 1836, as well as four years later during the Log Cabin and Hard Cider campaign.[35]

AN AFFECTING SCENE IN KENTUCKY.

FIGURE 7. Richard M. Johnson's vice-presidential nomination elicited many criticisms because of his alleged common-law marriage to Julia Chinn, an enslaved woman. *An Affecting Scene in Kentucky* [1836?] illustrates a Whig attack on Johnson and his two daughters by Chinn. Prints and Photographs Division, Library of Congress, http://www.loc.gov/pictures/item/2008661287/.

WOMEN'S ACTIVITY

As Lydia Maria Child observed in 1835, "The women of the United States have no direct influence in politics; and here, as in England, it is deemed rather un-feminine to take an earnest interest in public affairs." Yet, as they had in previous election cycles, women continued to play a visible, but still limited, role in the 1836 campaign.[36]

The presence of women in the Whig camp was widely acknowledged. One young woman wrote a pro-Harrison poem that led a newspaper editor to remark, "We are glad she is for Harrison—though we understand most of the Ladies are so." The poem said, in part,

'TIS not for martial glory,
For battles bravely won,
Fit themes of song and story,

We laud his name alone;
But for the noble heart and pure,
In *every station* tried,
And ever constant to endure;
A guardian and a guide.[37]

Whig women also made themselves visible in public settings. During Andrew Jackson's journey to his Hermitage plantation in July 1836, women in Dandridge, Tennessee, gathered alongside his route not just to honor him but to indicate their support of White. "The ladies dressed in white, waved their white handkerchiefs as he passed," a Nashville newspaper reported. "Every lady who had or could procure a white dress, waited on, and congratulated him on his arrival." Along with other symbols of White support (e.g., a white oak, white flags, etc.), the women of Dandridge were letting Jackson and the Democrats know that "they are immutably resolved to resist every influence which can be brought to bear upon them for the purpose of inducing them to desert the man of their choice, Judge White."[38]

Other Whig women participated in public meetings. One toast at a Portland, Maine, Whig meeting, "sent in by a Lady," read, "Martin Van Buren—Had his vote succeeded in muzzling the Press, it would have put a glorious finish to our land of Liberty, and Lynch laws, where ministers of the gospel are tarred and feathered by way of pasttime, and negroes are roasted with impunity." Another Whig toast "by a lady" remarked, "Bachelors and Van Burenism, alike selfish and unpatriotic, enemies to the *union* and *better-half* of the nation." Yet another woman at a Milford, Connecticut, Whig meeting made the following toast: "The Tree of Liberty; may it ever remain sound at heart, and every Jackson twig wither and fall to the ground like a canker worm." The newspaper editor made sure to note that this last toast was "delivered in person," an important signal to readers that by their physical presence, women were endorsing the Whig Party's activities. In almost every respect, Whigs appeared to more actively include women during the campaign, something they would replicate in the next presidential election.[39]

On the Democratic side, women generally took a less visible role. Arkansas women "participated in the festivities" of a Democratic event commemorating the Fourth of July, but their role was limited to an evening ball. Pro–Van Buren toasts by women are noticeably lacking from the newspapers, with the few recorded toasts instead trumpeting Jackson and his heroism at New Orleans. Even their songs focused on Jackson's martial victories, not Van Buren's candidacy. One

Columbia, Tennessee, newspaper printed the lyrics to "Welcome Jackson," which began,

> Welcome mighty Chief again!
> Thou hast number'd well thy slain;
> Hero of the battle plain,
> And of Liberty.[40]

The two notable exceptions on the Democratic side were Lucy Kenney and Frances Wright. Kenney, of Fredericksburg, Virginia, wrote glowingly of Jackson and Van Buren in a published pamphlet. "Gen. Jackson had been brought by the special interposition of Providence in due time, to remedy all the evils which would have resulted from a different administration," she said in 1835. His administration was "pure, noble, high-spirited, and unwavering." Van Buren, meanwhile, was "our next rising sun that will warm and light this lower world . . . whose meridian splendor will shine with such effulgent lustre as will illuminate the hemisphere in which his destiny is cast."[41]

Freethinking feminist Frances Wright, who founded an antislavery utopian community in Tennessee in the 1820s, took a very public role in supporting Van Buren's candidacy. It was an odd choice, considering Wright's public fight against slavery and her belief that the two-party system was corrupt. Nevertheless, she traveled across the country trumpeting the righteousness of the Democratic Party. At a wire factory located at the falls of the Schuylkill River north of Philadelphia, she railed, in a "sweet, rich" voice, against the Second Bank's recharter, calling it "the death knell of our freedom." Wright also argued that "the best remedies for Southern Slavery" would require "that the inhabitants of the North should reform their own Society first, and then the Southern would be induced to follow their example." She encountered significant opposition in finding venues that would host her lectures; in one editor's assessment, "the very course taken to put her down, has made her more notorious."[42]

Whigs reveled in vilifying Wright. They associated her with Abner Kneeland, a Universalist newspaper editor in Boston arrested for blasphemy for, among other things, writing that the Whigs were part of an aristocracy founded on "a Book [the Bible], which they call a revelation from this imaginary personage [God]," while Democrats pursued a rational "TRUTH." Whigs stripped Wright of her feminine identity by criticizing her as "a 'whole hog Van Buren man'" for giving political lectures in favor of the Democratic candidate. They also invoked the diminutive form of her name (Fanny) to indicate a host of Democratic shortcomings, including "Fanny Wright radicalism," "a man of infidel sentiments, a Fanny Wright man," "Fanny Wrightism and [racial] amalgamation," and "a thorough going *loco foco* Fanny Wright democrat."[43]

Whigs found Wright's speechmaking "a particularly vicious threat, one that combined irreligion, calls for sexual transformation, and working-class consciousness," according to historian Lori D. Ginzberg. One publication, which called Wright "that priestess of Infidelity . . . urged on by Satan," described her destructive influence:

> Wives, once happy in their husbands' arms, seduced by her diabolical doctrines, parted from the peaceful and lovely paths of virtue and affection at home, strayed into the mazy meanderings of sinful pleasure, abandoned themselves to indiscriminate indulgence in libidinous practices, and are now among the mass of moral putrefaction that tenant the temples of infamy.

In other words, Whigs argued, electing Van Buren, who deigned to associate himself with a woman such as Wright, was tantamount to destroying the moral foundations of the republic. The contrast with Jackson's reputation as the defender of female virtue twelve years earlier was glaringly obvious, and if Democrats were paying attention, they should have sensed the trouble that Van Buren was going to face following in Jackson's footsteps.[44]

One failed Democratic attempt to use women as moral representatives illustrated the stark contrast between the two parties. At a Van Buren meeting held on 8 January 1836, former US representative William Allen claimed that in 1813, the women of Chillicothe presented Harrison with a petticoat for ordering Major George Croghan to abandon Fort Stephenson when it came under British attack. The presentation of the petticoat implied that Harrison was a coward. As one Democratic newspaper reported, the truth of the story did not matter, only that "the 'heroine' of Tippecanoe . . . richly deserved" the petticoat.[45]

Whigs were livid at this challenge to Harrison's masculinity and military heroism, saying "a ruse so contemptible is only worthy of the parisites of the little Magician [Van Buren]." One Whig publicly called Allen "a Liar and a Scoundrel," comments that usually, but not in this case, led to a duel. But Whigs were also concerned with the insult to the Chillicothe women. At a September meeting of the Young Men's Harrison Convention, delegates approved a resolution that sought "to remove from the ladies an imputation injurious to their sense of propriety" by declaring that the petticoat story was "utterly false, and that nothing like it ever transpired." Whigs acknowledged, as one toast articulated, that "The Ladies—though personally excluded—are always remembered and spoken of on public occasions." In this instance, Democrats learned that using women as political pawns in a presidential campaign could backfire.[46]

A TEPID DEMOCRATIC VICTORY

The election's results seemingly confirmed the nation's support for the Democrats. Van Buren won with 170 electoral votes, while the three Whig candidates combined for 113 votes, with Harrison securing 73, White 26, and Webster 14. (In a show of defiance typical of South Carolina during this period, the state gave its 13 votes to native son Willie P. Mangum.) The popular vote showed the closeness of the election, however. While Van Buren's 762,765 votes easily outdistanced Harrison's 541,190, White's 138,250, and Webster's 40,149, the total Whig vote of 734,829 represented a 49.07 percent minority. Van Buren's winning margin of almost 28,000 popular votes and 50.93 percent majority against the combined Whig opposition fell well below Jackson's victorious margin of 161,950 popular votes and 54.1 percent majority four years earlier.[47]

Van Buren also struggled with the Jacksonian base. He lost support in every southern state that allowed voters to cast ballots in the 1832 election, and White defeated the New Yorker in two states in which Jackson had previously done well: Georgia and Old Hickory's home state of Tennessee. The vote was so close in 1836, in fact, that as Clay predicted, the House could easily have decided it, just as in 1824. If Van Buren had lost New York, Pennsylvania, or Virginia, then he would have failed to win the requisite 148 electoral votes needed to become president. His margin of victory in two of those three states was minimal: 4,326 in Pennsylvania and 6,883 in Virginia.[48]

The vice-presidential race also revealed the fractures present in the Democratic Party. Virginia electors refused to support Johnson, which prevented him from acquiring the necessary majority to become vice president. That left the decision to the Senate, which elected Johnson over Whig candidate Francis Granger 33 to 16. To the relief of Democrats, only one of their party broke rank and voted with the Whigs in opposition to Johnson. Whigs were less than thrilled with the prospect of Johnson in the vice-presidential seat. North Carolina representative James Graham wrote his brother, "Dick is dead weight to carry. He is not only a man of vulgar habits and loose morals, but destitute of talent and propriety."[49]

Van Buren's victory in the 1836 election allowed Democrats to argue that their party encompassed more than just Andrew Jackson's larger-than-life personality. While many recognized that Van Buren, not Jackson, was the architect of the Democratic Party, they understood that Americans would judge the New Yorker's success according to the standard set by Old Hickory. The Whigs failed to win the presidency in 1836, but the economic depression that consumed Van Buren's administration provided them with the very real prospect of electing their first president just six years into their existence.

CHAPTER 10

He Will Be a Party President

With the election settled, attention turned to Van Buren. The Little Magician faced obstacles in working his sorcery to unite the Democratic Party in the face of Whig opposition. Every indication suggested that the political operative who worked so masterfully behind the scenes would find success, but there were signs of pending doom if Van Buren and the Democrats chose to look closely. Unfortunately for them, they did not.

FROM OLD HICKORY TO SLY FOX

Interested observers were divided over the nation's future under Van Buren. James Buchanan called his election "emphatically the triumph of democratic principles." He went on to declare, "We have every thing to hope & nothing to fear from his character. We may anticipate comparative peace & quiet in his day; for nearly all the exciting questions of the time have been happily settled by the bold & commanding genius of General Jackson." Former New York City mayor Philip Hone celebrated "the end of General Jackson's administration, — the most disastrous in the annals of the country" and indicated his desire to give Van Buren "a fair chance." Hone wrote in his diary, "He will be a party President, but he is too much of a gentleman to be governed by the rabble who surrounded his predecessor and administered to his bad passions." John C. Calhoun was not as optimistic. "There is a fixed determination on the part of every branch of the opposition to wage war against the Usurper," he told Samuel D. Ingham. To another correspondent, the South Carolinian wrote, "Van Buren goes in very weak and may be easily crushed with any thing like a vigorous effort." Edward Everett wrote Daniel Webster that Massachusetts Whigs were experiencing "the fear of change which perplexes monarchs." Everett's only consolation was that conditions under Jackson had become so bad, "it is not easy to change for the worse."[1]

At Van Buren's inauguration on 4 March 1837, he used his initial address to remind the twenty thousand listeners present at the Capitol that "party exasperation has been often carried to its highest point; the virtue and fortitude of the people have sometimes been greatly tried; yet our system, purified and enhanced in value by all it has encountered, still preserves its spirit of free and fearless discussion, blended with unimpaired fraternal feeling." He also dedicated a lengthy paragraph to the issue of "domestic slavery." Reminding Americans of his opposition to ending slavery in the nation's capital and his desire to leave it untouched in the present slaveholding states, Van Buren promised "that no bill conflicting with these views can ever receive my constitutional sanction." He also informed them that "the principle that will govern me in the high duty to which my country calls me is a strict adherence to the letter and spirit of the Constitution as it was designed by those who framed it." Van Buren vowed, "To matters of domestic concernment which it has intrusted to the Federal Government and to such as relate to our intercourse with foreign nations I shall zealously devote myself; beyond those limits I shall never pass." Despite being "the first president to use the word slavery in an inaugural address," one historian has noted, Van Buren offered nothing new in his message. His inaugural address "was essentially a charter for inaction, a call to do nothing more than run the shop" in the same manner as Jackson. That Van Buren kept Jackson's existing cabinet intact spoke to his desire to maintain the status quo.[2]

One topic that received only superficial mention in Van Buren's inaugural address was the nation's economy. "Our commerce has been extended to the remotest nations; the value and even nature of our productions have been greatly changed; a wide difference has arisen in the relative wealth and resources of every portion of our country," he told listeners. "Yet the spirit of mutual regard and of faithful adherence to existing compacts has continued to prevail in our councils and never long been absent from our conduct." What Van Buren and the Democrats could not have predicted was that although they had control of the executive branch for the next four years, an economic depression would disrupt "the spirit of mutual regard," providing Whigs with the very real possibility of seizing the presidency for the first time in 1840.[3]

THE ECONOMICS OF THE VAN BUREN PRESIDENCY

The economic downturn that began shortly after Van Buren took office is often referred to as the Panic of 1837. Historian Jessica M. Lepler has argued, however, that American politicians and newspaper editors turned many individual panics in 1837 into a ten-week singular crisis. The use of the term "panic" to describe either individual economic choices or their national implication had meaning in Jacksonian America. During the Bank War of Jackson's presidency, the word came "to refer to a financial crisis with an illegitimate, politically inspired cause," according to Lepler. The choice of that term in 1837, she suggested, allowed Americans to blame "their troubles on collective forces beyond the control of all but political elites."[4]

The origins of the 1837 economic crisis were complex. An influx of foreign specie (i.e., gold and silver coins) into the United States in the latter part of Jackson's second term increased the money supply by more than 100 million dollars between 1834 and 1836. Combined with the surplus government revenue left over from paying off the national debt in 1834, banks were able to issue new loans using bank notes (i.e., paper money) instead of specie. In 1836, however, English banks began to reverse the flow of specie back to Europe. US banks, no longer able to guarantee their loans with specie, stimulated an economic contraction by not issuing new loans and by denying extensions on current ones.[5]

Exacerbating this contraction were two actions undertaken by Jackson and his congressional supporters in 1836. One was the Deposit-Distribution Act, which required the creation of more banks in which government deposits would be made and ordered the distribution of the surplus revenue to the states. The second was a Treasury order, called the Specie Circular, which stipulated that government land purchases were to be paid in specie, not bank notes. The movement of funds required by the Deposit-Distribution Act occurred as British banks were making their move to restrict credit to British companies invested in the United States, which added to the lack of available funds. The Specie Circular had the simultaneous effect of undermining confidence in bank notes.[6]

Facing a divided party and nation, Van Buren decided to continue the Specie Circular, believing that it provided the only way to save deposit banks in the West and Southwest. To do otherwise, he argued to William C. Rives, would lead to calls for a renewal of the BUS, which was unacceptable for true Jacksonian Democrats. As these varied economic circumstances came together in May 1837, some mercantile firms and one bank closed. In response, almost every bank in the nation followed the lead of their prominent New York peers in halting specie payments.[7]

The actual economic effects of these circumstances were short lived, but the social and political consequences were significant. Newspapers began discussing the economic "panic" that had overtaken the country, feeding the fear of average

Americans that a financial depression had fallen upon them. Both Democrats and Whigs used the opportunity to blame the other party for the economic distress. Democrats condemned "the bankites of Philadelphia and Washington" and Whig newspapers for creating the illusion of "an excessive panic, to destroy all confidence." Whigs responded by declaring, "The cry of panic is no party whoop. Distress is no phantom invoked for the promotion of special political ends and objects."[8]

Under pressure to respond to the economic crisis, on May 15, Van Buren called for a special session of Congress to meet in September. Prior to this special session, the new president decided to adopt Treasury clerk William M. Gouge's idea to place federal deposits in an independent treasury instead of trusting them to state banks. His September 4 message to the special session laid out his independent treasury plan. Of the three available alternatives, Van Buren argued, his idea made the most sense. Reviving the BUS was out of the question; to do so, the president argued, "would be to disregard the popular will, twice solemnly and unequivocally expressed." Neither were the pet banks favored by Jackson an option because, in Van Buren's estimation, they "stimulated a general rashness of enterprise and aggravate[d] the fluctuations of commerce and the currency." Instead, he outlined a system that would place government deposits in an independent treasury, with subtreasury branches spread across the nation. In essence, he sought to use the independent treasury as a replacement for the duties formally conducted by the Second Bank of the United States. The message, Blair's *Globe* declared, was "the boldest and highest stand ever taken by a Chief Magistrate in defence of the rights of the people."[9]

Van Buren's proposal to permanently separate, or divorce, the Treasury from the nation's banks "defined the central domestic issue of his entire presidency," according to historian Major Wilson. From late 1837 to early 1839, Van Buren and his allies tried and failed to pass an independent treasury bill three times. The first attempt to "divorce" the federal government from its reliance on banks for government deposits came in October 1837. The Senate ultimately passed an independent treasury bill by a party line vote, 26 to 20, but the House voted to postpone taking up the bill, 120–107. Indicating intraparty division about how best to address the economy, 16 Democrats broke ranks to vote for the bill's postponement, and 7 abstained.[10]

The second attempt to pass such a bill came in early 1838. After a tumultuous session marked by a duel between two congressmen, Democrat Jonathan Cilley of Maine and Whig William J. Graves of Kentucky, which resulted in Graves mortally wounding Cilley, the Senate narrowly passed the independent treasury bill, 27 to 25, on March 26. Highlighting the issue's divisiveness, several Democrats, including John C. Calhoun, James Buchanan, and Felix Grundy, were among the negative votes. On June 25, however, the House voted down the independent treasury bill 125 to 111. Once again, the president held the Senate and lost the House. Despite these setbacks, the economy improved enough that banks resumed specie payments, allowing Democrats to win back some of the previous year's political losses in the fall elections. Neither party, however, could claim to possess a mandate from the people.[11]

Without a clear Democratic victory in the fall elections, Democrats were unable to force through a divorce bill in the winter congressional session of 1838–39, the third such failure since Van Buren took office. Not until the election year of 1840 were Democrats successful in passing an independent treasury bill: 24–18 in the Senate in January and 124–107 in the House in June. Van Buren signed the bill, which allowed for federal regulation of banks and required specie payment for federal debts, on July 4, leading some Democrats to call it a "Second Declaration of Independence." In reality, as historian Donald B. Cole pointed out, the independent treasury bill of 1840 "simply made official" what Secretary of the Treasury Levi Woodbury had been doing all along: separating federal deposits from the nation's banks. By that point, however, the 1840 campaign had taken on a life of its own, and policy issues had been largely relegated to the background.[12]

NONECONOMIC ISSUES

While the nation's economic health drew much of Van Buren's attention, other issues also challenged his leadership. Several foreign policy crises called into question his political decision making. He also had to address the serious quandary posed by slavery, which continued to grow in political importance throughout his time in office.

Texas caused one of Van Buren's first foreign policy challenges. The Texas issue became verboten for Democrats in 1836 because of the questions about Van Buren's commitment to the "peculiar institution." Not wanting to jeopardize his vice president's chances of victory, Jackson, who had eyed Texas as a potential source of westward expansion for years, waited until the end of his administration to recognize the newly independent Texas republic. Upon taking office, Van Buren shied away from the Texas issue. In August 1837, Secretary of State John Forsyth publicly outlined Van Buren's decision: annexing a sovereign state was constitutionally questionable, and it risked putting the United States at war with Mexico. Though he did not say so publicly, Van Buren's primary concerns were to keep alive his independent treasury plan and to avoid fracturing the Democrats even further. While the president wanted to improve his standing in the South, he believed that favoring annexation would do more harm than good.[13]

Tensions with Great Britain also escalated during Van Buren's administration. In Canada, British citizens and former Americans who had moved into the British-controlled territory rose up in rebellion. Fearing that assistance for the rebels was coming from the US side of the border, in late December 1837, British troops boarded and sank an American steamship, the *Caroline*, that was operating on the Niagara River near Buffalo, New York. Upon receiving word of the potential international crisis, Van Buren sent General Winfield Scott to quell unrest among American citizens who were clamoring for war. Periodic disturbances continued to break out along the border, however. Later in 1838, a boundary dispute between Maine and New Brunswick over timber rights in the Aroostook Valley led to Governor John Fairfield ordering ten thousand militia into the field to defend Maine's honor. Van Buren responded by warning Fairfield that his state would fight alone if it continued to occupy the disputed territory, but he also cautioned Great Britain that the United States was willing to defend Maine if it were attacked. Once again, he sent Scott to the scene to work out a resolution, which he did successfully in March 1839. Three years later, the Webster-Ashburton Treaty of 1842, which defined the US-Canadian border, lessened the tension with the British on this issue.[14]

An additional situation that held both domestic and foreign policy implications was Native American relations resulting from Jackson's presidency. Van Buren came into office determined to carry out what he considered the "philanthropic and enlightened policy" of removing Indians to the West. This "settled policy of the country" included completing the removal of the Cherokees in 1838 along what became known as the Trail of Tears, which led to the deaths of one-quarter of that tribal group. Van Buren told Congress in his second annual message that the removal policy had produced "the happiest effects" and that the Cherokees had "emigrated without any apparent reluctance." He also continued prosecuting the Second Seminole War begun under Jackson. Van Buren repeatedly blamed the Seminoles for engaging in "acts of treachery and murder" that prolonged the war against them. The conflict, which ended after he left office, resulted in the deaths of at least several hundred Seminoles and nearly fifteen hundred US soldiers.[15]

Besides the nation's economy and Indian removal, the other major domestic issue facing Van Buren's administration was the debate over slavery. The president's mediocre showing in the South during the 1836 campaign convinced him that he needed to bolster his proslavery credentials. To that end, Van Buren made his strong defense of slavery in his inaugural address. He also supported Calhoun's proslavery resolutions, introduced in the winter 1837–38 congressional session. These resolutions, which comfortably passed the Senate with near-unanimous Democratic support, advocated for the right of states to their "domestic institutions" and pressed for the federal government to protect that right. They also called for the protection of slavery in the District.[16]

In 1839, the *Amistad* incident presented the president with another opportunity to demonstrate his fidelity to slavery. A group of enslaved Africans had killed their captors and seized control of the Spanish ship *Amistad*, mistakenly directing it to Long Island. These enslaved people were taken to Connecticut, where they awaited resolution of their status. In January 1840, Van Buren, supported by his attorney general, secretary of state, and secretary of the navy, issued an executive order instructing that the enslaved men be released to Spanish authorities. Abolitionists intervened, and the enslaved peoples' status eventually made its way to the US Supreme Court. In March 1841, the justices ruled that the enslaved men should return to Africa. Distracted by the need to appoint two new cabinet officers, Van Buren let the decision go by unremarked.[17]

These instances of proslavery support, along with Van Buren's continuation of Indian removal, seemed to bode well for his standing among white southern voters in 1840. He had also demonstrated his commitment to forcefully, yet peacefully, stand up to foreign threats to American sovereignty. What ultimately determined Van Buren's reelection chances, though, was the national economy. The question was, Would the Whigs be able to take advantage of this opportunity?

CHAPTER 11

Bring Out the Hurra Boys

Van Buren's struggle to solve the nation's economic issues gave Whigs hope for the 1840 election. With a level of activity unmatched by the Democratic Party, the Whigs' Log Cabin and Hard Cider campaign fully employed the cultural politics developed over the last several decades to significantly expand popular election-eering and create, for the first time, the exuberant presidential campaign cycle that remains to the present day.

THE CANDIDATES AND THEIR ORGANIZATIONS

Prior to meeting at the Whig national convention in late 1839, the party discussed several possible nominees. The most obvious choice was Senator Henry Clay, rejuvenated by his congressional fights with administration supporters. Daniel Webster also remained a well-respected senator, and William Henry Harrison had proved that his age and fade into obscurity prior to the 1836 campaign were not fatal political flaws. Van Buren's foreign policy had also elevated General Winfield Scott's reputation, making him a younger alternative to Harrison if the Whigs de-sired a military man.[1]

By 1839, the Whigs were also in the hands of new, younger party managers who wanted to take the election away from the old guard (Clay and Webster) and pursue a fresh strategy that would bring them victory. These new party managers, centered in New York and Pennsylvania, included Thurlow Weed, editor of the *Albany Evening Journal*; New York governor William H. Seward; *Log Cabin* edi-tor Horace Greeley; Pennsylvania canal commissioner Thaddeus Stevens; and former Pennsylvania governor Joseph Ritner. Others included Boston *Atlas* editor Richard Hildreth and Ohio congressman Thomas Corwin, nicknamed the "Wagon

Boy" and "King of the Stump." These individuals wanted anyone but Clay, someone new who was not associated with the party battles of the Jackson presidency, someone whom they could present as the champion of the common American. This person also had to be someone who could address what US representative Millard Fillmore saw as the Whigs' major challenge. "Into what crucible can we throw this heterogeneous mass of old national republicans, and revolting Jackson men; Masons and anti-Masons; Abolitionists, and pro-Slavery men; Bank men and anti-Bank men with all the lesser fragments that have been, from time to time, thrown off from the great political wheel in its violent revolutions," he wrote, "so as to melt them down into one mass of pure Whigs of undoubted good mettle?"[2]

Webster decided in the summer of 1838 not to participate in the race, so by the time the Whigs met in Harrisburg, Pennsylvania, on 4 December 1839, there were three potential nominees: Clay, Harrison, and Scott. Scott's appeal centered on his military career. While he, like Harrison, had fought in the War of 1812, he was thirteen years younger than his rival for the nomination. His military experiences were also more recent, as he had helped to quell the border conflicts with Canada during Van Buren's administration. Scott told Clay in early 1839 that Whigs had written him expressing their interest in putting his name forward as the party candidate, but he believed that each "individual had some doubt of the success of his own favorite candidate, & only looked to me as his *second* choice." Scott claimed that his response to each query was the same—he told "all & each:—'that I was no *politician*, & could not claim the high distinction of being a *statesman*; that I was absolutely indifferent whether I ever reached the office of President; that I made no pretensions to it, whatever, & that there were already presidential candidates enough before the public without the addition of my name.'"[3]

Harrison remained popular among Whigs despite his loss in the 1836 election. A young Abraham Lincoln summed up some Whigs' thinking about Old Tip in an 1838 editorial for Illinois's *Sangamo Journal*: "If the American People wish to honor a patriot and statesman; if they wish to reward a long-tried and faithful friend; if they wish to stimulate the youth of our country to emulation of noble examples, if they wish to proclaim to the world, that poverty shall never arrest virtue and intelligence on their march to distinction," he wrote, "they can, more effectually than in any other way, do all these by elevating Gen. Wm. H. Harrison to the Presidency." Harrison had sacrificed his health and his wealth in service to his country, Lincoln argued, and he deserved the chance to lead.[4]

Harrison recognized the challenges that he faced in winning over the Whig rank and file. He sought to smooth his path to the nomination by reaching out to the disparate factions within the party, such as the Anti-Masons, who remained a potent minority. He promised one former Anti-Masonic representative, Harmar Denny, that he would serve only one term, use the executive veto sparingly, "disclaim all right of control over the public treasure," and maintain constitutional separation between the executive branch and Congress. Harrison also expressed concern that Clay "stands no chance of success but by means of a packed convention one which will represent the politicians & not the people." Still, Harrison's supporters feared that Winfield Scott's age and military experience would pose a challenge to Old Tippecanoe. One New York Whig, John Bradley, expressed his confidence in the younger general's candidacy. Not only would Scott "bring out the Hurra boys," but he would also produce "an enthusiastic rally of all the fragments of the conservative, anti masonic, and abolition parties, and all the malcontents of our opponents." Bradley warned, however, that "the Generals lips must be hermetically sealed, and our shouts and Hurras must be long & loud" in order to produce victory.[5]

Clay entered the convention knowing that winning the nomination would prove difficult. During a tour of New York earlier in the summer, he had met with Thurlow Weed, who had outlined to the Kentuckian three reasons why he was not electable: he was pro-Bank, proslavery, and a Mason. In Weed's estimation, too many voters were anti-Bank to make him a viable option; the Whigs needed anti-slavery votes to win; and enough Whigs had started out in the Anti-Masonic Party that Clay's Masonic membership was a liability.[6]

Even more problematic for Clay, the new Whig leaders orchestrated the adoption of a convention rule that ordered each state to vote as a unit. This maneuver fatally undermined his nomination chances. Clay possessed a plurality of delegates, but winning a majority through the unit rule proved impossible. Out of the 254 available votes, the Kentuckian initially secured 103 to Harrison's 91 and Scott's 57. Clay's total dropped and Scott's rose slightly on the second ballot, with Harrison remaining steady. Perceiving the threat that Scott posed to Harrison's nomination, Thaddeus Stevens gave the pro-Clay Virginia delegation a letter that Scott had written to Francis Granger soliciting northern antislavery votes. This letter halted Scott's momentum among the Virginians. Realizing that his preferred nominee's chances were dead, Weed switched New York's votes to Harrison. On the final ballot, Harrison won 148, Clay 90, and Scott 16. Clay had already sent a letter announcing that if he did not win, then the nominee would "have my best wishes, and receive my cordial support."[7]

Clay's loss stemmed from many factors. Whigs had regressed during the 1839 elections, which suggested that the party required a new direction and figurehead.

The temporary economic uptick in 1839 convinced Whigs that they did not need the Kentuckian's policy experience as much as they needed a compelling personality. Finally, the absence of four southern states—Arkansas, Georgia, South Carolina, and Tennessee—from the convention deprived Clay of almost certain support. With those four delegations in attendance, the unit rule likely would not have passed. Even if it had, Clay probably would have possessed 143 votes of the necessary 148 majority on the first ballot. With that slim margin, his prospects for the nomination would have been much brighter.[8]

The Whigs' vice-presidential nod went to Clay's friend, forty-nine-year-old Virginian John Tyler. A strong advocate of states' rights, Tyler left the Democratic Party because of Jackson's opposition to nullification in 1832. He was out of step with the mainstream Whig Party, but he represented an important southern state and social class. He also balanced Harrison's connection with an antislavery state, Ohio. With the vice-presidential candidate chosen, the Whigs followed precedent by closing their proceedings without adopting a platform. Before leaving, however, the delegates called for a convention of young Whig men to meet in Baltimore in May 1840 to "aid the advancement of the Whig cause." Not coincidentally, the Democrats were scheduled to meet in the city at that same time.[9]

An "AVALANCHE OF THE PEOPLE," numbering approximately seventy-five thousand Whigs, descended on Baltimore prior to the Democratic convention in May 1840. They demonstrated outside the meeting hall, repeatedly declaring that "With Tip and Tyler, We'll bust Van's biler." Despite Philip Hone's pronouncement of the convention as "a sickly concern, a creeping plant, withering under the shade of the mighty Harrison tree," the proceedings went smoothly at first. Democrats faced little intrigue about their presidential nominee when they opened their proceedings. The 248 delegates in attendance nominated Van Buren without debate and adopted a platform emphasizing Jacksonian principles, the first platform officially adopted at a national party convention. The resolutions expressed support for a limited, constitutional federal government, a sound economy, and "the separation of the moneys of the government from banking institutions." They opposed internal improvements and a national bank. They also specifically alluded to the Democrats' support for the protection of slavery and criticized abolitionists for "endanger[ing] the stability and permanency of the union" by their actions. Finally, the platform invoked "the liberal principles embodied by Jefferson in the Declaration of Independence, and sanctioned in the constitution," particularly the protection of those seeking "the present privilege of becoming citizens, and the owners of soil among us." One historian believed that the platform "was designed to seal the return of Calhoun and his followers to the

Democratic ranks," a necessary move if Van Buren wanted to bolster his southern support.[10]

Just as in 1835, however, Democrats once again encountered questions about their vice-presidential nominee. The sitting vice president, Richard M. Johnson, provided Democrats with the opportunity to counter Harrison's military service with their own martial hero. Unfortunately, Johnson possessed the same deficiencies in 1840 that he had during the previous campaign. Some southerners were still upset about his relationships with enslaved women and his multiracial progeny. One of Amos Kendall's friends reported after visiting Johnson's Kentucky tavern in 1839 that the vice president "devotes most too much of his time to a young Delilah of about the complexion of Shakespears swarthy Othello." She reportedly was "his third *wife*; his second, which he sold for her infidelity, having been the sister of the present *lady*." Kendall's friend described the unnamed woman as "some eighteen or nineteen years of age and quite handsome." She "plays on the piano," he continued, "calls him my *dear Colonel* and is called *my dear* in return, and is said to be very *loving* and devoted." Andrew Jackson, who pushed for his Tennessee protégé, James K. Polk, to replace Johnson on the 1840 ticket, believed that the vice president's "family connection" would harm Democrats among "the whole religious portion" of Kentucky and Tennessee. "This, when we are fighting the great battle for principle, and for the perpetuation of our republican system[,] is unfortunate," Old Hickory pronounced.[11]

Ultimately, the Democrats declined to nominate a vice president, leaving it up to the states to make the choice. This decision did not sit well with Secretary of State Forsyth, who withdrew his name from consideration, "snarling and showing his teeth, and retreating tail foremost, like a disappointed cur who has been driven from the bone for which his mouth watered." Several delegates noted their states' preference for Johnson, but they also acknowledged that sufficient disagreement existed to let the states express their will separate from the national convention. Tennessean Felix Grundy observed, "If we could get the head [i.e., the president] along, the tail would not be far behind." Although Democrats never reached consensus on Johnson's candidacy, he overcame many of the objections to his personal life to become an effective campaign speaker, even if his fellow party members found him tiresome at times. As one Louisville editor commented, if "Rumpsy-Dumpsy" Johnson was truly responsible for Tecumseh's death, "he must have gone at him with *twaddle*."[12]

One additional political party emerged to contend for the presidency. The Liberty Party was born out of political abolitionists' frustration with the two-party political system, which they believed was beholden to the "Slave Power." Dismissing some abolitionists' claims that forming a national party would dilute their message, the Liberty Party's founders, who included New Yorkers Alvan Stewart and Myron P. Holley, argued, in the words of historian Reinhard O. Johnson, "that slavery was a political as well as a moral evil . . . [and] required both a political and a moral solution." They also suggested that they could purify the corruption within the nation's political system, perhaps even forcing one or both of the parties to support the end of slavery. Attempts to select a third-party Liberty ticket failed in the fall of 1839, but the Whigs' nomination of Harrison and Tyler in December revived the Liberty effort.[13]

With influential abolitionists such as AAS editor Joshua Leavitt now supporting the idea, a convention of abolitionists met in Albany, New York, in April 1840. Six northeastern states were represented by 121 delegates, most of whom came from New York. After a lively debate about the prudence of nominating a national ticket, the attendees selected James G. Birney and Thomas Earle to represent them in the election. The forty-eight-year-old Birney had abandoned his position as the scion of a wealthy slaveholding Kentucky family and joined the AAS, freeing the people whom he held in slavery in the mid-1830s. Earle, who turned forty-four years old three weeks after the convention, was a Massachusetts-born Quaker long active in the Pennsylvania abolitionist movement. While the Liberty Party would not engage in the same type or scope of campaigning as the Whigs and the Democrats, it played an important role in ensuring that slavery remained part of the national discussion.[14]

THE CAMPAIGN ISSUES

As the opposition party, the Whigs set the tone for the campaign. Foremost among their attacks on Van Buren was the economy. Whigs blamed the nation's "hard times" on Van Buren's reluctance to offer a true solution for the weak economy, namely, the reestablishment of the BUS. They also warned that the president's independent treasury bill was a step in the direction of monarchy.[15]

To bolster their argument, Whigs characterized Van Buren as an out-of-touch elitist. They made much of the twenty thousand dollars he spent on refurbishing the White House, a modest amount compared to the sixty-five thousand dollars Jackson had spent. Pennsylvania representative Charles Ogle, an Anti-Mason turned Whig, eviscerated Van Buren in one particularly effective speech. Calling the White House a "Presidential palace," Ogle outlined in detail what he considered to be the excesses of Jackson and Van Buren. The interior changes that Ogle described allegedly consisted of decorations and items found in a European palace, while the outside improvements painted Van Buren as a pretentious nabob, if not a little depraved. The so-called Democratic "reformers have constructed a number of clever sized hills, every pair of which, it is said, was designed to resemble and assume the form of AN AMAZON'S BOSOM, with a miniature knoll or hillock on its apex, to denote the n——ple." Dinnerware, lamps, mirrors, wallpaper, sofas—all came under criticism as wasteful, extravagant spending "of the PEOPLE'S CASH." If there was not enough federal funding for internal improvements, Ogle wondered, then how could there be money for remaking the White House and its grounds?[16]

The Whigs expanded Ogle's arguments to a more general claim that Van Buren and the Democrats were interested only in themselves and not the people. Accusations of the president's tyrannical and monarchical tendencies filled the mouths of Whigs and flowed from their pens. Van Buren's many nicknames— Martin Van Ruin, King Matty, the Little Magician of Kinderhook—all spoke to the president's desire to ignore or manipulate the people's will. Whigs indicated their belief that their opponents were prioritizing their party over the good of the nation by calling Democrats Van Buren's "'Spoils' Crew." One "Workingman" summarized the Whig position by indicating why Harrison was a better choice than Van Buren: "Because the administration party is a party without principles;— each of their radical leaders is speculating *on his own hook*, and torturing his imagination for new *experiments* to inflict upon the nation."[17]

A second substantive campaign issue was foreign relations. While overshadowed by the nation's economic troubles, the United States' several conflicts—within, along, and outside its borders—presented Van Buren in particular with problems. Whereas Harrison could point to his military career, the president possessed no such experience. Worse, the only Democrat who had proceeded Van Buren in the presidency was a military hero who acted decisively both on the battlefield and in the halls of Washington power. With a war against the Seminoles in Florida, seemingly annual conflagrations along the US-Canadian border, and recurring tensions with Mexico facing the nation, the Whigs had reason to be optimistic, and the Democrats pessimistic, about their respective candidates' chances when it came to that set of issues.[18]

Last, the issue of slavery hounded both Van Buren and Harrison. Despite Van Buren's proslavery statements during the 1836 campaign and his proslavery actions taken while president, white southerners still distrusted him on the issue. Thomas Morris, a US senator from Ohio, reportedly claimed that Harrison was "in feeling and principle, a more devoted pro-slavery man, than Mr. Van Buren, who, I believe, in feeling is anti-slavery." North Carolina's *Wilmington Advertiser* asked, "What do our southern friends think of this? If Mr. Van Buren is in feeling an abolitionist ought they to trust him!" The *Richmond Whig* asked, "Who is the *soundest* on the negro question?" Its editor noted, "Harrison is a Virginian—Van Buren is a Naw Yorker . . . Van Buren voted in the New York Convention to put a free negro on the same [f]ooting with a white man, as to suffrage—Harrison would have died sooner than give the vote." Some southerners still found Van Buren trustworthy, at least compared to Harrison. "The South owes to Mr. Van Buren a lasting debt of gratitude," one Charleston, South Carolina, newspaper argued. "She is bound to him for having given her new guarantees for the safety of her institutions and for the security of the life and property which their preservation involves."[19]

Harrison faced questions concerning slavery as well. He had belonged to an abolitionist society when he was younger, but he had favored the introduction of slavery into the Northwest Territory. During the Missouri Crisis of 1819–21, he supported proslavery forces, and he also owned enslaved people during his tenure as territorial governor there. "Throughout his political career," historian Reginald Horsman noted, Harrison "opposed interference with the rights of slaveowners." Despite Harrison's clear-cut support for slavery, Democrats labeled him an abolitionist and referred to Whigs as "the Abolition Party" and "Federalism and Abolition United." *Richmond Enquirer* editor Thomas Ritchie wanted to ensure that southern voters knew that the Whigs were presenting Harrison "to the South as Anti-abolitionist and to the West & North as the abolition Candidate." In reply to a query about a public letter Andrew Jackson had written about Harrison, the former president told two correspondents that he believed that the Whig candidate was not only a "black cockade Federalist" but also an abolitionist.[20]

Going into the 1840 presidential contest, many on both sides might have been confident in their predictions for the outcome, but few could have predicted how the campaign would unfold. More than substantive issues, cultural politics played an instrumental role in charting the political course of two very different candidates.

CHAPTER 12

Hard Cider, Coons, Log Cabins, and Big Balls

The nation's economy, foreign relations, and debate over slavery were substantive issues at play in the 1840 campaign, but cultural politics proved significant in shaping the election's outcome, too. Often remembered as expressions of entertainment and examples of unfettered democracy, these forms of cultural politics instead represented the culmination of a decades-long evolution of presidential campaigning that attested to the United States' rich political culture.[1]

MATERIAL CULTURE

The most memorable part of the 1840 election was undoubtedly its material culture. The decline in the production and use of material culture in the 1832 and 1836 campaigns reversed itself during Van Buren's administration, with Whigs employing it to criticize the president. During the 1840 campaign, this trend continued. Whigs used Harrison's military career and public image to become the main producers and consumers of campaign objects. Meanwhile, Democrats, perhaps because of complacency after previous successes or Van Buren's understated personality, paid little attention to creating their own on any widespread scale.[2]

The most familiar objects associated with the 1840 Whig campaign were the log cabin and the various representations of containers holding hard cider. The log cabin and hard cider imagery came from a Democratic critique of Harrison. In December 1839, the *Baltimore Republican* responded to a Clay supporter's question about how to "get rid of" the recently nominated Harrison by advising, "Give him a barrel of HARD CIDER, and settle a pension of two thousand a year on him, and my word for it, he will sit the remainder of his days in his LOG CABIN by the

side of a 'sea coal' fire, and study moral philosophy." Shortly thereafter, as Pennsylvania editor Richard S. Elliott recalled it, he visited fellow Pennsylvanian, banker
Thomas Elder, who suggested using the log-cabin reference to the Whigs' advantage. Elder "well knew that passion and prejudice, properly aroused and directed,
would do about as well as principle and reason in a party contest." Elliott sketched
the idea, and it became "the central formula of the Whig campaign." As Philip
Hone remarked, "Our opponents have, by their silly, disparaging epithets applied
to the Whig candidate, furnished us with weapons, the use of which is understood
by every man in our ranks."[3]

According to one historian, "a transparency showing a log cabin and a cider
barrel, with a woodpile and a coonskin," was first employed in 1840 by a Pennsylvania ratifying convention. Log-cabin floats, often accompanied by barrels of hard
cider for imbibing onlookers, began to appear frequently in Whig parades as the
campaign progressed. Whigs also built log cabins to serve as party headquarters,
the first one erected in Auburn, New York, William H. Seward's hometown. Describing the Baltimore Whig demonstration that took place before and during the
Democratic national convention, Tennessean Samuel H. Laughlin recorded in
his diary,

> We could see the whole procession of the Whigs with their Banners, and log
> cabins drawn on wagons, as they passed through Monument Square . . . The
> number of little cabins, built of poles, not by those who had them hauled
> through the streets, and marched in the array, for they were young and old
> aristocrats—lean, long waisted dandies,—loafers of all sorts of ages, and real
> silk-glove gentry who knew no more how to build one of these cabins, tho' not
> bigger than pig pens, than they did how to square a circle, or interpret Ezekiel's
> prophesies; but they were built and constructed, and hauled about by laboring
> men whom they despise at heart, and who despise them, but now worked for
> hire for these rich gentry.

Erecting log cabins even became routine in rural communities. In Lebanon,
Tennessee, located thirty miles east of Nashville, Virginia Campbell noted that
although her sister, Meg, did not dismiss her students for a Whig rally in the town,
"she is so warm a whig that the employment of her pupils during playtime, is
building *log cabins* & constructing some substitute for a barrel of *hard cider*."[4]

As one historian suggested about this imagery, Whigs created Old Tip as a
"political persona" for Harrison. They "surrounded it with various trappings such
as log cabins and cider barrels, offered it as packaged charisma, as the representa-

tive and savior of the common man, and sold it to the masses." Log cabins epito-mized the hard-working ethos of the western farmer, which was who Whigs wanted voters to think Harrison was, while "hard cider represented a hard working Amer-icanism by virtue of its rural production and its affordability compared to wine or beer which were considered European and too expensive to be consumed by regular citizens." That Harrison's home was not a log cabin but "a splendid resi-dence . . . beautiful—finer than Mount Vernon," according to one Democrat, was lost among the log-cabin representations foisted on voters.[5]

While the Whigs' log-cabin headquarters were supposed to serve multiple party functions, such as socializing and reading, Democrats labeled the log cabins "whig groggeries" and compared them to "the barracks of an army . . . quarters for the vicious and depraved, who were to be debauched with liquor, and stimulated with lying and inflammatory harrangues, and with vulgar and ribald songs, and corrupted with money when that should be found necessary." A Washington *Globe* correspondent called these log-cabin headquarters "a Federal trap, baited with hard cider to catch honest people's votes in! !" The log cabins merely rein-forced Democrats' arguments about their opponents' inebriated wantonness. As one observer wrote about a rally at Ohio's Fort Meigs, "never in my life have I been an eye witness to so much drunkenness, debauchery, rowdyism, and obscen-ity, or an ear witness to so much vulgarity, blasphemy and blackguardism." Dem-ocrats relied on a New York temperance leader to assess the contribution of alco-hol to the Whig campaign. In his judgment, "more than ten thousand men will be made drunkards in one year, by this 'hard cider enthusiasm.'"[6]

Another ubiquitous new object used by Whigs, the campaign ball, actually made its first appearance outside the Democratic national convention in May 1840. Whigs took the idea from Thomas Hart Benton's January 1837 comment during the debate about expunging Jackson's censure from the Senate journal: "Solitary and alone, and amidst the jeers and taunts of my opponents, I put this ball in motion. The people have taken it up, and rolled it forward, and I am no longer any thing but a unit in the vast mass which now propels it." Twisting Ben-ton's statement into partisan propaganda, Whigs rolled paper or buckskin balls covered with campaign slogans in parades or between towns to rally support for Harrison. For example, the following lines appeared on one Massachusetts ball:

> O'er every ridge we roll this Ball,
> From Concord Bridge to Faneuil Hall.
> Farewell, poor Van, you're not our man;
> To guide the ship, we'll try old Tip.

A group of Allegany County, Maryland, Whigs composed the following ditty to inscribe on their ball, which measured twelve feet in diameter:

> With heart and soul
> This ball we roll;
> May times improve
> As on we move.
> This democratic ball,
> Set rolling first by Benton,
> Is on another track
> From that it first was sent on . . .
> Ye officeholders, fed with pap,
> Have very saucy grown:
> We tell ye, sirs, we don't like that,
> And mean to make it known . . .
> As rolls the ball,
> Van's reign does fall;
> And he may look
> To Kinderhook;
> His former friends
> To other ends,
> Take care your toes
> Ye Loco Fo's . . .
> Having no bell,
> We roll your knell.[7]

Despite some local examples, surprisingly few national Whig campaign objects mentioned Van Buren's economic policies. Instead, they focused on other themes. For example, at an event commemorating the sixty-fifth anniversary of the Battle of Bunker Hill, campaign objects connected Harrison to the Revolution. Much of the Whig paraphernalia linked his military service to that of George Washington, while others presented him as a Napoleonic or Cincinnatus figure. These choices are especially interesting because of the contrast between the two military figures: Napoleon's overwhelming lust for power versus Cincinnatus's willingness to turn his back on military rule and retire to his farm. Harrison's alleged life as a farmer who was "The People's Friend" or "The Poor Man's Friend" was used on banners to contrast him with the Whigs' imagery of Van Buren as an out-of-touch elitist. Female supporters in McHenry County, Illinois, carried banners that captured many of these themes about Harrison. They proclaimed him "The Ohio

Farmer," "The Defender of our Homes and Children," and "The Friend of the West, and the Foe of the Savage." Democrats, however, mocked the Whigs' focus on accoutrements. Imagine, one remarked, a "reckless Western settler . . . decorated with a log cabin breast pin, one hand holding an axe-helve and the other resting on a hard cider rattan, his hair redolent with Tippecanoe extract and glossy as a soap lock." These were the "shallow humbugs" who thought they could secure Harrison the presidency, the *Albany Argus* exclaimed.[8]

Pro–Van Buren items were largely absent from the 1840 campaign. Unlike Harrison's image, Van Buren's was set in most Americans' minds, so Democratic campaign objects emphasized issues over personality. During his 1839 tour, for example, Van Buren witnessed an arch raised by the citizens of Greenbush, New York. "Resting upon hickory trees for columns," the arch bore the inscription, *"The People's Money, where the People can control it"* on one side, with *"The greatest good of the greatest number"* on the other. A Roxbury, Massachusetts, banner in 1840 read, "Shall the Banks or the People Rule?" One issue that appeared on Democratic campaign objects was the accusation that the Whigs wanted to sentence "poor white convicts to slave labor," an allusion to the rumor that Harrison proposed selling white debtors into slavery. Most of the party's silk ribbons referenced the independent treasury, such as one that read, "Martin Van Buren and The Independent Treasury. No Property Qualification, and No White Slavery." Another ribbon reminded voters of Harrison's questionable associations by hearkening back to the Federalist politics of the 1790s: "We Pledge Ourselves to a Firm and Uncompromising Opposition to all Alien and Sedition Gag Law and Black Cockade Candidates, Although Disguised by the Name of Whig." One exception to the policies-over-personality approach was the use of hickory poles, displayed to remind voters of Van Buren's connection to Andrew Jackson. This tactic backfired, as it allowed Whigs to argue gleefully, as they had in 1836, that Slippery Elm had replaced Old Hickory. "A slippery elm pole, the true Van Buren emblem, would have been an eyesore to everybody," one Ohio Whig editor observed.[9]

Democrats underestimated the Whigs' use of material culture. They thought that voters would not be enticed "to vote for this dumb candidate" by the use of "loud noise and drink; by banners and pictures; barrels and balls; by great assemblages and riotous parades, as if they were as ignorant and thoughtless as negroes and barbarians," as one 1840 editorial described the Whig campaign. Democrats believed that their "businesslike decorum" would carry more weight with voters than the Whigs' "Logg cabin hard cider and Coon humbugery," as Jackson called it.[10] They could not have been more wrong.

PUBLIC EVENTS

One of the most striking characteristics of the 1840 campaign was the spectacle of public events. Part of the inspiration for these large enthusiastic rallies came from the religious fervor and example of the Second Great Awakening, a series of Protestant revivals that swept the nation during the early 1800s. The Awakening not only produced reform movements, such as temperance and Sabbatarianism, and infused energy in others, such as abolitionism, but it also provided a camp-meeting model for political parties to follow.[11]

As the party of moral reform, social order, and evangelical Christianity, Whigs enthusiastically embraced this paradigm, while Democrats, who privileged religious diversity and separation of the sacred from the secular, generally avoided it. One Tennessee Whig, James Campbell, described the religious framework of the Whigs' strategy: he referred to Hugh Lawson White and Ephraim H. Foster as "bishops," the presidential electors as "presiding elders," and political speeches as "sermons." He wrote, "In each county we will have a sufficient number of local preachers, to make war upon the Heathen, & carry the glad tidings of our political salvation to every corner of their counties." If that was not enough, Campbell wrote, then "we will send missionaries." He continued, "We expect to hold political Camp-meetings in every County in the state—two & four day meetings—not to drink eat and revel, but to speak & to consider." Employing biblical language, he told Representative William B. Campbell, "every thing that is here written will come to pass. Not one jot, nor one tittle will fall to the ground." Another Whig predicted to William Campbell, "The coming contest may be called the battle of Armageddon. It will be the greatest political battle ever fought." He continued with a warning: "Should the Philistines [i.e., Democrats] succeed, and the ark of Liberty be taken by them, wo—wo is unto us—wo unto Israel."[12]

Harrison's candidacy was key to attracting evangelical voters, his supporters emphasizing his Christian fidelity. One campaign biographer, Isaac R. Jackson, recounted how he "more than once, on entering at day-break the chamber of General Harrison, found him on his knees at his bedside, absorbed in his devotions to his Maker." Another supporter, Jacob Moore, noted Harrison's opposition to dueling. This issue was especially pertinent because of the 1838 Cilley-Graves duel, which had resulted in Cilley's death. Harrison was the right choice for president, according to Moore, "because he is, like Washington, opposed to the unchristian practice of DUELLING, and has publicly stamped the offence as a crime against society, and the laws of God." Evangelical Whigs also appreciated his Sabbatarianism leanings. One correspondent praised Harrison for "honoring the Lord's day" and prayed that God would provide him "an instrument . . . for the removal of this great national sin" of violating the biblical mandate about the Sabbath. Harrison was astute enough to demonstrate publicly his religious dedication. In January 1840, shortly after being nominated, he attended a revival in Cincinnati and even went forward to the altar to show his repentant spirit.[13]

Incredibly, Whigs were also able to make Harrison into a Christian defender of Native Americans. Even though his national fame was based on victories over Tecumseh and his forces at the Battles of the Thames and Tippecanoe, evangelical Whigs argued that, "like a true hero, he tempered his victories with mercy, and when the smoke of battle was over, was the first to perform acts of kindness to the vanquished." They highlighted Harrison's compassion for Indians, whose removal he supervised as Indiana's territorial governor, as well as his concern that they not fall prey to the temptations presented by alcohol. Harrison himself took the fight directly to the Democrats in his own *Discourse on the Aborigines* (1838), which was turned into a campaign tract. He condemned his political opponents for their conduct of the Second Seminole War, particularly their use of bloodhounds against Indian forces. Democrats tried to counter this attack by spreading the rumor that Harrison fathered children with a Winnebago woman, but evangelicals were unconvinced. In their eyes, Harrison was the candidate who would help Native Americans survive and embrace white American civilization, including Christianity.[14]

Additionally, Whigs took advantage of the Democrats' stance against the intermingling of religion and politics. They pointed to Jackson, who helped to mark his party as un-Christian by arguing that instituting a national day of prayer and fasting during the 1832 cholera epidemic would "[transcend] the limits prescribed by the constitution for the President . . . [and] disturb the security which religion now enjoys in this country." Democrats also faced criticism from evangelicals for their opposition to Sabbatarianism. In 1829, for example, Richard M. Johnson criticized the movement to keep the Sabbath holy, pronouncing that "it is not the legitimate province of the Legislature to determine what religion is true, or what is false." Additionally, the Democratic Party's appeal to religious minorities such as Catholics and Mormons allowed Whigs to paint them as "atheists and religious perverts." They also associated Democrats with the "Loco foco doctrines" of reformers such as Orestes Brownson, Abner Kneeland, Robert Owen, Tom Paine, and Frances Wright, "the principles of the wildest Jacobins of revolutionary France . . . which strike at the very root of law, social order, morality and religion." Whigs argued that their opponents wanted to bring about "the OVERTHROW OF

THE CHURCH IN ALL ITS FORMS AND SECTS, and the *destruction of the ministers of religion.*" Whig minister Calvin Colton posed this question to fellow believers: Were they "willing to give up their rights of conscience, their religious ordinances, their holy temples, to the desolating sweep of an infidel, savage dynasty—and such a dynasty of lust, and fire, and blood"?[15]

Whether religious or political, successful rallies required large crowds. Although the number of attendees at these Whig rallies may have sometimes been exaggerated for effect, the events' sizable attendance was nonetheless remarkable. At a "Young Men's Convention and Old Soldiers' Meeting" held in Illinois in June 1840, approximately fifteen thousand attended. An August rally in Nashville attracted between forty thousand and one hundred thousand, depending on which account one reads. The largest gatherings tended to be the ones commemorating Harrison and his military victories, which the Whig candidate usually attended. For example, twenty-five thousand made their way to a May event at the Tippecanoe battlefield in Lafayette, Indiana. In June, Harrison spoke to twenty-five thousand people at Fort Meigs, which he had successfully defended while under siege in 1813. One of the largest rallies was held in September in Dayton, Ohio, where a reported one hundred thousand heard Harrison condemn the Democratic opposition. Lengthy rallies, with many attendees, helped to build the crowd's emotional investment in the message, binding them to the Whig candidate and to the party.[16]

PUBLIC SPEECHES

Surprisingly, Van Buren did not play a significant public role once the campaign began in 1840. This decision was ironic for two reasons. One was his part in creating the Jacksonian party system during the 1828 campaign, which witnessed the growing influence of cultural politics, such as auxiliary organizations and material culture. Considering his important role, one would have expected the Little Magician to maximize the use of campaign tactics that had worked so well for the party he had built. That was not the case in 1840.[17]

The second reason was that Van Buren had made a public tour in the spring of 1839. Like Washington, Monroe, and Jackson before him, the president thought it important to connect with the people to bolster his political support. He had originally planned to visit the southern and western states with an eye toward improving his "ability to execute, successfully, such duties as may devolve upon me, in connection with their interests." His fight with congressional Whigs led him to postpone the trip, however, especially after Tennessee congressman James K. Polk warned him that appearing in Tennessee would have "disastrous consequences."

Not until May did Van Buren decide to make his first visit to New York as president, on what was by all appearances a reelection tour.[18]

From June 20 to October 16, Van Buren traveled from Washington, DC, through Pennsylvania, New Jersey, New York, and Vermont. He visited dozens of towns and cities along the way, meeting thousands of American citizens. At the beginning of the tour, the president received invitations to public dinners, which he declined "in conformity to a rule which he . . . [had] prescribed to himself as most suitable to the circumstances under which he travels."[19]

Yet Van Buren's rule against attending public dinners in his honor did not extend to making public addresses. Over the tour's nearly four months, he made almost three dozen recorded speeches to the public. His first major address, given on July 2 in New York City's Castle Garden, set the tone for the rest of his trip. Responding to an address made by John W. Edmonds, chair of the committee of arrangements, Van Buren's speech delved into particular policy statements. The president devoted a paragraph to arguing that the independent treasury "may well be regarded as a question involving the nature, and to some extent, the existence of republican institutions, as well as a consideration of the main purposes for which our government was established." He then spent three paragraphs on foreign relations, particularly the border conflicts with Great Britain.[20]

For the rest of the tour, Van Buren's public addresses began with gratitude for the citizens' hospitality, then usually transitioned into a discussion of political topics. In late August, for example, he told the two to three thousand people in attendance at Oswego, New York, that their support for his administration's steps in the nation's border conflicts with Great Britain "affords me great satisfaction." Nearly two weeks later, he thanked the people of Onondaga for recognizing the "inveterate malignity" with which his opponents had treated him on the tour. "While justice and truth are all powerful," he observed, "falsehood and injustice serve only to depress those who practice them, and elevate the object they were intended to destroy." While Van Buren's public comments were often brief, it is not a stretch to imagine that he had an eye toward the next year's election when making them.[21]

Whigs enthusiastically criticized Van Buren's tour. One newspaper asked Americans to understand "that Mr. Van Buren is travelling upon an electioneering tour for himself." The idea that the president was openly using his trip to solicit votes for reelection was a consistent theme in the Whig papers. "A President of the United States, on a tour, making party speeches, the very moment he is receiving the honors of the constituted authorities of the whole city, is not only an act offensive, but uncivil and insulting," the *Washington (DC) Daily National*

Intelligencer observed. "Is not Mr. V.B. the very first President who thus avowedly started on an electioneering tour?" A Massachusetts newspaper argued, "He is not what he ought to be—the President of the people, and not of a party." Whigs also criticized Van Buren's perceived aristocratic pretensions. At Sing Sing, "*three of his faithful followers kissed his hand, with which he seemed highly gratified,*" one newspaper reported. "Should he ever visit Sing Sing again, there will probably be those sufficiently *embued with loyalty to kiss his great toe.*"[22]

Democrats responded to the Whigs' many criticisms with some of their own. "When Granny Harrison passed through our State on an *electioneering* tour, the federalists fell before his carriage, like deluded Hindoos," one New Jersey newspaper noted. "But when the President of a republican government, is about to pass through on a visit to his home, they would offer him a direct and unmerited insult." They also criticized the presumptive Whig nominee, Henry Clay, whose travels through New York overlapped with Van Buren's and appeared very much like an electioneering tour. "Is there a man of the smallest pretensions to common sense, who does not perceive his object?" the *Albany Argus* asked. "Mr. Clay's object is the Presidency."[23]

Democrats made sure to note Van Buren's popularity on his tour as well. At Sandy Hill, New York, his reception, attended by "many of the most respectable political opponents of the President . . . was such as American freemen will always give to their Chief Magistrate—plain, respectable and republican." His reception by the people of Rochester "exhibits in an admirable manner, the deep and strong hold which Mr. Van Buren has gained, and is constantly gaining upon the hearts and affections of his countrymen." The president's tour of New York "has been of the most gratifying nature," the *Albany Argus* reported. "The people have been anxious to testify their respect for his character, and have evinced a cordiality towards his person which has been any thing but pleasing to certain opposition editors."[24]

Despite his 1839 tour, Van Buren declined to attend public events during the election year of 1840. To a group of supporters in Milledgeville, Georgia, he cited "the obligations of official duty to deny myself that gratification." In declining an invitation offered by New York City Democrats, he wrote, "There is no portion of my Fellow Citizens with which it would afford me more satisfaction to unite . . . [I]f my public duties did not prevent it, I would not fail to be with you." It was an odd choice given his previous experiences.[25]

Van Buren was not unaware of the necessity of an active public campaign. In offering his thoughts on how to handle the 1840 New York state elections, for example, he outlined the party's weaknesses and recommended a course of action.

Democrats had become lazy, Van Buren argued. "By superior activity & a better organization on the part of the whigs, they laboring all the year round, both young & old, in season & out of season," the Democrats' opponents had seized the advantage in partisan activity. In his opinion, the New York, Ohio, and Pennsylvania state elections of 1838 and 1839 revealed the Whigs' strategy of "superior activity." Van Buren's recommendations were many, but they centered on New York, with the steps taken there "to be followed in all the States." He argued for the centralization of partisan efforts in the state legislature "instead of a central corresponding Committee." He also asked that "a Democratic association be found in each town in the State to be composed of the most active & young friends of the cause" to help counter Whig charges. The Democrats' responsibility, according to the president, was to use their party organization "to preserve & promote the purity & freedom of elections."[26]

Van Buren's seventy-five-page document reinforces the critical irony in his approach to the campaign. He saw the necessity of Democratic organization and activity that could match that of the Whigs, yet he failed to take an overly active role in assisting his own campaign during the election year. Unlike the previous summer, for example, Van Buren did not embark on a campaign tour in 1840. Whether his official duties, as he wrote some correspondents, or the impropriety of a nominated president actively campaigning during an election year kept him in Washington, Van Buren's absence from the campaign trail hampered Democratic efforts to hold on to the White House and may have dealt the fatal blow to his chances at a second term

Although lacking Van Buren's personal help in swaying voters, veteran party standard bearers still tried to rally their fellow Democrats. For example, when Jackson's health allowed, he made several appearances on the president's behalf. One of the most prominent was at New Orleans in January 1840, to commemorate the twenty-fifth anniversary of the victory over the British. Despite complaining about his health and the embarrassment of having "to borrow or travel as a pauper" because of his tenuous financial situation, Jackson made the trip down the Mississippi River to the Crescent City. He drew a crowd estimated at thirty to forty thousand people, including veterans who had fought with him and women with "radiant and beaming countenances," while making various stops in the city. Jackson did not speak publicly, but Democratic newspaper editors made sure to emphasize the people's adoration of "the old General." One New Orleans correspondent wrote the *Globe*, "The other party is making a great splutter about Harrison, but it is all talk; he has no standing here—is unknown." For most of the campaign, however, Jackson had to content himself with writing letters in an attempt to rally Democrats.[27]

Other Democratic stalwarts, including Thomas Hart Benton, James Buchanan, Richard M. Johnson, and Silas Wright Jr., took to the stump for Van Buren. Former US attorney general Felix Grundy and Governor James K. Polk, both known for their wit and speaking longevity, were effective spokesmen in Jackson's home state. Polk's efforts as a sitting governor especially earned him the Whigs' ire for being "the party missionary, stump speaker and circuit rider." State representative (and future US president) Andrew Johnson's speaking reputation was not as stellar. According to James Campbell, brother of Virginia governor David Campbell, Johnson was "a strong minded man . . . [who] cuts when he does cut not with a razor, but with a case knife [i.e., a dull kitchen knife]."[28]

As in the previous presidential election, William Henry Harrison injected himself into the campaign in unprecedented ways. He made approximately two dozen major campaign speeches, as well as many minor speeches, between his nomination in December 1839 and the end of the campaign. According to one scholar, several factors led Harrison to take such an active public-speaking role. His success in the previous campaign undoubtedly convinced him that public speeches were a necessary partisan weapon. The growth of large public events, such as parades and rallies, that incorporated multiple speakers made it easier and more logical for a presidential candidate to address the crowds as well. Finally, the Whig national convention did not adopt a platform, leaving it up to Harrison to define his party's stance on issues. His silence led Democrats to argue that he "remained mum because their charges about his senility, his stupidity, and all the rest were accurate." Failing to answer those charges would only substantiate their claims, and addressing them in writing, in personal letters or newspapers, allowed Democrats to allege that Harrison was not the author. Therefore, the most effective way to combat these accusations was for Harrison to speak in public.[29]

Harrison's speeches typically followed a pattern. He spoke often about his previous military experience, an understandable decision given that several of his speeches were at sites of his military victories or included large groups of veterans who had fought with him. Harrison's military career was also his most notable public achievement, much more appealing than his gubernatorial, congressional, or diplomatic careers. He infused his speeches with classical allusions as well. This choice reflected not only the tenor of the times but also showed Harrison's learning. Additionally, he spent considerable time defending himself from Democratic attacks on his age, health, and intellectual capacity. Finally, Harrison rarely engaged in detailed discussion of the major issues of the day, relying instead on general criticisms of Van Buren and the Democrats.[30]

Several examples from Harrison's extant campaign speeches during the summer months of 1840 convey the themes that he and his advisers considered important. On June 5, he gave his first major speech in the doorway of the National Hotel in Columbus, Ohio. Undoubtedly not as extemporaneous as the newspaper reporter believed, Harrison's speech responded to several "instances of gross misrepresentation, or absolute falsehoods, industriously and shamelessly propagated by a party press." He denied, for example, that he was beholden to "a committee of conscience-keepers" who did not trust him to answer his own correspondence, instead keeping him "in a cage, fastened with iron bars." Harrison also expressed surprise that the *Richmond Enquirer* accused him of being "a *Black Cockade Federalist*," given its previous support for him before he joined the Whigs. He defended himself as well against the rumor that he had been an abolitionist.[31]

Other speeches highlighted additional Whig lines of attack, many of them reminiscent of the class warfare language later used by William Jennings Bryan in the 1890s and Bernie Sanders in the years leading up to the 2016 election. At Fort Meigs in mid-June, Harrison urged listeners to exercise caution regarding their leaders, calling the United States under Van Buren "a monarchy in spirit if not in name." He used Edward Gibbons's definition of a monarchy as an "executive [who] has command of the army, the execution of the laws and the control of the purse," remarking that "power is insinuating," and that "few men are satisfied with less power than they are able to procure." On July 28, Harrison spoke at Fort Greeneville, where in 1795, as a lieutenant, he had served as Major General Anthony Wayne's aide-de-camp in negotiating an important US-Indian treaty. Harrison reiterated his warning about Van Buren's monarchical tendencies and reminded the crowd, in ironically quintessential Jacksonian fashion, that "power is always stealing from the many to the few." Harrison then declared, "Destroy the poor man's credit, and you destroy his capital."[32]

As the campaign neared its climax, Harrison increased the vigor of his attacks on his Democratic opponents and his own defense. At a Dayton, Ohio, rally in September, Harrison compared the Democrats to "false Christs," who were so devious that "even the elect will be deceived." He argued, "The Presidency has been put up to the highest bidder in promises, . . . and we see the result." By contrast, Harrison promised to serve only one term and not to endorse his successor, a blatant reference to Jackson's preference for Van Buren in 1836. He also denounced "the violence of party spirit" that had overtaken the country, which allowed Democrats to fashion themselves the protectors of the lower classes against the aristocracy. "The natural antagonist of Democracy is not aristocracy," Harrison argued. "It is monarchy." He concluded, "I have detained you fellow-citizens, longer than I intended. You now see that I am not the old man on crutches, nor the imbecile they say I am,—[cheering]—not the prey to disease,—[a voice cried here,—nor the bear in a cage,] nor the caged animal they wittily describe me to be. [Great laughter and cheering.]."[33]

In a speech given in September in Chillicothe, Ohio, as well as in his Dayton speech, Harrison reminded Whigs of the horrors of excessive democracy during the French Revolution. It was "run-mad democracy," he exclaimed. "Who forgets the square in Paris, where ran rivers of the people's blood, shed in the name of democracy at the foot of the statue of liberty!" The same terror potentially existed in the United States, he intimated, if the Democrats continued to lead the nation. Once again appealing to class distinctions and positioning himself as the true democratic defender of the common man, Harrison proclaimed, "I am in favor of every system, which will make the poor man richer, and will do the greatest good to the greatest number. I do not believe in making the rich richer, and the poor poorer, but in aiding the poor from emerging from their poverty and attaining wealth, and it is credit that is the capital of the poor man."[34]

Other Whig speakers during the campaign included not only well-known statesmen such as Henry Clay and Daniel Webster but also less-prominent politicians, including John W. Bear and Thomas Corwin of Ohio and Abraham Lincoln of Illinois. These younger men brought a new energy to the campaign trail. Bear was a prolific political stumper, giving over three hundred speeches in eight states and the nation's capital. Nicknamed the Buckeye Blacksmith because of his profession, Bear provoked different responses from both sides. Whigs lauded his "strong sagacity, accurate information, and . . . effective eloquence," while Democrats condemned him for his "low and vulgar ribaldry, stale jokes, and the manners of the Harlequin." Whig congressman Thomas Corwin, the Wagon Boy, was known for his humor and colloquial speaking style. One Whig editor proclaimed him "the ablest, best, most eloquent, and successful speaker in the American Congress." Lincoln, a state representative from Springfield, possessed a knack for public speaking that fit well with the Whigs' electioneering strategy. At one speaking engagement in Tremont, Illinois, for example, a newspaper reporter observed that Lincoln "related many highly amusing anecdotes which convulsed the house with laughter; and concluded his eloquent address with a successful vindication of the civil and military reputation of the Hero of Tippecanoe." Unlike some Whig orators, however, Lincoln also spoke seriously about issues, such as the economy.[35]

As expected, the reaction to the Whigs' stumping depended on which party one supported. Whigs, of course, presented Harrison and his speechmaking in the most positive light. One Whig who saw him during the 1840 canvass described Harrison as "very slender and thin in flesh, with a noble and benignant expression of countenance—a penetrating eye, expansive forehead and Roman nose. He is not bald but gray, and walks about very quick, and seems to be active as a man of 45." The report continued, "He appears better in the social circle than he does in public.—There is nothing of the 'Old Granny' about him, I assure you." Even some of those who were skeptical changed their minds about Old Tippecanoe. Following the Carthage, Ohio, meeting in August, one elderly man commented on his conversion to the Whig cause. "I have done General Harrison great injustice. I have opposed him and abused him," the man explained. "He has been vilified and shamefully wronged. I will do him justice in [the] future. He is the man to save the country."[36]

Democratic editor Thomas Ritchie, on the other hand, described the Whig electors in his state as "travelling orators, who . . . traverse their districts, mount the stumps, abuse the Administration, puff the military chieftan, and gull the people." He told Van Buren, "I have never seen a Junto so fanatical, so desperate in their purposes, or so reckless in their means." Andrew Jackson denounced the spectacle of the Whig campaign as well. He believed that the Whigs were telling the people "in emphatic Language, that they are unfit for self government and can be led by hard cider, coons, Log cabins and big balls."[37]

AUXILIARY ORGANIZATIONS

The proliferation of campaign events and speeches demonstrated that the Whigs had learned how to organize their campaign much more efficiently in 1840 than they had in 1836. They established a central committee in Washington, which consisted of several US House members: Rice Garland of Louisiana, the chair; John C. Clark of New York, the secretary; and members John Bell (TN), John M. Botts (VA), Thomas Corwin (OH), Moses H. Grinnell (NY), Leverett Saltonstall (MA), and Truman Smith (CT). This central committee distributed Whig publications, leading Democratic editor Thomas Ritchie to complain that the Whigs were misleading "honest voters . . . by humbugs and misrepresentations—by handbills . . . and by caricatures and pamphlets and speeches." The Whig central committee also sent orders to county-level committees, instructing them to identify eligible voters as pro-Whig or pro-Democrat and to cajole loyal and independent voters to vote for Harrison. This activity led Democrats to charge the Whigs with "transporting the vagabonds and perjured hirelings from State to State to give fraudulent and illegal votes." Historian Robert Gunderson noted that the Whigs also formed "a personal campaign committee . . . to advise Harrison and to handle his troublesome correspondence." *Cincinnati Republican* editor Colonel Charles S. Todd served as chair, with *Cincinnati Gazette* editor John C. Wright, Major David Gwynne, O. M. Spencer, and H. E. Spencer as members. Democrats referred to this group disparagingly as "the conscience-keeping committee."[38]

Building on the precedent set by the formation of Hickory Clubs in previous campaigns, Harrison's supporters began founding Tippecanoe Clubs even before their candidate received the official Whig nomination. The organization of these clubs led Clay men to "[make] a prodigious squalling among them." Harrison's official nomination only increased the number of clubs. Their members took an active role in the campaign, passing resolutions that reinforced the importance of defeating Van Buren. "Our Republican institutions, and that Liberty which we value above all price, will be put to imminent hazard, if not utterly lost" if Van Buren won, according to the Richmond Tippecanoe Club. The Straight-Out Tippecanoe Club of Franklin County, Ohio, pledged "to meet the *people* of the party opposed to them, on the stump or the rostrum," excepting officeholders, a group that they did not believe had "any common interest with the people."[39]

Many Tippecanoe Clubs met in log cabins with readily available hard cider. A Mobile, Alabama, newspaper announced the building of a thirty-by-eighty-foot log cabin, deeming it "a commodious and appropriate place for meetings." When the floor of the hotel in which they were meeting partially collapsed, members of a Detroit Tippecanoe Club proved their commitment to their candidate by passing a resolution "to proceed to the woods to procure timber for the log cabin, when there will be no danger of tumbling into the cellar." In describing the building of an Ohio log cabin for a Tippecanoe Club, a reporter noted that in one corner was "placed a barrel of hard cider, the honest old Hero's beverage." He observed, "That hard cider story is giving the Locos awful *gripes*, but the cider itself sets capitally on healthy Harrison stomachs." At the cabin's inaugural dedication, Tippecanoe Club members sang and proclaimed their Whig loyalty "in a draught of hard cider."[40]

These meetings led Democrats to call Tippecanoe Club members "hard cider fops" and to remark that "gambling, betting, bragging, boasting and cheating, is there [sic] true game." Van Buren supporters expressed outrage at the actions taken by a Macon, Georgia, Tippecanoe Club. Its members reportedly "BURIED THE CONSTITUTION *six feet deep, and reared over it a pole of some eighty feet high, with a* CIDER BARREL *at its top, as an* EMBLEM OF THEIR PRINCIPLES!" Tippecanoe Clubs were not always able to hold their ranks. J. C. Welty, a club member in

Hagerstown, Maryland, publicly renounced his affiliation. His decision centered on his impression of Harrison and the Whigs' transparency. "I would rather go with the democrats who are not disposed to conceal their principles," Welty wrote, "than with the whigs who conceal every thing, and have brought out a candidate who appears to have a great many bad principles."[41]

On the other side, Democrats continued to exploit Andrew Jackson's reputation in organizing their own auxiliary groups. As they had since the 1824 election, they founded and convened Hickory Clubs. In Middletown, Connecticut, a group of "active, intelligent, and independent young men" formed one to combat the Whigs' determination "to restore the reign of intolerant and oppressive federalism." Kinderhook and OK Clubs were also organized, although their numbers paled in comparison to those named for Jackson. The clubs called meetings and participated in parades and conventions, like the one held in Poughkeepsie, New York, in September 1840. Whigs found pleasure in pointing out the president's inability to establish his political independence even when it came to auxiliary organizations. In an editorial entitled "Wearing Daddy's Clothes," a Galena, Illinois, editor wondered why Van Buren's supporters "continually try to keep their man out of sight. Why try to disguise him in another man's garments, and run upon another man's popularity? Why do they name their political papers 'Old Hickory,' and societies 'Hickory Clubs'?" The writer concluded, "You cannot make the people believe that Martin Van Buren is 'Old Hickory,' though you dress him up in Jackson's old clothes." The very thing that had helped elevate Van Buren to the presidency—his connection to Jackson—was now a major line of attack for the Whigs.[42]

PUBLIC CORRESPONDENCE

Since Van Buren did not take to the stump as Harrison did, the most significant public contribution the president made to his 1840 campaign was writing letters to allies and interested groups. When interested citizens in Elizabeth City, Virginia, asked him a series of questions about "each one of those momentous questions which now agitate the public mind," including slavery, banking, and the tariff, Van Buren sent a lengthy reply addressing each of their questions. The president wrote another notable letter to a group of Kentucky Democrats. Written on July 4, the same day Van Buren signed the Independent Treasury Act, the letter focused on placing the major economic issues of the day within the context of previous party battles. He resurrected one of Jackson's mantras by arguing that the bill would prevent the practice by which "the few were enabled to enrich themselves by using the money which belonged to the many." Overall, Van Buren's letters tended to be dry and uninspiring, characteristic of his dense, overly verbose writing style.[43]

Slavery was a particularly important issue that prompted both candidates to engage in public correspondence with voters. To James Lyons, who wrote asking about Harrison's alleged abolitionism, Harrison replied that his views on the subject were well known and that his friends viewed "with scorn and contempt, the charge of my being an abolitionist, and truly assert that I have done and suffered more to support southern rights than any other person north of Mason & Dixon's line." Delegates at one North Carolina Democratic meeting asked both Van Buren and Harrison to express their opinions on abolitionism and passed resolutions that stated, in part, "We cannot, nor will not support any man for the Presidency, who does not give the South Satisfactory assurances, that he is opposed to the bold and mischievous movements of the Abolitionists." The president, about whom southerners still retained doubts, responded by referring these writers to his previous remarks, including his inaugural address. The pro-Democratic *North Carolina Standard* maintained that Van Buren's previous statements regarding slavery "speak a language that the people of the South will understand and approve." Harrison also referred those making inquiries to his previous statements, but that tactic left them unsatisfied. "Where is Gen. Harrison, and why does he not answer, too?" one North Carolina paper asked. "Freemen of North Carolina, will you support such a man?"[44]

The Log Cabin and Hard Cider slogan handed to Whigs by their opponents provided them with a theme they fully exploited in their campaign for Harrison. Whigs used it to good effect in these five forms of cultural politics—material culture, public events, public speeches, auxiliary organizations, and public correspondence—clearly giving them an advantage over the Democrats.

CHAPTER 13

Doggerel Rhymes and Vulgar Pictures

Unlike the Whigs, Democrats never found a unifying theme around which to rally their supporters. That deficiency showed in the four remaining manifestations of cultural politics: print culture, political music, visual culture, and women's activity. Van Buren's unwillingness to use his long-revered political sagacity in maximizing Democratic participation in cultural politics also helped produce an outcome that few would have foreseen just a few years earlier.

PRINT CULTURE

Newspapers continued to grow in both numbers and influence following the 1836 election. By 1840, there were nearly 1,400 newspapers in the nation, with a total circulation of almost one hundred and fifty thousand copies annually. New York (245), Pennsylvania (187), Ohio (123), Massachusetts (91), and Indiana (73) produced the most papers. More important than the number of newspapers was the partisan breakdown of their production. Between 1836 and 1840, Democrats increased the number of their newspapers from 10 to 58, while Whig newspapers grew from 14 in 1836 to 101 in 1840.[1]

Needless to say, Whigs seized the opportunity presented by the medium of print. James Gordon Bennett's *New York Herald* was the Whigs' first "penny press," or cheap mass-produced newspaper. With Thurlow Weed's encouragement, Horace Greeley, later a famous newspaper publisher and presidential candidate, founded *Log Cabin*, a special campaign newspaper that both engaged serious issues and disseminated party propaganda. Greeley printed eighty thousand weekly copies of his paper at the height of the campaign. Other new Whig newspapers included the Athens (Georgia) *Harrisonian*, the Baltimore *Pilot*, the Brattleboro (Vermont) *Flail*, the Chicago *Hard Cider Press*, the Cleveland (Ohio) *Axe*, the Elvira (Ohio) *Old Tip's Broom*, the Springfield (Illinois) *Old Soldier*, and the Raymond (Mississippi) *Snag Boat*. These joined old Whig stalwarts, such as former Clay biographer George Prentice's Louisville (Kentucky) *Daily Journal*, which had on its masthead the slogan "Union of the Whigs for the sake of the Union." In Jackson's backyard, Caleb C. Norvell edited the *Nashville Whig*, while Allen A. Hall edited the city's other Whig newspaper, the *Daily Republican Banner*. Additionally, Nashville Whigs published the *Spirit of '76*, a booklet focused exclusively on bolstering their cause through speeches and other means of propaganda.[2]

Like Whigs, Democrats relied on established newspapers and temporary campaign publications to convey their message to voters. The Washington *Globe* continued to be the leader that other Democratic editors followed. Other prominent Democratic papers included Edwin Crosswell's *Albany (NY) Argus*, Samuel Medary's *Ohio Statesman* (Columbus), and Thomas Ritchie's *Richmond Enquirer*. New campaign weeklies also appeared. One example was Amos Kendall's *Extra Globe*, which supplemented Francis P. Blair's paper. One of Crosswell's coworkers, Thomas M. Burt, edited the Albany (New York) *Rough Hewer*. Other Democratic papers established solely for the campaign included the Springfield (Illinois) *Old Hickory*, the Xenia (Ohio) *Kinderhook Dutchman*, and the Harrisburg (Pennsylvania) *Magician*. In Tennessee's capital city, the *Nashville Union* was the party's newspaper. Nashville Democrats also published the *Advance Guard*, a weekly pamphlet devoted exclusively to politics.[3]

Democrats relied heavily on Amos Kendall, who had proved his mettle in partisan warfare, to set their campaign tone. He asked the thirteen thousand postmasters under his authority to solicit subscribers for the *Extra Globe* campaign newspaper, implying that they might be rewarded with patronage. After resigning his cabinet post, following the national convention in May, to concentrate on helping Van Buren, Kendall issued an address to potential voters. In it, he eviscerated Harrison and the Whigs in his usual style. He accused Whigs of abandoning "their unceasing denunciations of 'military chieftains'" to nominate Harrison "merely because he had once been a general." Kendall mocked the "senseless excitement" of their rallies, with their "doggerel rhymes and vulgar pictures." Added to this "mummery and mockery" were "abuses and outrages a thousand times more aggravated than any they charge against the Administration," all to elect a "sham hero." He concluded that "CONTEMPT FOR THE PEOPLE lies at the bottom of this whole scheme of electioneering." From the Hermitage, Andrew Jackson encouraged Kendall to use his pen to discredit "the hard cider system fairly before the people."[4]

Along with newspapers, a bevy of new campaign biographies appeared during the 1840 election. Combined with those produced in 1836, many of which still circulated, these campaign biographies were the most significant attempt yet to use this type of print media to create presidential candidates' images.

Unsurprisingly, given the Whigs' embrace of cultural politics, most of the biographies focused on Harrison, predictably portraying him as a humble commoner, a military hero, and the cure for the nation's ills. The 1839 edition of Richard Hildreth's *The People's Presidential Candidate; or The Life of William Henry Harrison, of Ohio*, for example, concluded by stressing Harrison's plain living. "No true republican, certainly, will ever think it a matter of reproach," Hildreth wrote, "that after passing so many years in public service, and enjoying so many opportunities to enrich himself, General Harrison should still remain poor." Hildreth went on to note that Harrison, while serving his country, had "not only risked his life, . . . but he contributed also a considerable portion of his small estate to sustain his country in that hour of peril." Likewise, Isaac R. Jackson's *The Life of William Henry Harrison* (1840) focused largely on Harrison's military career to highlight his strengths. Jackson called the Whig candidate "one of those bright beacon lights destined to shine as long as the annals of our nation endure." The biographer also noted that Harrison's "manners are plain, frank, and unassuming," and claimed, "No other commander has ever been more popular with our militia."[5]

Harrison executive committees in Cincinnati and Louisville asked Charles S. Todd and Benjamin Drake to coauthor a campaign biography, which they published in March 1840. Entitled *Sketches of the Civil and Military Services of William Henry Harrison*, Todd and Drake's work provided a more comprehensive look at Harrison's life. They emphasized his genealogy, especially noting his father, Benjamin Harrison, who had signed the Declaration of Independence. The authors also compared the Whig presidential candidate to George Washington. Both men "sought no laurels by the wanton sacrifice of their soldiers, but regulated all their movements with a single aim to the public good. Both exercised the extensive powers with which they were invested, without any invasion of the laws, or the rights of the citizen."[6]

Whigs even produced a campaign biography for young people. Entitled *"Hero of Tippecanoe": Or the Story of the Life of William Henry Harrison*, its audience

was "*the youthful* PATRIOTS *and rising* STATESMEN *of the United States.*" Through
the character of Captain Miller, the anonymous author described the nation's
current "times of perplexity" by asserting, "Our country suffers. Business is suspended. Confidence is gone." Captain Miller then asked his "young friends" a
series of rhetorical questions: "Whom shall we call to the rescue? Where find the
man, around whom we can rally confidence? . . . One who will be the friend of
the poor—who will bring back the prosperity of former days, when children did
not cry for bread? . . . Where shall we find such a man? . . . WILLIAM HENRY
HARRISON—he is the man."[7]

Of the several new biographies of Van Buren that appeared in 1840, only one
full-length book depicted him in a positive light: Moses Dawson's *Sketches of the
Life of Martin Van Buren, President of the United States* (1840). Dawson, ironically enough, had written a glowing defense of Harrison's military career in 1824.
In subsequent years, however, the Cincinnati newspaper editor had parted ways
with Harrison, a breach that was apparent in the 1840 campaign. In Dawson's
Sketches of the Life of Martin Van Buren, he argued that Van Buren's "private
conduct is not only unexceptionable, but highly praiseworthy" and that his "political career has been consistent and patriotic." He encouraged voters to choose
Van Buren in part because the president had freed them "from the despotism
of the great money power [i.e., the Bank]." Dawson dedicated his biography to
Andrew Jackson, "the greatest man as a hero, a patriot and a citizen, the world
now contains." The former president "stands as steady as the rock of Gibralter" in
his support of Van Buren, Dawson told his readers, despite the venomous rumors
spread by "designing demagogues or corrupt editors."[8]

As in 1836, Whigs produced their own biographies of Van Buren, which were
harsh in their assessment of his character and accomplishments. As Robert Mayo
explained in the preface to his *A Word in Season* (1840), he wanted to expose Van
Buren's many faults, including "the uses and abuses he has made of those CON-
CENTRATED POWERS" that he encouraged during Jackson's administration, which
allowed him to place "the elective franchise of twelve millions of freemen at the
feet of a military despot in the civic garb, for the benefit of a favorite POLITICAL
ADVENTURER." Mayo warned readers that even though Van Buren adjusted his
political opinions to the circumstances, one truth about the president had remained consistent throughout his public career: he always undertook "THE PUR-
SUIT OF THE SPOILS OF OFFICE AND THE CONCENTRATION OF POWER." Another,
anonymous Whig biographer caustically noted that in Van Buren's career, he had
supported many candidates, such as William H. Crawford, only to abandon them

for the opposition when they lost. "According to his creed," this observer remarked, "the party that wins is always the democratic party."[9] Van Buren was a "Slippery Elm" indeed.

POLITICAL MUSIC

In an 1843 diary entry, Philip Hone recalled that "General Harrison was sung into the Presidency." Although electing Harrison took more than music, Hone's impression was apropos: both Whigs and Democrats generated a tremendous outpouring of music in the 1840 campaign.[10]

Regardless of whether they were read or sung, lyrics highlighted for both singers and readers the themes that the parties deemed important. Whig songs, for example, emphasized Harrison's positive characteristics and Van Buren's negative attributes, as in the popular "A Harrison Song":

> What has caused the great commotion, motion, motion
> Our country through?
> It is the ball a rolling on, on.
> For Tippecanoe and Tyler too—Tippecanoe and Tyler too,
> And with them we'll beat little Van, Van,
> Van, Van is a used up man,
> And with them we'll beat little Van.

Another song, "Old Tip," trumpeted Harrison's military heroism:

> And now since the men have so long held the nation,
> Who trampled our rights in their scorn to the ground,
> We will fill their cold hearts with a new trepidation,
> And shout in their ears the most terrible sound—
> The people are coming resistless and fearless,
> To sweep from the white-house the reckless old crew;
> For the woes of our land, since its rulers are tearless,
> We look for relief to old Tippecanoe.
> The iron-armed soldier, the true-hearted soldier,
> The gallant old soldier of Tippecanoe.[11]

Democrats tried to counter Whig charges about Van Buren's aristocratic tendencies by presenting him as the champion of the common man:

> Van's popularity fills the Great West;
> His firmness and honesty none can contest;

His measures considered, approved, and are seal'd
By the hard-fisted yeoman that toils in the field.

In the song "When This Old Hat Was New," Democrats also stressed the president's perseverance in the face of incessant Whig criticism.

When this old hat was new, they thought the people fools—
And still they hope for Fed'ral ends, to find them willing tools;
But though they've often changed their names as knaves are wont to do—
Their doctrines look just as they did,
When this old hat was new! . . .
When this old hat was new, Van Buren was the man,
The people loved—altho' abused by all the Fed'ral clan,
A Democrat, unmoved, unchanged;—still to his country true,
He's ever been her friend and guard—
Since this old hat was new![12]

Democrats sought to undermine the popular campaign imagery of log cabins and hard cider that they had inadvertently given Whigs by now accusing them and their candidate of encouraging alcohol use. One such song was meant to be sung to the tune of "Rock-a-Bye Baby":

Hushaby baby;
Daddy's a whig,
Before he comes home,
Hard cider he'll swig,
Should he get tipsey,
Together we'll fall,
Down will come daddy,
Tip, cradle and all.

Whigs responded by portraying hard cider as the remedy for the nation's many problems under Van Buren's leadership. One verse of "Good Hard Cider," for example, addressed the independent treasury bill:

There's a favorite hobby of Matty and Co.,
The Sub Treasury scheme as all of us know,
Which should it succeed, he'll unite sword and purse,
And make the rich richer, the poor ten times worse:
But good hard cider, etc. will banish that curse.

Sung to the tune of "Auld Lang Syne," the Whig song "Log Cabin and Hard Cider Candidate" framed hard cider as the drink on which the nation had been founded:

> Should good old cider be despised,
> And ne'er regarded more?
> Should plain log cabins be despised
> Our father built of yore?
> For the true old style, my boys!
> For the true old style.
> Let's take a mug of cider now
> For the true old style.[13]

As historian Kirsten E. Wood observed, both parties intended their music to highlight interparty discord and produce intraparty unison. In that way, the 1840 campaign further hindered the use of music "to evoke national integration," using it instead to encourage political dissonance. Music also served as the soundtrack to the campaign, imprinting in voters' minds useful themes that could guide their decisions as they cast their votes.[14]

VISUAL CULTURE

Lithography remained a major partisan tool used throughout Van Buren's admin- istration and during the 1840 campaign. Whigs particularly enjoyed tweaking Van Buren and the Democrats for their economic policies. One illustration, entitled *Fifty Cents. Shin Plaster* (1837), depicts Andrew Jackson, on a pig, and Thomas Hart Benton, on a jackass, chasing the "Gold Humbug" butterfly, which rep- resents their commitment to specie. In another lithograph, *Uncle Sam Sick with La Grippe* (1837), Uncle Sam lies sick in a chair, with "Dr. Jackson," "Apothecary Benton," and "Aunt Matty" attempting to heal him. Outside the house, "Brother Jonathan" (a common euphemism for New England) tells "Docr. Biddle" that "Uncle Sam's in a darned bad way." Biddle reassures him that he has "sent for Dr. John Bull [i.e., Great Britain] for his assistance," a reference to the connection between the Bank of the United States and British bankers, such as Baring Broth- ers. A bust of George Washington, the "Pater Patriæ" (or Father of the Country), lies shattered on the floor, an indication of the nation's fragile fate.[15]

Once the election cycle began in earnest in 1840, lithography visually captured the partisan fight, with Whigs continuing to take full advantage of the medium to ridicule Van Buren and the Democrats. A work by Henry R. Robinson, *Granny Harrison Delivering the Country of the Executive Federalist* (1840), shows Harrison

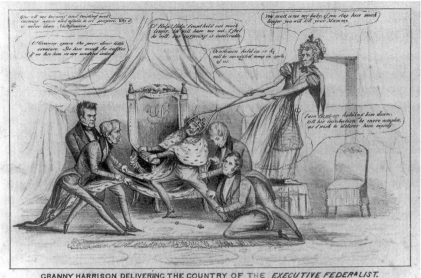

FIGURE 8. Whigs often accused Van Buren of elitism. In *Granny Harrison Delivering the Country of the Executive Federalist* (1840), the Whig presidential candidate appears as a midwife who is attempting to remove Van Buren from his presidential throne. Democratic leaders, including Benton, Blair, Calhoun, and Kendall, try to keep Harrison from making the "delivery." Prints and Photographs Division, Library of Congress, http://www.loc.gov/pictures/item/2008661374/.

using forceps to "deliver" Van Buren from his throne. Harrison tells him, "You must come my baby; if you stay here much longer you will kill your Mammy." Another Robinson creation, *A Political Movement* (1840), depicts Harrison and Clay watching Van Buren head out of Washington, with the assistance of the usual Democratic suspects. "Push a head Blair," the vacating president says, "let's get out of this ungrateful City. This is the reward of all my patriotic service."[16]

One Robinson lithograph summed up the imagery Whigs wanted to convey to voters. *The North Bend Farmer and His Visitors* (1840) places Harrison, dressed like a farmer, at a plow on his Ohio farm. He welcomes a host of Democratic visitors: Van Buren, Blair, Calhoun, and Kendall. He offers them "a mug of good cider" and describes himself as "a plain backwoodsman" who has "cleared some land, killed some Indians, and made the Red Coats fly in my time." Blair tells Kendall, "I will state in my paper that we found him drinking Rye Whiskey and that will kill him with the Temperance men and reading Abolition tracts settles him in the South. Our readers you know will swallow anything. I must make the most of this interview as our case is desperate indeed." Van Buren tells Calhoun,

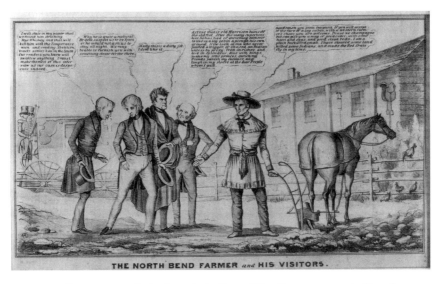

THE NORTH BEND FARMER *and* HIS VISITORS.

FIGURE 9. In contrast to their characterization of Van Buren as an out-of-touch elitist, Whigs portrayed Harrison as a common man. *The North Bend Farmer and His Visitors* (1840) shows Democratic leaders, including Van Buren, approaching the Whig candidate, who is farming his fields. Prints and Photographs Division, Library of Congress, http://www.loc.gov/pictures/item/2008661371/.

"As I live that is old Harrison himself the old fool. After the many opportunities he has had of enriching himself to live in a log cabin and plough his own ground. Now look at me who never pulled a trigger, or chased an Indian unless by proxy: I roll in riches, and live in splendour, dine with kings, make my sons princes, enrich my friends, punish my enemies, and laugh in my sleeve at the dear People whom I gull." The contrast between the image of Harrison as a rough-hewn man of the people and Van Buren as the pretentious aristocrat was unmistakable.[17]

As before, Democrats used lithography less frequently than their opponents, and their examples were once again distinctly less dramatic. Thomas Moore's *Independence Declared 1776. The Union Must Be Preserved* (1839) connected Van Buren to both the revolutionary generation and Jackson, possibly an attempt to bolster the president's standing in the North. Revolutionary heroes Joseph Warren and the Marquis de Lafayette appear, as does a scene depicting the Battle of Bunker Hill. George Washington is prominently displayed, grasping a scroll containing the words "We declare ourselves free and independent." Van Buren and Jackson clasp hands above Old Hickory's famous line: "Our Union Must Be Preserved." A similarly bland offering, *Martin Van Buren* (1840), by Benjamin W.

FIGURE 10. *Going Up Salt River* (1840) was one of the few positive portrayals of Van Buren during the 1840 campaign. Its depiction of Whig leaders such as Clay and Webster using Harrison to win the presidency, however, makes it more anti-Whig than pro–Van Buren. Prints and Photographs Division, Library of Congress, http://www.loc.gov/pictures/item/2008661384/.

Thayer, displays a head-and-shoulders portrait of Van Buren prominently in the center. On either side stand two columns. Jackson appears on the left column, holding his 1832 Second Bank recharter veto, with several snakes representing the BUS hanging dead underneath him. A farmer stands on the right column, holding a paper entitled "Ten Hours," a reference to Van Buren's executive order instituting a ten-hour workday for "persons employed on the public works under the immediate authority" of the executive branch.[18]

One notable exception to the usual Democratic lithography is the more visually stimulating pro-Democratic *Going Up Salt River* (1840). Harrison appears as a donkey carrying Clay, Webster, and Virginia representative Henry A. Wise. As Harrison steps into "Salt River," Webster asks Wise, "Do you think we have enough hard cider to last us to the Hedd of Navigation?" Wise replies, "Dont be frightened we have plenty lashed on to the stern!" indicating the whiskey barrel tied to Harrison's tail. Clay, holding Harrison's ears, says, "I'm content!" Hands on his hips, Van Buren stands on the shore, saying, "Gentlemen I wish you a quick voyage, take care you don't spill your valuable cargo!" While more graphically interesting than other Democratic campaign images, the lithograph's message was still rather pedestrian.[19]

WOMEN'S ACTIVITY

More so than in any previous election, women played a significant role in the 1840 campaign. Their activity primarily occurred under the Whig name, since the party gave its politics a religious flavor, and many Whigs clearly believed that women's very presence or participation imbued partisan activities with moral dignity. Women still could not vote, of course, but they performed other tasks that benefited the party, in effect creating their own political culture. They made and bought campaign objects and, befitting expected gender roles of the time, housed and fed rally attendees. Yet Whig women also contravened traditional expectations by attending rallies; sometimes, they even "made speeches, conducted political meetings, and wrote pamphlets." As one historian noted, the Whig Party incorporated women into its political activities "in part to normalize the still unseemly spectacle of partisan rallies and to provide visible testimony to the idea that the public good was served. If disinterested women lent support by their presence, the party had to be concerned with principle, not mere spoils."[20]

Whig politicians made certain to appeal to women at partisan events. At the large Bunker Hill convention held in September, Philip Hone acknowledged the significant female presence. "The balconies and windows were filled with women, well dressed, with bright eyes and bounding bosoms, waving handkerchiefs, exhibiting flags and garlands, and casting bouquets of flowers upon us," he recorded in his diary. "Mothers and daughters, old women and beautiful young ones, seemed delighted that their share in the jubilee was recognized."[21]

When Webster visited Richmond in October 1840, he not only gave two public addresses to the party faithful but also addressed one specifically to Richmond women, 1,200 of whom attended. He told his female audience, "The rough contests of the political world are not suited to the dignity and the delicacy of your sex; but you possess the intelligence to know how much of that happiness which you are entitled to hope for, both for yourselves and for your children, depends on the right administration of government, and a proper tone of public morals." He reassured the women in attendance that he rejected the notion of "one morality for politics, and another morality for other things," and reminded them that "a mother's plastic hand" shaped the minds of future citizens, "for good or evil."[22]

Other Whigs weighed in on women's role as well. Former Virginia governor

James Barbour said that Whig women were "animated with the one holy purpose of redeeming from destruction those liberties earned for us by our fathers, which are equally dear to woman as to man, and which she, with us, is equally bound to transmit untarnished to our children for ages to come." Richmond lawyer James Lyons believed that Whig women provided a "shield of female purity." The *Richmond Whig* observed that the "better part of creation were and are, almost unanimously Whig," and their presence "ought to silence Loco Focoism, and sanctify the inevitable Revolution which is about to occur."[23]

Even in Jackson's home state of Tennessee, women often attended Whig rallies. A reported three to four hundred women were present at Whig events in Jefferson and Greene Counties in June. The following month, five hundred women took part in a Whig gathering of three thousand people. One of the women, carrying a banner, led a procession of women on horseback until they reached the meeting place. She then proceeded to place "the flagstaff firmly in the centre of a large pound cake, '*a real forty pounder*,' which the provident care of the good ladies of Morristown and its vicinity had prepared for the occasion." One newspaper editor asked, "Did any body ever hear of the ladies paying similar honors to the *hero* of Kinderhook?"[24]

In Lebanon, Tennessee, Virginia Campbell wrote about one Whig meeting in the final weeks of the campaign. On October 7, she and several other women ventured into town, where their "ears were saluted by the ringing of bells, the buzz of the multitude & the martial music of the Harrison Guards & the Straight Outs, two companies approaching from Nashville." She described their reaction to the sight: "Our eyes were charmed by the Liberty Pole & banners floating in the breeze but the grandest of all—by a sight of the *great Ball*, which was made at Muskingham, Ohio, & has travelled from Baltimore to Nashville & thence brought to Lebanon for this parade . . . it is 15 feet in diameter." Campbell and her friends moved to a house on a nearby hill to give themselves a better perspective. "After seeing the *ball* slowly turning on its *axles* drawn by four horses, immediately followed by the Harrison Guards in beautif[ul] uniforms—not unlike the Riflemen of Richmond—then came the Straight Outs, a very new company & entirely unique in their uniforms." This company of Whig men wore "white trousers, plaid surtout (or hunting shirt) trimmed entirely around skirt & collar with crimson fringe, white wool hats, turned up in three places & fastened over the top with *coon tails*, a butcher knife or *buck horn* dirk hung at their side and a *keg of cider* & hatchet swung across their shoulders. They really looked more like indians than white men—yet we admired them exceedingly as they are really *Harrison fashion*." According to Campbell, "the sound of rejoicing & exultation was kept up all night and very early next morning[.] [T]he different roads leading to this village seemed alive with multitudes of living beings, of whom the greater portion were ladies (at least it seemed so)."[25]

Not content to allow men to speak for them, Whig women expressed their opinions about the campaign. "I never saw any thing like the excitement here," Virginian Sarah Pendleton Dandridge commented. "We hear of nothing but Gen. Harrison. It is said many lifelong Van Buren men in this region have joined the Whig ranks." Richmond resident Sara Pryor later recalled young girls (although not herself) who loved "singing the campaign songs of the hero of the log cabin." Another Richmond woman, Mary Steger, wrote a relative, "I really think the Whigs here deserve great credit for their exertions[.] Our Log Cabin is open almost every few nights, . . . and it is always full" to its capacity of 1,500. Steger continued, "I never took so much interest in politics in my life[.] The fact is you have to know something about them for nobody here thinks of any thing else."[26]

Massachusetts women also related their perspective on the political events of the day. Eliza Davis of Worcester served as liaison between her husband, Senator "Honest John" Davis, and Whig Party committee members. During the "Great Harrison Gathering" that took place in Worcester in mid-June 1840, she hosted twenty "good & true whigs," offering them beds that could hold "two good natured people each." On the day of the rally, she watched the procession from a window. "What a show!" Eliza exclaimed. "Never, never shall I forget the deep and solemn feelings that agitated me as I beheld this magnificent spectacle!" She described the sights and sounds in a letter to her husband: "With its banners, its music, the greetings & huzzas that resound on every side, one felt there was power for good or for evil in such a living mass." The excitement of the day led Eliza to declare, "I shall be a lover of the people—shall ever believe and trust them."[27]

Mary Pierce of Brookline, Massachusetts, corresponded with her future husband, Henry Poor, about the Whigs' political activity in the fall election season. Poor acknowledged to Pierce, whom he called "a good Whig," the political importance of the female presence. "We owed a great deal to the whig young ladies in this state at the last September election," he wrote. He also related a story about "a young lady, a good Whig," who was able to influence her betrothed. "When Election day approached," Poor reported, the young woman "declared she would never *marry* a Loco, and unless her lover changed his politics, and voted the whig ticket, she would have nothing more to do with him." Poor concluded, "He could not withstand this, and voted for the whig candidate, who was elected by this vote." Surprisingly, Pierce responded with displeasure to Poor's story. "I do not *al-*

together approve of the means the young lady you mentioned took to change her lover's political opinions," she told him. "It was not right for him . . . to vote the whig ticket to please all the ladies in the world." Instead, Pierce preferred changing men's minds by using "the Socratic mode of reasoning," as she had with her Democratic brother-in-law. If he voted the Whig ticket, she wrote, "I shall flatter myself so much as to attribute it in *some measure* to the wonderful eloquence I have been displaying for the few last evenings in sundry discussions," during which she admitted having "in a most astonishingly dexterous manner contrived to conceal my ignorance."[28]

The most active public female voice espousing the Whig cause was that of Virginian Lucy Kenney. Once an outspoken supporter of Van Buren, by early 1838, Kenney had changed her mind. While she still respected Jackson, she had only negative things to say about his successor. "You lack the one thing needful, you want soul: noble, expounding, true, firm, unwavering Jeffersonian principles," she addressed Van Buren publicly in a pamphlet. "Thank God, the scales are fallen from the People's eyes, and be assured you will soon fall like Lucifer, to rise *no more.*" Kenney's disaffection stemmed from an incident that had occurred shortly after Van Buren took office. She had visited him at the White House and left him one of her pamphlets, for which the president had given her a shinplaster, or a paper banknote worth one dollar. When she pointed out that she had spent vastly more of her own money to distribute her pro-Democratic writings and had even used one thousand dollars given to her by the Whigs, Van Buren dismissively said, "Miss Kenney we must keep still on that subject." Kenney suggested that he was afraid that people would think he had paid her to help him win the election. While she denied that "money was my greatest object," she told Van Buren shortly after he received the presidential nomination in 1835 that "when he should fill the office of our Chief Magistrate," she hoped that "he would remember" her.[29]

Whatever her motivation, Kenney chose to "discard close-fisted Van the mean, and turn [her] muse to gallant Harry [Clay]," whom she considered "the bright star of the West, that will guide this distressed nation, once more to prosperity, union, peace, concord, and its wanted dignity among other nations." To help Clay "break the Van Buren enchantment," Kenney continued to use her pen to criticize the president. In *A Letter Addressed to Martin Van Buren* (1838), she lambasted new Secretary of the Navy James K. Paulding's public criticism of the navy's disorder under his predecessor, which appeared in the pages of the *Globe*. Kenney believed that Van Buren's aristocratic pretensions had led him to allow Paulding's critiques. "You seem to have forgotten your origin, and think the public will do the same, by your attempting to cover with infamy and disgrace all those who occupy the place in society which you once did," she remarked.[30]

Her pamphlet elicited a response from a Democratic woman, Eliza B. Runnells, who called Kenney "a political bully, flourishing her weapon of diabolic destruction against the President" and his administration. Runnells also drew attention to Kenney's hypocrisy in claiming to support wholeheartedly Jackson's policies while opposing Van Buren's. "Mr. Van Buren persues the same course, adopts the same measures, sustains the same principles," she wrote, "yet he is obnoxious in all points, wherein he agrees with his predecessor." Kenney responded, "Because I was an admirer of General Jackson is no reason that I should be one of Mr. Van Buren." From her perspective, "the two characters are entirely distinct, the one being honorable and high-minded, the other, low, groveling, and intriguing." Van Buren's "whole life, since he entered upon the field of politics, has been made up of inconsistencies," she concluded.[31]

By 1840, Kenney had moved completely into the Harrison camp. Her two pamphlets published in that year, A History of the Present Cabinet and An Address to the People of the United States, reflected many of the themes of the broader Whig campaign. She accused Van Buren of using the poorly executed Second Seminole War to distract Americans from his administration's shortcomings. "He is general-in-chief, and in three years he cannot whip 500 Indians in Florida," she jeered. She ridiculed his "regal pomp and splendor," noting that "his table is such, no poor man can approach it—decked out in all the ornaments that the richest jewelry can produce." By contrast, Harrison was, in her estimation, "emphatically the man of the people." He was "an honest and upright man," and only he could "unite every party of the Union." Although now supporting the official Whig candidate, Kenney still thought highly of Clay, whose patriotism she compared to Patrick Henry's. Two years later, she was still beating the drum against Van Buren, notwithstanding her pronouncement that Andrew Jackson remained "the god of my idolatry."[32]

Unlike the Whigs, Democrats failed to involve women in any meaningful way during the campaign, confining them to traditional female duties such as cooking and feeding the men who attended political events. A politically engaged woman such as Sarah Childress Polk, who kept her husband, Tennessee governor James K. Polk, informed about partisan news while he was away, appeared to be the rare Democratic exception in the 1840 election. In some cases, Democrats openly mocked the female presence among their opponents. Following Webster's speech, for example, one reader of the Richmond Enquirer asked acerbically, "Are the ladies of Virginia so destitute of religious and moral instruction, that they need a thorough politician to enlighten them on the subject of the training of their children?" That same newspaper ran a notice sarcastically suggesting that Whigs should place an advertisement in line with their emphasis on maternal influence: "A meeting of the Babies of Richmond, with their Nurses, is respectfully requested This Evening, at the Log Cabin, in order to form a Tippecanoe Infant Club." For a Democratic Party that valued "a strict boundary between the private and the public spheres and resented attempts to politicize domestic life," as one historian described it, women had virtually no political standing.[33]

WHIG SUCCESS

As the election's end drew near, both parties expected victory. Despite the negative reports coming in from early returns, Andrew Jackson held on to the belief that God "has not so early doomed us to fall by bribery, and corruption." Whigs, on the other hand, had more reason to be optimistic given the tenor of the campaign. "The greatest excitement prevails," Philip Hone wrote. "Men's minds are wrought up to a pitch of frenzy, and, like tinder, a spark of opposition sets them on fire."[34]

The Whigs' campaign strategy proved successful. Harrison won the election 234 to 60 votes, with Whig victories in nineteen states testifying to his national appeal. Conversely, the geographically scattered spread of the seven states in which Van Buren triumphed (Alabama, Arkansas, Illinois, Missouri, New Hampshire, South Carolina, and Virginia) indicated the Democrats' lack of a cohesive and effective strategy to address the president's many weaknesses. In addition to Harrison's victory, Whigs also captured both congressional chambers.[35]

The electoral vote was misleading, however. Harrison's 1,274,304 popular votes exceeded Van Buren's total by only 145,956. (The Liberty Party's James Birney accumulated a mere 6,946 popular votes.) The close nature of many state contests belied the belief that the people had given the Whigs a mandate. In only three states (Kentucky, Rhode Island, and Vermont) did Harrison's total surpass 60 percent. In twelve of the sixteen remaining states that he won, his percentage did not exceed 56 percent. The other four states were closely contested. A shift of 239 votes in Pennsylvania, for example, would have given the Keystone State to Van Buren. While it would have taken changes in several close states to have reelected the president, Democrats had little reason to believe that their future prospects were dim. As Jackson told Van Buren, "I trust, still, in the virtue of the great working class, that they will rally and check at once this combined corrupt coalition and on their native dunghills set them down."[36]

Once the election results were in, Democrats identified what had helped the Whigs succeed. They had created a network that was "a stupendous system . . . commencing in the smallest subdivisions of localities, and successively combining and centralizing itself till it ascended, through town, county, and State, to the central and controlling head which remained in perpetual session and incessant activity, in the federal capital itself." Van Buren, recalling his lengthy analysis earlier in the year, which highlighted the need for Democratic organization, blamed his loss on the Whigs' use of cultural politics, although he preferred to call it "the instrumentalities and debaucheries of a political Saturnalia, in which reason and justice had been derided."[37]

Horace Greeley's *New York Log Cabin* taunted Democrats after the loss by contrasting their pre- and postelection attitudes:

> *Blarney Before Election*: Dear People! Nobody but *us* can imagine how pure, patriotic, shrewd, and sagacious you are. *You* can't be humbugged! You can't be misled! You always see right straight through a millstone, whether there's a hole in it or not. You are always right as a book, and nobody can gum you. In short, you are O.K.

> *Raving After Election*: You miserable, despicable, know-nothing, good-for-nothing rascals! Bought up by British Gold! Led away by Log Cabin fooleries! Gummed by coon-skins! Blinded by skunk-skins! Dead drunk on hard cider! Senseless, beastly, contemptible wretches! Go to the devil!

With control of the executive and legislative branches, the Whigs had every reason to gloat. They appeared set to enact their political agenda, whatever that might be, and Harrison was going to be their champion.[38]

Epilogue

On Tuesday, 26 January 1841, before boarding the steamboat *Ben Franklin* that would begin Harrison's journey from Cincinnati to Washington, he spoke to several thousand people. One diarist, John Findlay Torrence, recorded that Harrison "closed his speech by saying: 'Gentlemen and fellow-citizens; perhaps this may be the last time I may have the pleasure of speaking to you on earth or seeing you. I will bid farewell, if forever, fare the well." Torrence observed, "Joy beamed in every eye; a smile was on every face. The roar of cannon and the shouts of joy were beyond description, from my pen. It was a beautiful sight to see the hats, caps, handkerchiefs streaming from every person on the wharf, as well as from those in the windows and on the housetops." As the steamboat navigated along the Ohio River, "the banks were crowded, at every town as well as at every country road, and each farm would have a few" who wanted to catch a glimpse of Harrison. "We could see the old farmers on the bank with their guns," Torrence wrote. They "would fire them, throw up their hats and 'huzza for "Tip,"' the people's President of the West." Throughout the journey, it was clear that Harrison was beloved.[1]

A snowstorm blanketed Washington as Harrison arrived on 9 February 1841, the day of his sixty-eighth birthday. He spent the next few weeks assembling his cabinet, celebrating with Whigs, and preparing his inaugural address. Two days before Harrison's inauguration, Philip Hone reported seeing him walking along Pennsylvania Avenue, "stooping a little, bowing to one, shaking hands with another, and cracking a joke with a third." Hone wrote, "There he was, unattended, and unconscious of the dignity of his position,—*the man* among men, the sun of the political firmament."[2]

The March 4 inauguration recalled some of the cultural politics associated with the Whig campaign. Members of Tippecanoe Clubs marched, women stood on the sidelines "waving their handkerchiefs," and "a large log cabin (the emblem of a sturdy yeomanry)" accompanied Harrison as he rode to the Capitol. Tens of thousands witnessed his inauguration, but very few attendees heard the entirety of Harrison's speech, the longest until Ronald Reagan's inaugural address in January 1981. In it, the new president renewed his commitment to serve only one term and outlined the dangers of an overly active chief executive, essentially pledging to act passively while in office. Like Van Buren had four years earlier, Harrison mentioned slavery. "The attempt of those of one State to control the domestic institutions of another can only result in feelings of distrust and jealousy, the certain harbingers of disunion, violence, and civil war, and the ultimate destruction of our free institutions," he informed listeners. In addition to encouraging national unity, Harrison discouraged partisanship. "If parties in a republic are necessary to secure a degree of vigilance sufficient to keep the public functionaries within the bounds of law and duty, at that point their usefulness ends," he argued. "Beyond that they become destructive of public virtue, the parent of a spirit antagonist to that of liberty, and eventually its inevitable conqueror."[3]

In fact, the harmony that Harrison envisioned was already failing within his own party. Some prominent Whigs, no doubt taking their lead from the president's insistence that he would be a passive president, pushed to seize control over Harrison's administration. Henry Clay was the main violator of protocol. He suggested that the new president call an extra congressional session to discuss "the great and general embarrassments in the Commerce, Currency, and Business of the Country" and provided him with a proposed proclamation to that effect. Clay implied that neglecting to heed his advice would make the new president look weak. Harrison responded with a biting rebuke. "You use the priviledge of a friend to lecture me & I will take the same liberty with you," he wrote. "You are too impetuous. Much as I would rely on your judgement there are others whom I must consult." Clay waited two days to respond. "I was mortified by the suggestion you made to me on saturday, that I had been represented as dictating to you or to the new administration," the Kentucky senator wrote. "Mortified, because it is unfounded in fact, and because there is danger of the fears, that I intimated to you at Frankfort, of my enemies poisoning your mind towards me." Clay continued, "If to express freely my opinion, as a Citizen and as a Senator, in regard to public measures be dictation, then I have dictated, and not otherwise." He left Washington without seeing Harrison and resolving their differences.[4]

Almost two weeks later, on Friday, March 26, Thomas Miller was summoned to the White House to treat Harrison for a severe cold he had contracted. Over the next eight days, Miller and several other physicians attempted to care for the president and help him recover. His condition worsened, however, and by the evening of Saturday, April 3, Harrison was dying. At 8:45 p.m., he uttered his last words: "Sir, I wish you to understand the true principles of the government; I wish them carried out, I ask nothing more." At 12:30 the following morning, one month after his inauguration, William Henry Harrison succumbed to what his doctors diagnosed as pneumonia.[5]

Harrison's death, the first of any sitting US president, rocked the nation. The *Niles' National Register* sorrowfully remarked, "The hopes of a nation are withered, and high and confident expectation has given place to grief and despondency." Philip Hone lamented Harrison's loss after only "one month of unremitted labour and ceaseless anxiety." Whigs generally interpreted Harrison's death, in the words of historian Richard Carwardine, as "God's punishment for those public sins they had so frequently lamented: Sabbath-breaking, intemperance, abuse of racial minorities, the worship of money and, in the recent election, the 'volcanic and subterranean thunderings of party strife.'"[6]

Democrats reacted less sympathetically but still attributed Harrison's death to divine intervention. "Providence in his mercy . . . [has] removed the president whose election we believe was consummated by delusion, deception and fraud," Henry Horn wrote Andrew Jackson. Old Hickory told Francis P. Blair, "A kind and overruling providence has interfered to prolong our glorious Union and happy republican system which Genl. Harrison and his cabinet was preparing to destroy under the dictation of that profligate demagogue, Henry Clay."[7]

Vice President John Tyler, whom Whigs had added as a way to balance their ticket, took over for Harrison. His lack of belief in true Whig principles doomed him with the party that had elevated him to his position. The next forty-seven months witnessed Tyler and the Whigs at odds with one another over numerous major issues, including the economy. By the time the party's national convention met in May 1844, Henry Clay, whom the Whigs had spurned in favor of Harrison in the 1840 campaign, was the clear Whig presidential candidate. Unfortunately for the Kentuckian and his supporters, Andrew Jackson's protégé, James K. Polk, overcame Van Buren for the Democratic presidential nomination and used the issue of westward expansion to narrowly secure the White House.[8]

In 1848, the Whigs returned to the model of nominating a war hero. Zachary Taylor, who won fame in the Mexican-American War, defeated Democrat Lewis Cass to become president. Incredibly, Whigs again lost their president prematurely—Taylor died of an intestinal sickness twenty-eight months into his administration. In the face of increasing sectional division within the party, his successor,

Millard Fillmore, proved incapable of holding the Whigs together. The 1852 presidential election was the last in which a Whig candidate ran. Winfield Scott, who had been denied the Whig nomination in 1839, lost to New Hampshire's Franklin Pierce. By 1856, the Whig Party had disintegrated, replaced by the antislavery Republicans and the nativist, anti-Catholic Know Nothings. The second American party system was dead, and the nation was on the road to civil war.[9]

The Whigs' march into the political graveyard did not end the political electioneering techniques that they had perfected. American political culture was never the same after the 1840 presidential campaign. Political rallies became ever larger in number throughout the nineteenth century and into the twentieth century, and voters became more comfortable with the practice of candidates soliciting their support in person. Campaign biographies proliferated as managers sought to connect their candidates with voters, enabling men such as Abraham Lincoln, a relative political unknown nationally in 1860, to build a compelling narrative attractive to voters. Visual media, such as lithography and political cartoons, became a mainstay, and changing printing technology allowed for more intricate and complex representations. Likewise, music continued to play an important part in entertaining prospective voters and giving meaning to political slogans. Material culture remained an essential part of campaigns as well, identifying voters' loyalty. Women's roles also increased as they secured more political rights throughout the nineteenth century, culminating in passage of the Nineteenth Amendment in 1920, which granted them the vote.

All these forms of cultural politics radically changed American presidential campaigns, and their influence can be seen today. Political rallies that accompany the caucuses and the primaries preceding the national nominating conventions are ubiquitous in the months leading up to a presidential election. Music accompanies the staging of these events, with artists and songs often deliberately chosen to reflect the campaign's values. Not only are candidates now required to meet voters in person, but they are also supposed to use visual and social media to spread their political messages and to interact with voters virtually. All candidates have stories to tell that connect them to voters, which they disseminate in various formats, including the traditional campaign biography. Even when presidential candidates are multimillionaires or come from privileged backgrounds, voters expect them to identify themselves in some way with the average American. Some forms of material culture, such as campaign buttons and ribbons, play a less-prominent role today, but others, such as bumper stickers and t-shirts, still routinely appear. The role of women represents one of the most significant changes in presidential campaigning. Not only do women constitute a key voting bloc for aspiring candidates, but they have also received vice-presidential nods from both major parties and, in Hillary Rodham Clinton's case in 2016, have been a major party's presidential nominee.

While multiple factors contributed to the high voter participation rates in presidential elections between 1840 and 1908, when every election exceeded 65 percent participation, the cultural politics of the 1840 campaign clearly made a difference. That election marked the first widespread appearance of all types of cultural politics surveyed in this book. Despite the growth of this kind of election-eering and the advent of other forms, such as radio, television, and the Internet, the voter participation rate of 80.2 percent in the 1840 election still stands as the third-highest total to date, surpassed only by the hotly contested 1860 election, which precipitated the Civil War, and the controversial 1876 election, which included disputed electoral votes and required a political compromise to decide the result. Since 1968, only two presidential elections (2004 and 2008) have topped 60 percent in voter participation rate, a testament to Jacksonian-era partisan organizations and their ability to use cultural politics to energize the voting population.[10]

The cultural politics of the 1840 campaign also illustrate the downside of popular electioneering. Personal attacks on presidential ticket candidates increased in 1840. The intrusive character assassinations on candidates and their families, which often overwhelm analysis of candidates' ideologies and policies, have visibly influenced modern politics. Simplistic slogans, pandering to the lowest common denominator, and outright lying to win votes was a clear campaign strategy in 1840. Similarly, today, candidates routinely offer sound bites as a substitute for clear and detailed policy statements, and Americans are well acquainted with the concepts of "truthiness," "fake news," and "alternative facts" as means of political disinformation. Dismissing women's voices and contributions is no longer permissible today, although female candidates are often held to a different standard than their male counterparts in such areas as physical appearance, fashion choices, and dedication to traditionally defined gender roles.

All these negatives can be seen in modern politics; none can be considered a positive contribution to the campaign experience. Whether because of tradition or apathy, voters are just as culpable as candidates when it comes to expecting, and accepting, these undesirable displays. Like their counterparts in 1840, many people today become enamored of those candidates who titillate instead of challenge them and are willing to reward these candidates for their condescending treatment of voters.

Far from being an inconsequential election, the Log Cabin and Hard Cider campaign of 1840 represented the culmination of decades of the early republic's cultural politics and signaled the full-fledged transition to modern-day politics. "Tippecanoe and Tyler Too" may be all that many people today remember about the 1840 election, but Americans would do well to acquaint themselves with how that election illustrates the weaknesses of political democracy. Most Americans today do not want a return to the time when upper-class paternalists ruled over a much smaller population of eligible voters. But if the elite few are able to maintain power by distracting a much larger number of voters with the same basic, if updated, campaigning tools wielded during the presidential elections held between 1824 and 1840, is the United States any better off than it was during the earliest days of its existence? It is a question worth asking when considering the future of American democracy.

Notes

INTRODUCTION

1. Thomas B. Alexander, "The Presidential Campaign of 1840 in Tennessee," *Tennessee Historical Quarterly* 1 (March 1942): 36–37; and *Nashville (TN) Whig*, 1 June 1840.

2. *Nashville (TN) Whig*, 1 June 1840. The "coon" symbology used by the Whigs referenced their employment of frontier identity and had no obvious connection to the current racist connotations of the word. See David R. Roediger, *The Wages of Whiteness: Race and the Making of the American Working Class*, rev. ed. (Brooklyn, NY: Verso, 1999), 98.

CHAPTER 1: Competing Blueprints for Democracy

1. Mark R. Cheathem, *Andrew Jackson and the Rise of the Democrats* (Santa Barbara, CA: ABC-CLIO, 2015), 6.

2. Ibid., 8–9.

3. Ibid., 15–26.

4. Ronald P. Formisano, "Deferential-Participant Politics: The Early Republic's Political Culture, 1789–1840," *American Political Science Review* 48 (June 1974): 478, 474; and Reeve Huston, "Rethinking the Origins of Partisan Democracy in the United States, 1795–1840," in *Practicing Democracy: Popular Politics in the United States from the Constitution to the Civil War*, ed. Daniel Peart and Adam I. P. Smith (Charlottesville: University of Virginia Press, 2015), 46–65.

5. William G. Morgan, "The Origin and Development of the Congressional Nominating Caucus," *Proceedings of the American Philosophical Society* 113 (April 1969): 184–87.

6. Ibid., 184–95; William G. Morgan, "The Decline of the Congressional Nominating Caucus," *Tennessee Historical Quarterly* 24 (Fall 1965): 245–48; James McHenry to John McHenry, 20 May 1800, in *Memoirs of the Administrations of Washington and John Adams, Edited from the Papers of Oliver Wolcott, Secretary of the Treasury*, ed. George Gibbs, 2 vols. (New York: n.p., 1846), 2:347; Albert Gallatin to Hannah Nicholson Gallatin, 12 May 1800, in Henry Adams, *The Life of Albert Gallatin* (Philadelphia: J. B. Lippincott, 1879), 243; and William Plumer Jr., to William Plumer Sr., 10 April 1820, in *The Missouri Compromises and Presidential Politics, 1820–1825, From the Letters of William Plumer, Junior, Representative from New Hampshire*, ed. Everett S. Brown (St. Louis: Missouri Historical Society, 1926), 49.

7. An Act Relative to the Election of a President and Vice President of the United States, 1 Stat. 239 (1792); and An Act to Establish a Uniform Time for Holding Elections for Electors of President and Vice President in All the States of the Union, 5 Stat. 721 (1845).

8. Alexander Keyssar, *The Right to Vote: The Contested History of Democracy in the United States* (New York: Basic Books, 2000), 328–36, 342; and Rosemarie Zagarri, *Revolutionary Backlash: Women and Politics in the Early American Republic* (Philadelphia: University of Pennsylvania Press, 2007), 30–37.

9. Michael J. Dubin, *United States Presidential Elections, 1788–1860: The Official Results by County and State* (Jefferson, NC: McFarland, 2002), 6–31. Population figures come from the Historical Census Browser, University of Virginia Library, accessed 13 January 2015, http://mapserver.lib.virginia.edu/.

10. Thomas Jefferson to Albert Gallatin, 16 June 1817, General Correspondence, 1651–1827, Thomas Jefferson Papers, Library of Congress, https://www.loc.gov/item/mtj bib022897/.

11. Andrew W. Robertson, "Jeffersonian Parties, Politics, and Participation: The Tortuous Trajectory of American Democracy," in Peart and Smith, *Practicing Democracy*, 101–5.

CHAPTER 2: Exercising the Right of Freemen

1. David Waldstreicher, Jeffrey L. Pasley, and Andrew W. Robertson, introduction to *Beyond the Founders: New Approaches to the Political History of the Early American Republic*, ed. Jeffrey L. Pasley, Andrew W. Robertson, and David Waldstreicher (Chapel Hill: University of North Carolina Press, 2004), 9–11; and Jean H. Baker, "Politics, Paradigms, and Public Culture," *Journal of American History* 84 (December 1997): 898–99.

2. Andrew W. Robertson, "'Look at this Picture . . . And on This!' Nationalism, Localism, and Partisan Images of Otherness in the United States, 1787–1820," *American Historical Review* 106 (October 2001): 1263–80; David Waldstreicher, *In the Midst of Perpetual Fetes: The Making of American Nationalism, 1776–1820* (Chapel Hill: University of North Carolina Press, 1997), 53–245; and Alan Taylor, "'The Art of Hook and Snivey': Political Culture in Upstate New York during the 1790s," *Journal of American History* 79 (March 1993): 1374–75.

3. *Frederick (MD) Republican Gazette and General Advertiser*, 28 October 1803; *Charles Town (VA) Farmers' Repository*, 28 August 1812; Daniel Dupre, "Barbecues and Pledges: Electioneering and the Rise of Democratic Politics in Antebellum Alabama," *Journal of Southern History* 60 (August 1994): 483; and Taylor, "The Art of Hook and Snivey," 1386–89.

4. M. J. Heale, *The Presidential Quest: Candidates and Images in American Political Culture, 1787–1852* (New York: Longman, 1982), 4; Richard J. Ellis, *Presidential Travel: The Journey from George Washington to George W. Bush* (Lawrence: University Press of Kansas, 2008), 20–25; and *Virginia Gazette and Alexandria Advertiser*, 11 July 1793.

5. Sandra Moats, "The Limits of 'Good Feelings': Partisan Healing and Political Futures during James Monroe's Boston Visit of 1817," *Proceedings of the American Antiquarian Society* 118 (April 2008): 155–58; Jeremiah Mason to Rufus King, 26 June 1817, in *Memoirs of Jeremiah Mason*, ed. G. S. Hillard (1873; repr. ed., Boston: Boston

Law Book, 1917), 155; James Monroe to Henry Dearborn et al. [10 July 1817], in *The Papers of James Monroe*, ed. Daniel Preston, Marlena C. DeLong, and Cassandra Good, 6 vols. to date (Westport, CT: Greenwood Press, 2003–), 1:233; and Henry Clay to Jonathan Russell, 18 August 1817, in *The Papers of Henry Clay*, ed. James F. Hopkins, Robert Seager II, and Melba Porter Hay, 11 vols. (Lexington: University Press of Kentucky, 1959–92), 2:372 (hereafter *PHC*).

6. Robert L. Brunhouse, ed., "David Ramsay, 1749–1815: Selections from His Writings," *Transactions of the American Philosophical Society* 55 (August 1965): 190; Waldstreicher, *In the Midst of Perpetual Fetes*, 26, 100–101, 115; *Carlisle (PA) Gazette*, 9 July 1788; *Providence (RI) Gazette: And Country Journal*, 12 July 1788; and *Federal Intelligencer and Baltimore (MD) Daily Gazette*, 12 March 1795.

7. Heale, *Presidential Quest*, 49.

8. James Maxwell et al. to George Washington, 12 May 1791, and George Washington to James Maxwell et al. [12 May 1791], in Archibald Henderson, *Washington's Southern Tour, 1791* (Boston: Houghton Mifflin, 1923), 216–17.

9. Address of Danbury Baptist Association to Thomas Jefferson, ca. 7 October 1801, in James P. McClure, ed., *The Papers of Thomas Jefferson, Volume 35: 1 August to 30 November 1801* (Princeton, NJ: Princeton University Press, 2008), 407–9, https://jeffersonpapers.princeton.edu/selected-documents/danbury-baptist-association; Thomas Jefferson to Danbury Baptist Association, 1 January 1802, in James P. McClure, ed., *The Papers of Thomas Jefferson, Volume 36: 1 December 1801 to 3 March 1802* (Princeton, NJ: Princeton University Press, 2009), 258, https://jeffersonpapers.princeton.edu/selected-documents/danbury-baptist-association-0; and James L. Hutson, "Thomas Jefferson's Letter to the Danbury Baptists: A Controversy Rejoined," *William and Mary Quarterly* 56 (October 1999): 775–90.

10. James Hillhouse et al. to James Monroe, 11 March 1811, General Correspondence, 1723–1859, James Madison Papers, Library of Congress, https://www.loc.gov/item/mjm016191/; and James Monroe to the inhabitants of the town of New Haven, 24 May 1811, in *Castine (ME) Eagle*, 2 July 1811.

11. Deed of William Read to William Ellery et al., 14 April 1766, quoted in Roderick Terry, "The History of the Liberty Tree of Newport, Rhode Island," *Bulletin of the Newport Historical Society* 27 (October 1918): 9; and Arthur M. Schlesinger, "Liberty Tree: A Genealogy," *New England Quarterly* 25 (December 1952): 442, 454.

12. *New York Herald*, 25 September 1794; *Baltimore (MD) Daily Intelligencer*, 10 September 1794; and Schlesinger, "Liberty Tree," 454–55.

13. Everit Brown and Albert Strauss, *A Dictionary of American Politics* (New York: A. L. Burt, 1892), 552; Gordon S. Wood, *Empire of Liberty: A History of the Early Republic, 1789–1815* (New York: Oxford University Press, 2009), 262; and *Boston Independent Chronicle*, 17 January 1799.

14. Roger A. Fischer, *Tippecanoe and Trinkets Too: The Material Culture of American Presidential Campaigns, 1828–1984* (Champaign: University of Illinois Press, 1988), 2.

15. Edward Countryman, *The American Revolution* (New York: Hill and Wang, 1985), 100–101, 113–15; Gordon Wood, *The Creation of the American Republic, 1776–1787* (Chapel Hill: University of North Carolina Press, 1993), 321–22; Wood, *Empire of Liberty*, 134–39, 415–18; and Robert Middlekauff, *The Glorious Cause: The American Revolution, 1763–1789* (New York: Oxford University Press, 1982), 214–15, 222, 600–601.

16. John L. Brooke, "Ancient Lodges and Self-Created Societies: Voluntary Association and the Public Sphere in the Early Republic," in *Launching the "Extended Republic": The Federalist Era*, ed. Ronald Hoffman and Peter J. Albert (Charlottesville: University of Virginia Press, 1996), 307; and Matthew Schoenbachler, "Republicanism in the Age of Democratic Revolution: The Democratic-Republican Societies of the 1790s," *Journal of the Early Republic* 18 (Summer 1998): 243, 254, 238.

17. DeWitt Clinton, *An Address Delivered before Holland Lodge, December 24, 1793* (New York: Childs and Swaine, 1794), 10; and Brooke, "Ancient Lodges," 359.

18. Brooke, "Ancient Lodges," 320–22, 326, 354, 358; and Dr. Erskine to Jedidiah Morse, January 1797, in William B. Sprague, *The Life of Jedidiah Morse, D. D.* (New York: Anson D. F. Randolph, 1874), 234.

19. Vera Brodsky Lawrence, *Music for Patriots, Politicians, and Presidents* (New York: Macmillan, 1975), 27; and "Gen. Washington, A New Favourite Song, At the American Camp," American Song Sheets, Rare Books and Special Collections, Library of Congress, accessed 28 March 2016, https://www.loc.gov/resource/amss.as104310.

20. "From George Washington to the Ladies of Trenton, 21 April 1789," Founders Online, National Archives, last update 29 June 2017, http://founders.archives.gov /documents/Washington/05-02-02-0095, originally published in Dorothy Twohig, ed., *The Papers of George Washington*, Presidential Series, vol. 2, *1 April 1789–15 June 1789* (Charlottesville: University Press of Virginia, 1987), 108–9; and Lawrence, *Music for Patriots*, 115.

21. *Baltimore (MD) Federal Gazette*, 29 June 1798; and *Washington (PA) Herald of Liberty*, 23 February 1801.

22. *Baltimore (MD) Patriot*, n.d., in *Albany (NY) Advertiser*, 30 November 1816.

23. Robert W. T. Martin, *Government by Dissent: Protest, Resistance, and Radical Democratic Thought in the Early American Republic* (New York: New York University Press, 2013), 59–62, 68–69.

24. Pierce W. Gaines, "Political Writings in the Young Republic," *Proceedings of the American Antiquarian Society* 76 (October 1966): 271; Abraham Bishop, *Connecticut Republicanism: An Oration, on the Extent and Power of Political Delusion, Delivered in New-Haven, on the Evening Preceding the Public Commencement, September 1800* (Philadelphia: William Carey, 1800), 51, 47, http://quod.lib.umich.edu/e/evans/N27748 .0001.001?rgn=main;view=fulltext; A New-England Farmer [John Lowell], *Mr. Madison's War: A Dispassionate Inquiry into the Reasons Alleged by Mr. Madison for Declaring an Offensive and Ruinous War against Great Britain; and Together with Some Suggestions as to a Peaceable and Constitutional Mode of Averting that Dreadful Calamity* (Boston: Russell and Cutler, 1812), x, 3, http://purl.dlib.indiana.edu/iudl /general/VAC1867.

25. John L. Brooke, "To Be 'Read by the Whole People': Press, Party, and Public Sphere in the United States, 1789–1840," *Proceedings of the American Antiquarian Society* 110 (April 2000): 63–67.

26. Jeffrey L. Pasley, *The First Presidential Contest: 1796 and the Founding of American Democracy* (Lawrence: University Press of Kansas, 2013), 112, 285–95, 354; *Potomak Guardian and Berkeley Advertiser* (Shepherdstown, VA), 4 July 1795; *New York Register of the Times*, 4 November 1796; "Address by Pennsylvania Republicans," 3 October 1796, in Noble E. Cunningham Jr., ed., *The Making of the American Party*

System, 1789–1809 (Englewood Cliffs, NJ: Prentice-Hall, 1965), 150; *Albany (NY) Register*, 19 September 1796; and *Gazette of the United States* (Philadelphia), 19 October 1796.

27. *Newport (RI) Mercury*, 28 September 1802; and *Boston Independent Chronicle*, 7 May 1798.

28. James Roger Sharp, *The Deadlocked Election of 1800: Jefferson, Burr, and the Union in the Balance* (Lawrence: University Press of Kansas, 2010), 111; *Washington (DC) Federalist*, 30 September 1800, and *Connecticut Courant* (Hartford), 15 September 1800, in Carol Sue Humphrey, ed., *The Revolutionary Era: Primary Documents on Events from 1776 to 1800* (Westport, CT: Greenwood, 2003), 340.

29. R. B. Bernstein, *Thomas Jefferson* (New York: Oxford University Press, 2005), 154–55; "The President . . . Again," *Richmond (VA) Recorder* [1 September 1802], in, *Salem (MA) Register*, 13 September 1802; and Annette Gordon-Reed, *Thomas Jefferson and Sally Hemings: An American Controversy* (Charlottesville: University Press of Virginia, 1997), 123–24.

30. *The Able Doctor, or, America Swallowing the Bitter Draught*, 1774, Prints and Photographs Division, Library of Congress, http://www.loc.gov/pictures/item/97514782/.

31. Jeffrey L. Pasley, "The Devolution of 1800: Jefferson's Election and the Birth of American Government," in *America at the Ballot Box: Elections and Political History*, ed. Gareth Davies and Julian E. Zelizer (Philadelphia: University of Pennsylvania Press, 2015), 25; and *The Providential Detection*, ca. 1797–1800, *Thomas Jefferson: Establishing a Federal Republic*, online exhibit, Library of Congress, http://www.loc .gov/exhibits/jefferson/images/vc136.jpg.

32. *A Philosophic Cock*, 1804, *Thomas Jefferson: Establishing a Federal Republic*, online exhibit, Library of Congress, http://www.loc.gov/exhibits/jefferson/images/vc140 .jpg; and David Dzurec, "Of Salt Mountain, Prairie Dogs, and Horned Frogs: The Louisiana Purchase and the Evolution of Federalist Satire, 1803–1812," *Journal of the Early Republic* 35 (Spring 2015): 100.

33. Lawrence, *Music for Patriots*, 115.

34. Rosemarie Zagarri, "Women and Party Conflict in the Early Republic," in Pasley, Waldstreicher, and Robertson, *Beyond the Founders*, 107–28; Zagarri, "The Rights of Man and Woman in Post-Revolutionary America," *William and Mary Quarterly* 55 (April 1998): 220–24; Zagarri, "Gender and the First Party System," in *Federalists Reconsidered*, ed. Doron Ben-Atar and Barbara B. Oberg (Charlottesville: University of Virginia Press, 1998), 118–34; Zagarri, *Revolutionary Backlash*, 47, 70; and Judith Sargent Murray, "Conclusion," *The Gleaner*, vol. 3 (Boston: I. Thomas and E. T. Andrews, 1798), accessed online at Judith Sargent Murray Society, http://www .jsmsociety.com/Gleaner_Conclusion.html.

35. Zagarri, *Revolutionary Backlash*, 5.

36. Fredrika J. Teute, "Roman Matron on the Banks of Tiber Creek: Margaret Bayard Smith and the Politicization of Spheres in the Nation's Capital," in *A Republic for the Ages: The United States Capitol and the Political Culture of the Early Republic*, ed. Donald R. Kennon (Charlottesville: University of Virginia Press, 1999), 93; and Catherine Allgor, "Margaret Bayard Smith's 1809 Journey to Monticello and Montpelier: The Politics of Performance in the Early Republic," *Early American Studies* 10 (Winter 2012): 31, 35–55.

37. Allgor, "Margaret Bayard Smith's 1809 Journey," 55–68.

38. Catherine Allgor, *Parlor Politics: In Which the Ladies of Washington Help Build a City and a Government* (Charlottesville: University Press of Virginia, 2000), 94–99; Zagarri, *Revolutionary Backlash*, 98–102; and Harriet Livermore, *A Narration of Religious Experience* (Concord, NH: Jacob B. Moore, 1826), 69.

CHAPTER 3: A New Mode of Electioneering

1. *Columbian Centinel* (Boston), 12 July 1817. On the Panic of 1819, see John Lauritz Larson, *The Market Revolution in America: Liberty, Ambition, and the Eclipse of the Common Good* (New York: Cambridge University Press, 2010), 39–45; Daniel Walker Howe, *What Hath God Wrought: The Transformation of America, 1815–1848* (New York: Oxford University Press, 2007), 142–47. On the Missouri Crisis, see John R. Van Atta, *Wolf by the Ears: The Missouri Crisis, 1819–1821* (Baltimore, MD: Johns Hopkins University Press, 2015); and Robert Pierce Forbes, *The Missouri Compromise and Its Aftermath: Slavery and the Meaning of America* (Chapel Hill: University of North Carolina Press, 2007).

2. On the 1824 election and its candidates generally, see Donald J. Ratcliffe, *The One-Party Presidential Contest: Adams, Jackson, and 1824's Five-Horse Race* (Lawrence: University Press of Kansas, 2015).

3. Morgan, "Decline of the Congressional Nominating Caucus," 253–54; and Chase C. Mooney, *William H. Crawford, 1772–1834* (Lexington: University Press of Kentucky, 1974), 241–42.

4. On Calhoun, see John C. Niven, *John C. Calhoun and the Price of Union: A Biography* (Baton Rouge: Louisiana State University Press, 1988). On Clay, see David S. Heidler and Jeanne T. Heidler, *Henry Clay: The Essential American* (New York: Random House, 2010).

5. Donald R. Hickey, *Glorious Victory: Andrew Jackson and the Battle of New Orleans* (Baltimore, MD: Johns Hopkins University Press, 2015), 133; John Reid and John Henry Eaton, *The Life of Andrew Jackson*, ed. Frank L. Owsley Jr. (Tuscaloosa: University of Alabama Press, 1974), lxxxi; and James Parton, *Life of Andrew Jackson*, 3 vols. (New York: Mason Brothers, 1859–61), 1:384. On Jackson, see Mark R. Cheathem, *Andrew Jackson, Southerner* (Baton Rouge: Louisiana State University Press, 2013).

6. Ratcliffe, *One-Party Presidential Contest*, 17–21.

7. Heale, *Presidential Quest*, 51, 43–44; and Niven, *John C. Calhoun*, 100–102.

8. Heale, *Presidential Quest*, 41–43, 51–52; Charles N. Edel, *Nation Builder: John Quincy Adams and the Grand Strategy of the Republic* (Cambridge, MA: Harvard University Press, 2014), 197–99, and John Quincy Adams, comp., *The Duplicate Letters, the Fisheries and the Mississippi: Documents Relating to Transactions at the Negotiation of Ghent* (Washington: Davis and Force, 1822), 10.

9. Heale, *Presidential Quest*, 53–56.

10. Ibid., 51; Reid and Eaton, *The Life of Andrew Jackson*, viii, v, 396, 395. The Wyoming River Valley, located north of Philadelphia in the Scranton/Wilkes-Barre area, had been the site of an Iroquois-Loyalist attack on Patriot soldiers and citizens in 1778. George Washington had ordered a devastating attack against the Iroquois in return. Eaton likely used the "Wyoming" pseudonym to remind voters in the swing state of Pennsylvania of the Jackson-Washington connection. J. M. Opal, *Avenging the*

People: Andrew Jackson, the Rule of Law, and the American Nation (New York: Oxford University Press, 2017), 39–40, 201. On the use of pseudonyms during the early republic, see Eran Shalev, "Ancient Masks, American Fathers: Classical Pseudonyms during the American Revolution and Early Republic," *Journal of the Early Republic* 23 (Summer 2003): 151–72.

11. Robert P. Hay, "The Case for Andrew Jackson in 1824: Eaton's *Wyoming Letters*," *Tennessee Historical Quarterly* 29 (Summer 1970): 140–41; [John H. Eaton], *The Letters of Wyoming, to the People of the United States, on the Presidential Election, and in Favour of Andrew Jackson* (Philadelphia: S. Simpson and J. Conrad, 1824), 11; and Heale, *Presidential Quest*, 57–58.

12. [Eaton], *Letters of Wyoming*, 103; and Heale, *Presidential Quest*, 58–59, 62.

13. Culver H. Smith, *Press, Politics, and Patronage: The American Government's Use of Newspapers, 1789–1875* (Athens: University of Georgia Press, 1977), 56–59.

14. Ibid., 56–59.

15. Ibid., 58–59.

16. Heale, *Presidential Quest*, 45–46; and Heidler and Heidler, *Henry Clay*, 165–76.

17. Andrew Jackson to Littleton H. Coleman, 26 April 1824, in Sam B. Smith, Harriet Chappell Owsley, Harold D. Moser, et al., eds., *Papers of Andrew Jackson* (hereafter *PAJ*), 10 vols. to date (Knoxville: University of Tennessee Press, 1980–), 5:398; Heale, *Presidential Quest*, 49; Ratcliffe, *One-Party Presidential Contest*, 261; *Raleigh (NC) Star*, 28 May 1824, in *Salem (MA) Gazette*, 8 June 1824; and *New York Statesman*, 15 June 1824.

18. *Hallowell (ME) Gazette*, 14 April 1824; and Cheathem, *Andrew Jackson, Southerner*, 99–100.

19. Ratcliffe, *One-Party Presidential Contest*, 198–99; *Washington (DC) Daily National Journal*, 4 September 1824; *Providence (RI) Gazette*, 16 October 1824; and Robert Williamson to Bartlett Yancey, 26 July 1824, in J. G. de Roulhac Hamilton and Henry M. Wagstaff, eds., "Letters to Bartlett Yancey," *James Sprunt Historical Publications* 10, no. 2 (1911): 46.

20. *Independent Chronicle and Boston Patriot*, 7 April 1824; *Richmond (VA) Enquirer*, 27 April 1824; and *Rhode Island American* (Providence), 6 August 1824.

21. *Caucus Curs in Full Yell, or a War Whoop, to Saddle on the People, a Pappoose President*, 1824, Prints and Photographs Division, Library of Congress, http://www.loc .gov/pictures/item/2002708979/; *A Foot-Race*, 1824, Prints and Photographs Division, Library of Congress, http://www.loc.gov/pictures/item/2008661728/; Kenneth Cohen, "'Sport for Grown Children': American Political Cartoons, 1790–1850," *International Journal of the History of Sport* 28 (May–June 2011): 1301–3, 1305–6; and Ratcliffe, *One-Party Presidential Contest*, 20–21, 52, 236.

22. Fischer, *Tippecanoe and Trinkets Too*, 1–2; *Washington (PA) Review and Examiner*, 7 February 1824; and *Portsmouth (NH) Journal of Literature and Politics*, 13 March 1824.

23. Edel, *Nation Builder*, 185–87; and Margaret Bayard Smith to Jane Bayard Kirkpatrick, 28 June 1824, in Margaret Bayard Smith, *The First Forty Years of Washington Society*, ed. Gaillard Hunt (New York: Scribner's, 1906), 165.

24. *Western Carolinian* (Salisbury, NC), n.d., in *Newbern (NC) Sentinel*, 19 June 1824; *Schenectady (NY) Cabinet*, 20 April 1824; *Columbian Observer* (Philadelphia),

21 August 1824, quoted in Thomas M. Coens, "The Formation of the Jackson Party, 1822–1825" (PhD diss., Harvard University, 2004), 196; and *New York Spectator*, 5 October 1824.

25. *New York National Advocate*, 5 January 1824; *Baltimore (MD) Patriot*, n.d., in *New York National Advocate*, 23 August 1824; and *Milton (NC) Gazette and Roanoke Advertiser*, 19 August 1824.

26. Andrew Jackson to the New Orleans citizens and soldiers, 15 December 1814, in *PAJ*, 3:204; Donald R. Hickey, "'What We Know That Ain't So': Myths of the War of 1812," in *The Battle of New Orleans in History and Memory*, ed. Laura Lyons McLemore (Baton Rouge: Louisiana State University Press, 2016), 24; *Baltimore (MD) Patriot*, 22 October 1824; and *Connecticut Herald* (New Haven), 26 October 1824.

27. *Berks and Schuylkill Journal* (Reading, PA), 20 March 1824.

28. *Schenectady (NY) Cabinet*, 17 August 1824; *Petersburg (VA) Intelligencer*, n.d., in *Boston Commercial Gazette*, 26 July 1824; and *Berks and Schuylkill Journal* (Reading, PA), 3 July 1824.

29. *Columbian Star* (Washington, DC), n.d., in *Middletown (CT) Sentinel and Witness*, 25 August 1824.

30. Dubin, *United States Presidential Elections*, 31–42; Ratcliffe, *One-Party Presidential Contest*, 279–81; and Donald Ratcliffe, "Popular Preferences in the Presidential Election of 1824," *Journal of the Early Republic* 34 (Spring 2014): 45–77.

31. Heidler and Heidler, *Henry Clay*, 178–80, 199–205; and Edel, *Nation Builder*, 206.

32. Heale, *Presidential Quest*, 31, 63.

33. Ratcliffe, "Popular Preferences," 63; and Daniel Peart, *Era of Experimentation: American Political Practices in the Early Republic* (Charlottesville: University of Virginia Press, 2014), 136.

CHAPTER 4: **We Must Always Have Party Distinctions**

1. Cheathem, *Rise of the Democrats*, xx–xxi.

2. Ibid., 93–94.

3. Ibid.

4. Ibid., 94–98; and Donald B. Cole, *Martin Van Buren and the American Political System* (Princeton, NJ: Princeton University Press, 1984), 4–5.

5. Andrew R. L. Cayton, "The Debate over the Panama Congress and the Origins of the Second American Party System," *Historian* 47 (February 1985): 220–22, 227–38; Cole, *Martin Van Buren*, 147–49; and diary entry, 8 February 1825, in Charles Francis Adams, ed., *Memoirs of John Quincy Adams, Comprising Portions of His Diary from 1795 to 1848*, 12 vols. (Philadelphia: J. B. Lippincott, 1876), 6:501.

6. Cole, *Martin Van Buren*, 149–51.

7. Ibid., 149–50; and Martin Van Buren to Thomas Ritchie, 13 January 1827, Martin Van Buren Papers, Library of Congress (hereafter VLC).

8. Cheathem, *Rise of the Democrats*, 93–94.

9. Hugh Lawson White to Andrew Jackson, 7 August 1827, in *PAJ*, 6:310; *United States Telegraph*, 11 May 1826, 6 September 1826; and Cheathem, *Andrew Jackson, Southerner*, 98.

10. First annual message, 6 December 1825, in James D. Richardson, ed., *The*

Messages and Papers of the Presidents, 1789–1897, 10 vols. (Washington, DC: GPO, 1896–99), 2:316 (hereafter Richardson, *M&P*); Andrew Jackson to John Branch, 3 March 1826, in *PAJ*, 6:142–43; and *United States Telegraph*, 4 May 1827.

11. Edwin A. Miles, "President Adams' Billiard Table," *New England Quarterly* 45 (March 1972): 31–43; and *United States Telegraph*, 26 May 1827 and 11 September 1828.

12. Cheatham, *Rise of the Democrats*, 102.

13. Speech to the citizens of Baltimore, 13 May 1828, in *PHC*, 7:272–73; *United States Telegraph*, 20 May 1828; and *United States Telegraph Extra*, 30 April 1828, 128.

14. Cheatham, *Andrew Jackson, Southerner*, 42–45.

15. *Richmond (VA) Whig*, 22 June 1827, quoted in *Alexandria (VA) Gazette*, 3 July 1827; and *Alexandria (VA) Gazette*, 18 December 1827.

16. Cheatham, *Andrew Jackson, Southerner*, 51–53; and [Andrew Erwin], *Gen. Jackson's Negro Speculations, and His Traffic in Human Flesh, Examined and Established by Positive Proof* (n.p., 1828), 1.

17. Cheatham, *Andrew Jackson, Southerner*, 110; and *National Banner and Nashville (TN) Whig*, 2 August 1828.

18. Cheatham, *Andrew Jackson, Southerner*, 46–48.

19. *Washington (DC) Daily National Journal*, 28 June 1828, 29 July 1828.

20. Cheatham, *Andrew Jackson, Southerner*, 46–48; *Washington (DC) Daily National Journal*, 28 July 1828; and *Cincinnati (OH) Daily Gazette*, 12 August 1828.

21. *United States Telegraph*, 20 March 1827; *Washington (DC) Daily National Intelligencer*, 7 March 1827; and *Washington (DC) Daily National Journal*, 18 October 1827.

CHAPTER 5: Drums and Fifes and Hickory Clubs

1. Cheatham, *Andrew Jackson, Southerner*, 108; W. Stephen Belko, *The Invincible Duff Green: Whig of the West* (Columbia: University of Missouri Press, 2006), 71; and Smith, *Press, Politics, and Patronage*, 57, 287n1.

2. *United States Telegraph*, 10 July 1827; Belko, *Invincible Duff Green*, 100–101; Culver H. Smith, "Propaganda Techniques in the Jackson Campaign of 1828," *East Tennessee Historical Society's Publications* 6 (1934): 62–63; and A Free Man [William J. Snelling], *A Brief and Impartial History of the Life and Actions of Andrew Jackson, President of the United States* (Boston: Stimpson and Clapp, 1831), 193.

3. Smith, "Propaganda Techniques," 48–50; John L. Wooldridge, ed., *History of Nashville, Tenn.*, [. . .] (Nashville, TN: H. W. Crew, 1890), 344; and W. W. Clayton, *History of Davidson County, Tennessee* (Nashville, TN: J. W. Lewis, 1880), 238.

4. Smith, "Propaganda Techniques," 47–48; and *We the People*, 12 April 1828.

5. *United States Telegraph*, 9 February 1826.

6. Brooke, "Press, Party, and Public Sphere," 91–92.

7. Smith, "Propaganda Techniques," 46; Richard John, *Spreading the News: The American Postal System from Franklin to Morse* (Cambridge, MA: Harvard University Press, 1998), 51, 31–32; and Smith, *Press, Politics, and Patronage*, 72.

8. Brooke, "Press, Party, and Public Sphere," 95.

9. Cheatham, *Rise of the Democrats*, 97–98.

10. Ibid., 96–98.

11. Heale, *Presidential Quest*, 73–74; Robert V. Remini, *Andrew Jackson*, 3 vols.

(New York: Harper and Row, 1977–84), 2:144–45; and Lynn Hudson Parsons, *The Birth of Modern Politics: Andrew Jackson, John Quincy Adams, and the Election of 1828* (New York: Oxford University Press, 2009), 137–38.

12. Harry L. Watson, *Liberty and Power: The Politics of Jacksonian America*, 2nd ed. (New York: Hill and Wang, 2006), 90–91; and Heale, *Presidential Quest*, 73.

13. Robert V. Remini, *The Election of Andrew Jackson* (New York: J. B. Lippincott, 1963), 83–86.

14. Heale, *Presidential Quest*, 66–68; Donald B. Cole, *Vindicating Andrew Jackson: The 1828 Election and the Rise of the Two-Party System* (Lawrence: University Press of Kansas, 2009), 24; Parsons, *Birth of Modern Politics*, 138–39; *United States Telegraph*, 22 April 1828; and *Newark (NJ) Centinel of Freedom*, 25 December 1827.

15. *Boston Statesman*, n.d., in *United States Telegraph*, 13 November 1827; *Carolina Sentinel* (Newbern, NC), 1 December 1827; *Portsmouth (VA) Palladium*, n.d., in *United States Telegraph*, 22 April 1828; and *Boston Statesman*, n.d., in *United States Telegraph*, 13 November 1827.

16. *Kennebec Journal* (Augusta, ME), n.d., in *Gazette of Maine* (Portland), 8 July 1828; and *Literary Cadet and Saturday Evening Bulletin* (Providence, RI), 6 August 1828.

17. Cheathem, *Andrew Jackson, Southerner*, 20–23.

18. Ibid., 112–13.

19. *A Letter from the Jackson Committee of Nashville, in Answer to One from a Similar Committee at Cincinnati, Upon the Subject of Gen. Jackson's Marriage: Accompanied by Documents in an Appendix, Thereto Annexed* (Nashville: Hall and Fitzgerald, 1827), reprinted in Major L. Wilson, ed., *Mississippi Valley Collection Bulletin* 1 (Summer 1968); John H. Eaton to Andrew Jackson, 22 December 1826, in *PAJ*, 6:245–46. Sworn statement of Elizabeth Craighead, 2 December 1826; sworn statement of Sally Smith, 10 December 1826; sworn statement of Mary H. Bowen, 21 December 1826, in John Spencer Bassett and J. Franklin Jameson, eds., *Correspondence of Andrew Jackson*, 7 vols. (Washington, DC: Carnegie Institute of Washington, 1926–35), 3:321, 323, 326 (hereafter *CAJ*); and Norma Basch, "Marriage, Morals, and Politics in the Election of 1828," *Journal of American History* 80 (December 1993): 911–12.

20. *Truth's Advocate and Monthly Anti-Jackson Expositor* (Cincinnati: Lodge, L'Hommedieu, and Hammond, 1828), 14; Andrew Jackson to Duff Green, 13 August 1827, in *PAJ*, 6:375; and Cheathem, *Andrew Jackson, Southerner*, 112.

21. *United States Telegraph Extra*, 28 March 1828, 45.

22. *Frankfort (KY) Argus*, n.d., in *N. Carolina Chronicle* (Murfreesboro), 12 May 1827; *Washington (DC) Daily National Journal*, 3 September 1828; and *Kentucky Gazette* (Lexington), 18 July 1828.

23. *Gloucester (MA) Telegraph*, 14 July 1827; and *Daily Cincinnati (OH) Republican*, 17 June 1828.

24. *Signs of the Times* (Albany, NY), 13 October 1827; and *United States Telegraph*, 5 August 1828.

25. Adams, *Memoirs of John Quincy Adams*, 8:76, 49; and *Washington (DC) National Journal*, n.d., in *Alexandria (VA) Gazette*, 8 July 1828.

26. Edel, *Nation Builder*, 236–37; and *Baltimore (MD) Gazette and Daily Advertiser*, 17 October 1827.

27. *Boston Daily American Statesman*, 26 October 1827; *New-Hampshire Patriot and State Gazette* (Concord), 5 November 1827; and *Lancaster (PA) Journal*, n.d., in *United States Telegraph*, 5 November 1827.

28. *Berks and Schuylkill Journal* (Reading, PA), 14 January 1826; *Gloucester (MA) Telegraph*, 14 July 1827; and *Troy (NY) Budget*, n.d., in *Daily Cincinnati (OH) Republican*, 17 June 1828.

29. M. C. Jenkins to William K. Ruffin, 11 September 1827, in J. G. de Roulhac Hamilton, ed., *The Papers of Thomas Ruffin*, 2 vols. (Raleigh, NC: Edwards and Broughton, 1918), 1:403; "Alexander McKim," *Biographical Directory of the United States Congress, 1774–Present (BDUSC)*, accessed 24 January 2017, http://bioguide. congress.gov/scripts/biodisplay.pl?index=M000515; Remini, *Andrew Jackson*, 2:319; and John Robb to Andrew Jackson, 28 August 1827, Andrew Jackson Papers, Library of Congress.

30. Andrew Jackson to Samuel Swartwout, 22 February 1825, in *PAJ*, 6:40; Henry Clay to George McClure [28 December 1824] and Henry Clay to Francis P. Blair, 8 January 182[5], in *PHC*, 3:906, 4:9–11; and Remini, *Andrew Jackson*, 2:104–5.

31. [Carter Beverly] to [Richard Shippey Hackley], 8 March 1827, in *Fayetteville (NC) Observer*, n.d., quoted in *United States Telegraph*, 13 April 1827; report of interview [ca. 15 April 1827], Henry Clay to Charles H. Hammond, 25 June 1827, and "Address to the Public," 29 June 1827, in *PHC*, 6:448, 719, 729; and Andrew Jackson to Carter Beverly, 5 June 1827, in *PAJ*, 6:330.

32. A Republican [Andrew Jackson], "General Jackson" [ca. 4 September 1827], editorial note; Andrew Jackson to William B. Lewis, 28 July 1828; A Subscriber [Andrew Jackson] to Stephen Simpson, 27 December 1827; and A Volunteer [Andrew Jackson] to the editors of the *Nashville Republican* [5 August 1828], in *PAJ*, 6:391, 485, 484–85, 598, 615.

33. William B. Lewis to Martin Van Buren, 8 August 1828 and 27 September 1828, in Lucy Fisher West, Walter L. Ferree, and George W. Franz, eds., *The Papers of Martin Van Buren*, microfilm ed. (Alexandria, VA: Chadwyck-Healey, 1987), reel 6.

34. M. C. Jenkins to William K. Ruffin, 11 September 1827, in Hamilton, *Papers of Thomas Ruffin*, 1:403; "Huzza! For General Jackson" [1828], American Song Sheets, Rare Books and Special Collections, Library of Congress, https://www.loc.gov/item /amss.as105670/; "The Hickory Tree," American Song Sheets, Rare Books and Special Collections, Library of Congress, accessed 26 May 2015, http://www.loc.gov/resource /amss.as105330.0; and *Washington (PA) Review and Examiner*, 31 May 1828.

35. John William Ward, *Andrew Jackson: Symbol for an Age* (New York: Oxford University Press, 1955), 13–29; "Hunters of Kentucky, or Half Horse and Half Alligator," American Song Sheets, Rare Books and Special Collections, Library of Congress, accessed 26 May 2015, https://www.loc.gov/item/amss.as105650; and *United States Telegraph*, 2 July 1828.

36. Andrea Maxeiner, "Sing America! Using Folk Songs to Teach American History," *Common-Place* 5 (July 2005), http://www.common-place-archives.org/vol -05/no-04/school/; *Cincinnati (OH) Daily Gazette*, 30 July 1828; and *Saratoga (NY)*

Sentinel, 5 August 1828. Some online sources list "Little Know Ye Who's Comin'" as being used in the 1824 campaign, but in my judgment, it almost certainly appeared during the 1828 campaign. Sara Georgini at the Adams Papers concurs, noting, "If it was used in 1824, then it must have been infrequent, for we see no ready evidence of it in play before 1828." E-mail to author, 5 May 2016.

37. Fischer, *Tippecanoe and Trinkets Too*, 8–17; and textile print, ca. 1829, MSS 557,The William C. Cook War of 1812 in the South Collection, Williams Research Center, the Historic New Orleans Collection, http://hnoc.minisisinc.com/thnoc /catalog/3/9575.

38. Fischer, *Tippecanoe and Trinkets Too*, 15; Parton, *Life of Andrew Jackson*, 3:144; and *Salisbury (NC) Journal*, 10 June 1828.

39. *Marylander*, n.d., in *Easton (MD) Gazette*, 2 August 1828; and *Washington (PA) Reporter*, n.d., in *New Orleans (LA) Argus*, 29 August 1828.

40. Fischer, *Tippecanoe and Trinkets Too*, 17.

41. Erika Piola, "The Rise of Early Lithography and Antebellum Visual Culture," *Winterthur Portfolio* 48 (Summer/Autumn 2014): 126–27.

42. John Sullivan, "The Case of 'A Late Student': Pictorial Satire in Jacksonian America," *Proceedings of the American Antiquarian Society* 83 (October 1973): 277–86; *The Crack'd Joke: A Late Student*, 1827, American Antiquarian Society, https://gigi.mwa .org/netpub/server.np?preview=49401&site=public&catalog=catalog&aspect&width: 4000; *United States Telegraph*, 3 January 1828 and 28 February 1828; and *Kennebec Journal* (Augusta, ME), 8 February 1828.

43. William C. Cook, "The Coffin Handbills—America's First Smear Campaign," *Imprint* 27 (Spring 2002): 23–37; *Monumental Inscriptions!*, 1828, Rare Books and Special Collections, Library of Congress, http://www.loc.gov/pictures/item/2007680069/; and coffin broadside, folder 197 [1828], MSS 557, William C. Cook War of 1812 in the South Collection, the Williams Research Center, the Historic New Orleans Collection, http://www.hnoc.org/BNO/william_cook.html#6.

44. Cook, "Coffin Handbills," 27–28; and *The Pedlar and His Pack or the Desperate Effort, an Over Balance*, 1828, Prints and Photographs Division, Library of Congress, http://www.loc.gov/pictures/item/2008661735/.

45. John Sullivan, "Jackson Caricatured: Two Historical Errors," *Tennessee Historical Quarterly* 31 (Spring 1972): 39–44; *Symptoms of a Locked Jaw*, [1827], Prints and Photographs Division, Library of Congress, http://www.loc.gov/pictures/item /2008661773/; and speech at Lexington public dinner [12 July 1827], in *PHC*, 6:766.

46. Sullivan, "Jackson Caricatured," 44.

47. *Washington (DC) Daily National Journal*, 12 January 1827 and 6 October 1828.

48. *United States Telegraph*, 18 September 1828, 8 February 1828, and 5 February 1828.

49. Dubin, *United States Presidential Elections*, 42–51; and Gerhard Peters and John T. Woolley, "Voter Turnout in Presidential Elections: 1828–2012," *The American Presidency Project*, accessed 20 February 2015, http://www.presidency.ucsb.edu/data /turnout.php. Delaware and South Carolina, the only states in 1828 to assign electoral votes via the state legislature rather than by voters, endorsed Adams and Jackson, respectively.

CHAPTER 6: A Disastrous, Perhaps a Fatal Revolution

1. Howe, *What Hath God Wrought*, 275; Sean Wilentz, *The Rise of American Democracy: Jefferson to Lincoln* (New York: Norton, 2005), 277–79; *Springfield (MA) Republican*, 1 October 1828; *Connecticut Herald* (New Haven), 28 October 1828; *Philadelphia National Gazette*, n.d., in *Washington (DC) Daily National Intelligencer*, 22 February 1831; and *United States Telegraph*, 30 January 1830 and 13 February 1830.

2. John, *Spreading the News*, 212–13; and Cheathem, *Rise of the Democrats*, 139–47.

3. Cheathem, *Rise of the Democrats*, 145–46.

4. On the Eaton affair, see John F. Marszalek, *The Petticoat Affair: Manners, Mutiny, and Sex in Andrew Jackson's White House* (New York: Free Press, 1997).

5. On Jackson's relationship with his nephew and niece, Andrew Jackson Donelson and Emily Tennessee Donelson, see Mark R. Cheathem, *Old Hickory's Nephew: The Political and Private Struggles of Andrew Jackson Donelson* (Baton Rouge: Louisiana State University Press, 2007); and Pauline Wilcox Burke, *Emily Donelson of Tennessee*, ed. Jonathan M. Atkins (Knoxville: University of Tennessee Press, 2001).

6. Marszalek, *Petticoat Affair*, 76–77, 116–19.

7. Ibid., 158–66.

8. Andrew Jackson to John Overton (with William B. Lewis note appended), 31 December 1829, in *PAJ*, 7:655–58; Cheathem, *Andrew Jackson, Southerner*, 124–28; Marszalek, *Petticoat Affair*, 208–9, 221–25; Jonathan Atkins, *Parties, Politics, and the Sectional Conflict in Tennessee, 1832–1861* (Knoxville: University of Tennessee Press, 1997), 37–38; and Parton, *Life of Andrew Jackson*, 3:287.

9. Cheathem, *Rise of the Democrats*, 172; and Cheathem, *Andrew Jackson, Southerner*, 125–26. On the Jackson-Calhoun relationship during the First Seminole War, see David S. Heidler and Jeanne T. Heidler, *Old Hickory's War: Andrew Jackson and the Quest for Empire* (Mechanicsburg, PA: Stackpole, 1996).

10. Cheathem, *Andrew Jackson, Southerner*, 126, 134–35; and toast at Jefferson birthday dinner [13 April 1830], in *PAJ*, 8:190–91. The version published in newspapers, "Our Federal Union—*It must be preserved*," reflected Jackson's inadvertent omission.

11. Cheathem, *Rise of the Democrats*, 175–77; and James W. Wyly to James K. Polk and James Standifer, 11 January 1833, in Herbert Weaver, Wayne Cutler, Tom Chaffin, et al., eds., *Correspondence of James K. Polk*, 12 vols. to date (Nashville, TN: Vanderbilt University Press; Knoxville: The University of Tennessee Press, 1969–), 2:16 (hereafter *CJKP*).

12. Cheathem, *Rise of the Democrats*, 179–81.

13. Cheathem, *Andrew Jackson, Southerner*, 59–60, 69–76, 152. On Jackson's relationship with Native Americans generally, see Robert V. Remini, *Andrew Jackson and His Indian Wars* (New York: Viking Penguin, 2001).

14. Ronald N. Satz, *American Indian Policy in the Jacksonian Era* (Lincoln: University of Nebraska Press, 1975), 25, 30; "The Removal Act of May 28, 1830," in Satz, *American Indian Policy*, 296–98; Remini, *Andrew Jackson and His Indian Wars*, 235; Donald B. Cole, *The Presidency of Andrew Jackson* (Lawrence: University Press of Kansas, 1993), 73–74, 291n46; Cheathem, *Andrew Jackson, Southerner*, 154; and speech, 9 April 1830, and speech, 17 May 1830, in 6 Reg. Deb. 318–20, 1020 (1830).

15. Cheatham, *Rise of the Democrats*, 158–59; and Cheatham, *Andrew Jackson, Southerner*, 159.

16. Cheatham, *Rise of the Democrats*, 147, 173–74; and 6 Reg. Deb. 80 (1830).

17. Cheatham, *Rise of the Democrats*, 148–50; and 28 May 1830, 6 Reg. of Deb. 1145 (1830).

18. John Lauritz Larson, *Internal Improvement: National Public Works and the Promise of Popular Government in the Early United States* (Chapel Hill: University of North Carolina, 2001), 191.

19. Cheatham, *Rise of the Democrats*, 185–92.

20. Ibid., 192–94, 199–202; Nicholas Biddle to Charles J. Ingersoll, 11 February 1832, in Reginald C. McGrane, ed., *The Correspondence of Nicholas Biddle Dealing with National Affairs, 1807–1844* (Boston: Houghton Mifflin, 1919), 181; Andrew Jackson to Martin Van Buren, 14 June 1832, VLC; and veto message, 10 July 1832, in Richardson, *M&P*, 2:590–91.

21. James S. Chase, *Emergence of the Presidential Nominating Convention, 1789–1832* (Urbana: University of Illinois Press, 1973), 3–40, 121–81; and *Niles' Weekly Register* 41 (29 October 1831): 172.

22. Chase, *Emergence of the Presidential Nominating Convention*, 185–226; Robert V. Remini, *Henry Clay: Statesman for the Union* (New York: Norton, 1991), 369–70; and *Niles' Weekly Register* 41 (24 December 1831): 307, 305, 308, 311–12.

23. Richardson, *M&P*, 2:447–48; Andrew Jackson to Richard Riker, 25 February 1830, in *PAJ*, 8:93; *Washington (DC) Globe*, 4 December 1830; and Andrew Jackson to Thomas Rigdon et al., 9 February 1831, in *PAJ*, 8:93, 9:70.

24. Cole, *Martin Van Buren*, 227–28; and Andrew Jackson to John Overton, 31 December 1829, in *PAJ*, 7:656.

25. *Washington (DC) Globe*, 8 December 1831; Chase, *Emergence of the Presidential Nominating Convention*, 229–75; *Richmond (VA) Enquirer*, 23 March 1832; and William S. Belko, *Philip Pendleton Barbour in Jacksonian America: An Old Republican in King Andrew's Court* (Tuscaloosa: University of Alabama Press, 2016), 169–76.

CHAPTER 7: Freemen, Cheer the Hickory Tree

1. William Wirt to John McLean, 17 April 1832, in Samuel Rhea Gammon Jr., *The Presidential Campaign of 1832* (Baltimore, MD: Johns Hopkins Press, 1922), 143; Henry Clay to the citizens of Vincennes, Indiana, 18 October 1831, in *Niles' Weekly Register* 41 (19 November 1831): 226–27; Heale, *Presidential Quest*, 110–12; and *Washington (DC) Globe*, n.d., in *Frankfort (KY) Argus*, 18 April 1832.

2. Andrew Jackson to Andrew J. Donelson, 19 August 1832, 5 October 1832, and 10 October 1832, in *PAJ*, 10:466, 517, 521.

3. *New York Commercial Advertiser*, 25 September 1832; *LeRoy (NY) Gazette*, n.d., in *Jamestown (NY) Journal*, 17 October 1832; and John C. Niven, *Martin Van Buren: The Romantic Age of American Politics* (New York: Oxford University Press, 1983), 312–15.

4. "Letter XXV," 7 August 1835, in Michel Chevalier, *Society, Manners and Politics in the United States: Being a Series of Letters on North America* (Boston: Weeks, Jordan, 1839), 317–18.

5. *Washington (DC) Daily National Intelligencer*, 5 October 1832 and 4 October 1832; and *Portland (ME) Advertiser*, 29 October 1832.

6. Diary entry, 22 October 1833, in Adams, ed., *Memoirs of John Quincy Adams*, 9:25.

7. *Ithaca (NY) Journal*, 28 September 1831; *Richmond (VA) Enquirer*, 27 July 1832; *Albany (NY) Argus*, 24 July 1832; *Eastern Argus* (Portland, ME), 24 October 1832; *Baltimore(MD) Republican*, 4 August 1831; *Trenton (NJ) Emporium and True American*, 29 September 1832; *Jefferson Democrat and Farmers' and Mechanics' Advocate* (Steubenville, OH), 12 September 1832; *Albany (NY) Argus*, 18 September 1832 and 23 October 1832; and *American Advocate* (Hallowell, ME), 7 December 1832.

8. *Niles' Weekly Register* 41 (24 December 1831): 305; and *Boston Weekly Messenger*, 26 April 1832.

9. *Washington (DC) Daily National Intelligencer*, 11 May 1832 and 1 June 1832.

10. *Philadelphia National Gazette*, 7 January 1832; *Albany (NY) Argus*, 11 May 1832; and *Columbian Register* (New Haven, CT), 9 June 1832.

11. *Alexandria (VA) Gazette*, 3 October 1832; *Bridgeport (CT) Spirit of the Times*, 19 September 1832; and *Eastern Argus* (Portland, ME), 26 June 1832.

12. Editorial note, Andrew Jackson to Josiah Nichol et al., 16 August 1832, and Andrew Jackson to William B. Lewis, 18 August 1832, in *PAJ*, 10:452n2, 827, 461–63; and Andrew Jackson to Joel Clark et al., 25 May 1832, in *Newark (NJ) Emporium and True American*, 14 July 1832.

13. Heidler and Heidler, *Henry Clay*, 225–26, 237–38, 248–49; Clay to citizens of Vincennes, 18 October 1831, 226–27; and Henry Clay to Joseph M. Sheppard et al., 3 July 1832, in *Lynchburg Virginian*, 16 July 1832.

14. Niven, *Martin Van Buren*, 299–301; Cole, *Martin Van Buren*, 226–27; and Martin Van Buren to Walter Bowne et al., 24 February 1832, in *Frankfort (KY) Argus*, 25 April 1832.

15. Martin Van Buren to Prosper M. Wetmore et al., 17 October 1832, in *Niles' Weekly Register* 43 (27 October 1832): 139; Martin Van Buren to Joseph H. Bryan et al., 4 October 1832, in *Albany (NY) Argus*, 16 October 1832; and John C. Fitzpatrick, ed., *The Autobiography of Martin Van Buren*, vol. 2 of *Annual Report of the American Historical Association for the Year 1918* (Washington, DC: GPO, 1920), 562.

16. *Washington (DC) Daily National Journal*, 18 May 1831.

17. *Washington (DC) Daily National Intelligencer*, 28 July 1832; and *New Jersey Advocate*, n.d., in *Poulson's American Daily Advertiser* (Philadelphia), 1 September 1832.

18. *Alexandria (VA) Gazette*, 9 October 1832; *Vermont Gazette (Bennington, VT)*, 23 October 1832; and *Daily Georgian* (Savannah), 8 September 1832.

19. Fischer, *Tippecanoe and Trinkets Too*, 16–17.

20. *Philadelphia Gazette*, 14 January 1832, in *Alexandria (VA) Gazette*, 17 January 1832; Andrew Jackson to Andrew Jackson Jr. and Sarah Y. Jackson, 13 June 1832, and John R. Burke to Andrew Jackson, 7 September 1832, in *PAJ*, 10:304–5, 831; and Fischer, *Tippecanoe and Trinkets Too*, 15, 17–18.

21. James L. Haley, *Sam Houston* (Norman: University of Oklahoma Press, 2002), 81–86; *New York Commercial Advertiser*, 31 October 1832; and *New York Evening Post* [23 April 1832], in *Albany (NY) Argus*, 1 May 1832.

22. Nancy R. Davison, "E. W. Clay and the American Political Caricature Business," in *Prints and Printmakers of New York State, 1825–1940*, ed. David Tatham (Syracuse, NY: Syracuse University Press, 1986), 91–110; .00001 *the Value of a Unit with Four*

Cyphers Going Before It, 1831, Prints and Photographs Division, Library of Congress, http://www.loc.gov/pictures/item/2008661747/; speech, 13 May 1828, in *Hagerstown (MD) Torch Light and Public Advertiser*, 22 May 1828; *The Rats Leaving a Falling House*, 1831, Prints and Photographs Division, Library of Congress, http://www.loc .gov/pictures/item/2008661748/; and diary entry, 25 April 1831, in Allan Nevins, ed., *The Diary of John Quincy Adams, 1794–1845* (New York: Scribner's, 1951), 418–19.

23. *Uncle Sam in Danger*, America on Stone: 19th Century American Lithographs, the Harry T. Peters Collection, Smithsonian National Museum of American History, accessed 7 April 2015, http://amhistory.si.edu/petersprints/lithograph.cfm?id=325655 &Keywords=flag&Results_Per=10&search_all=false.

24. Betty C. Congleton, "George D. Prentice: Nineteenth Century Southern Editor," *Register of the Kentucky Historical Society* 65 (April 1967): 94–99; and George D. Prentice, *Biography of Henry Clay* (Hartford, CT: Hanmer and Phelps, 1831), v, 236.

25. Lucille B. Emch, "An Indian Tale by William J. Snelling," *Minnesota History* 26 (September 1945): 211–15; and [Snelling], *Brief and Impartial History*, iv, 29, 85, 173.

26. Philo A. Goodwin, *A Biography of Andrew Jackson* (Hartford, CT: Clapp and Benton, 1832), 164, 310, 321; and Reid and Eaton, *Life of Andrew Jackson*, xii.

27. Belko, *Invincible Duff Green*, 196–237; and Andrew Jackson to William B. Lewis, 26 June 1830, in *PAJ*, 8:396.

28. Smith, *Press, Politics, and Patronage*, 114–35; *Washington (DC) Globe*, 7 December 1830; Duff Green to Ninian Edwards, 8 October 1830, in E. B. Washburne, ed., *The Edwards Papers* (Chicago: Fergus Printing, 1884), 547–48; and Belko, *Invincible Duff Green*, 196–201.

29. *New-Hampshire Patriot and State Gazette* (Concord), 2 January 1832 and 27 August 1832.

30. *Washington (DC) Globe*, 26 January 1832 and 30 August 1832.

31. *Washington (DC) Globe*, 30 August 1832.

32. *Washington (DC) Extra Globe*, 8 October 1832; and *Washington (DC) Globe*, 27 October 1832.

33. William S. Belko, "Toward the Second American Party System: Southern Jacksonians, the Election of 1832, and the Rise of the Democratic Party," *Ohio Valley History* 14 (Spring 2014): 28–50; and *United States Telegraph*, 23 May 1832, 9 March 1832, and 31 August 1832.

34. Elizabeth J. Clapp, *A Notorious Woman: Anne Royall in Jacksonian America* (Charlottesville: University of Virginia Press, 2016), 96–97, 127–28, 158–59; and *Paul Pry* (Washington, DC), 3 December 1831.

35. *Paul Pry* (Washington, DC), 6 October 1832 and 28 April 1832; and Jeffrey N. Bourdon, "Compassionate Protector: The Symbolism of Old Hickory in a Jackson Woman's Mind," *American Nineteenth Century History* 12 (June 2011): 191.

36. *Paul Pry* (Washington, DC), 24 March 1832 and 18 February 1832; and *Newark (NJ) Daily Advertiser*, 13 July 1832.

37. Clapp, *A Notorious Woman*, 156–57, 165, 193–94; Bourdon, "Compassionate Protector," 196; and *New England Weekly Review*, n.d., in *Paul Pry* (Washington, DC), 28 April 1832.

38. *Albany (NY) Argus*, 2 October 1832; and *Washington (DC) Globe*, n.d., in *Baltimore (MD) Republican*, 14 December 1832.

39. *American Advocate* (Hallowell, ME), 20 July 1832; *Miller's Weekly Messenger* (Pendleton, SC), 16 May 1832; *Portland (ME) Advertiser*, 14 February 1832; and Marszalek, *Petticoat Affair*, 174, 181, 198.

40. *United States Telegraph*, 13 September 1832; *Jerseyman* (Morristown, NJ), 14 November 1832; and *Boston Courier*, 22 November 1832.

41. *Baltimore (MD) Republican*, 26 September 1832.

42. Dubin, *United States Presidential Elections*, 51–60; Richard E. Ellis, *The Union at Risk: Jacksonian Democracy, States' Rights, and the Nullification Crisis* (New York: Oxford University Press, 1987), 74; and Peters and Woolley, "Voter Turnout in Presidential Elections."

43. *Washington (DC) Globe*, 12 November 1832; James K. Polk to John Coffee, 27 November 1832, in *CJKP*, 1:537; and "Letter XXV," in Chevalier, *Society, Manners and Politics*, 318–19.

44. Henry Clay to Francis T. Brooke, 7 November 1832; Henry Clay to Charles P. Dorman, 3 November 1832; Henry Clay to Charles Hammond, 17 November 1832, in *PHC*, 8:596, 595, 599. William Wirt to John T. Lomax, 15 November 1832, in John P. Kennedy, ed., *Memoirs of the Life of William Wirt, Attorney General of the United States*, 2 vols. (Philadelphia: Lea and Blanchard, 1849, 1856), 2:381–82; and *Niles' Weekly Register* 43 (17 November 1832): 177.

CHAPTER 8: We Are in the Midst of a Revolution

1. Michael F. Holt, *The Rise and Fall of the American Whig Party: Jacksonian Politics and the Onset of the Civil War* (New York: Oxford University Press, 1999), 33–34.

2. Robert V. Remini, *Andrew Jackson and the Bank War* (New York: Norton, 1967), 109–26.

3. Holt, *Rise and Fall of the American Whig Party*, 19–28; and speech, 26 December 1833, in Calvin Colton, ed., *The Works of Henry Clay, Comprising His Life, Correspondence and Speeches*, 10 vols. (New York: Henry Clay Publishing, 1904), 5:576, 620.

4. Remini, *Bank War*, 137–48, 155–69; "Protest" message, 15 April 1834, in Richardson, *M&P*, 3:90; and Andrew Jackson to John D. Coffee, 6 April 1834, in *CAJ*, 5:260.

5. Remini, *Bank War*, 173–75; and Cheathem, *Rise of the Democrats*, 213.

6. Holt, *Rise and Fall of the American Whig Party*, 25–30; 14 April 1834, 10 Reg. Deb. 1314 (1834); Remini, *Bank War*, 129–30; Fred Kaplan, *John Quincy Adams: American Visionary* (New York: HarperCollins, 2014), 476; and Cheathem, *Andrew Jackson, Southerner*, 170–71.

7. Remini, *Henry Clay*, 459–60; *Washington (DC) Globe*, 5 August 1834 and 6 November 1834; and Holt, *Rise and Fall of the American Whig Party*, 59.

8. Remini, *Andrew Jackson*, 2:215.

9. Cheathem, *Old Hickory's Nephew*, 65–66; William G. Shade, "'The Most Delicate and Exciting Topics': Martin Van Buren, Slavery, and the Election of 1836," *Journal of the Early Republic* 18 (Fall 1998): 465–69; *Washington (DC) Daily National Intelligencer*, 31 March 1835; *United States Telegraph*, n.d., in *New York American*, 14 June 1834; and *United States Telegraph*, 3 February 1835.

10. Joel H. Silbey, "Election of 1836," in *History of American Presidential Elections*, ed. Arthur M. Schlesinger and Fred L. Israel, 4 vols. (New York: Chelsea House, 1971),

584; Andrew Jackson to James K. Polk, 12 May 1835, in *CAJ*, 5:345–46; and Major Wilson, *The Presidency of Martin Van Buren* (Lawrence: University Press of Kansas, 1984), 16.

11. Wilson, *Presidency of Martin Van Buren*, 16; Robert M. Owens, *Mr. Jefferson's Hammer: William Henry Harrison and the Origins of American Indian Policy* (Norman: University of Oklahoma Press, 2007), 227–29; Donald Hickey, *The War of 1812: A Forgotten Conflict* (Urbana: University of Illinois Press, 2012), 132; and David Curtis Skaggs, *William Henry Harrison and the Conquest of the Ohio Country: Frontier Fighting in the War of 1812* (Baltimore, MD: Johns Hopkins University, 2014), 212–13, 281n56.

12. Thomas Brown, "The Miscegenation of Richard Mentor Johnson as an Issue in the National Election Campaign of 1835–1836," *Civil War History* 39 (March 1993): 6; and *Providence (RI) Journal*, 2 June 1835.

13. *Hagerstown (MD) Torch Light*, 11 June 1835; and *Richmond (VA) Whig*, 20 July 1835 and 2 June 1835.

14. Silbey, "Election of 1836," 16; and *Niles' Weekly Register* 48 (30 May 1835): 228.

15. Heidler and Heidler, *Henry Clay*, 270–73; Remini, *Henry Clay*, 478–79; Henry Clay to Francis T. Brooke, 27 June 1835; Henry Clay to William B. Rose, 4 July 1835; and Henry Clay to [John M. Bailhache], 14 July 1835, in *PHC*, 8:775, 779, 782.

16. Wilson, *Presidency of Martin Van Buren*, 17; and Reginald Horsman, "William Henry Harrison: Virginia Gentleman in the Old Northwest," *Indiana Magazine of History* 96 (June 2000): 128–43.

17. Horsman, "William Henry Harrison," 144; "Letter XVIII," in Chevalier, *Society, Manners and Politics*, 196; and William Henry Harrison to Solomon Van Rensselaer, 15 January 1835, in Catharina V. R. Bonney, ed., *A Legacy of Historical Gleanings*, 2 vols. (Albany, NY: J. Munsell, 1875), 2:55–56.

18. Cheathem, *Andrew Jackson, Southerner*, 82–84, 99–100, 108, 112, 119, 140, 153; and Atkins, *Parties, Politics, and the Sectional Conflict*, 37–38.

19. A. O. P. Nicholson to James K. Polk, 5 December [1833], in *CJKP*, 2:157–58; Jonathan M. Atkins, "The Presidential Candidacy of Hugh Lawson White in Tennessee, 1832–1836," *Journal of Southern History* 58 (February 1992): 34–37; and *Nashville (TN) Republican*, 10 February 1835.

20. *Nashville (TN) Republican*, 2 June 1835; Hugh Lawson White to William Ledbetter et al., 24 October 1835, in *Journal of the House of Representatives of the State of Tennessee, at the Twenty-first General Assembly, Held at Nashville* (Knoxville, TN: Ramsey and Craighead, 1836), 121; and Andrew Jackson to James K. Polk, 3 August 1835, in *CAJ*, 5:358.

21. Norman D. Brown, "Webster-Jackson Movement for a Constitution and Union Party in 1833," *Mid-America* 46 (July 1964): 147–71; and Richard P. McCormick, "Was There a 'Whig Strategy' in 1836?" *Journal of the Early Republic* 4 (Spring 1984): 56. On Webster's life generally, see Robert V. Remini, *Daniel Webster: The Man and His Time* (New York: Norton, 1997).

22. McCormick, "Was There a 'Whig Strategy' in 1836?" 56–58; Daniel Webster to Edward Everett [8 December 1834], in Charles M. Wiltse and Harold D. Moster, ed., *The Papers of Daniel Webster: Correspondence*, 7 vols. (Hanover, NH: University Press

of New England, 1974–86), 3:375 (hereafter *PDW*); and Remini, *Daniel Webster*, 444–45, 448–49.

23. Henry Clay to Samuel L. Southard, 31 July 1835, in *PHC*, 8:794.

CHAPTER 9: A Movement of the People

1. *Richmond (VA) Whig*, 11 August 1835; *Philadelphia (PA) Inquirer*, 18 June 1835; *Illinois Weekly State Journal* (Springfield), 27 June 1835; and *Niles' Weekly Register* 51 (24 September 1836): 59.

2. Nicholas Biddle to Herman Cope, 11 August 1835, in McGrane, ed., *Correspondence of Nicholas Biddle*, 256; and William H. Harrison to Solomon Van Rensselaer, 25 August 1836, in Bonney, *Legacy of Historical Gleanings*, 2:56.

3. *Crawfordsville (IN) Record*, 18 July 1835; *Vincennes (IN) Gazette*, 11 July 1835; Freeman Cleaves, *Old Tippecanoe: William Henry Harrison and His Time* (New York: Scribner's, 1939; Norwalk, CT: Easton Press, 1986), 296 (page citations refer to the 1986 edition); and *New York Commercial Advertiser*, 9 July 1835. Harrison also failed to mention that immediately after the Battle of Tippecanoe, his leadership and decision making there had been questioned.

4. Cleaves, *Old Tippecanoe*, 305; Harrison to Van Rensselaer, 25 August 1836; and *Norwich (CT) Courier*, 28 September 1836.

5. Harrison to Van Rensselaer, 25 August 1836; *Baltimore (MD) Chronicle*, 23 September 1836, in *Washington (DC) Daily National Intelligencer*, 24 September 1836; *Pennsylvania Inquirer*, 26 September 1836, in *Washington (DC) Daily National Intelligencer*, 28 September 1836; and Cleaves, *Old Tippecanoe*, 307–9.

6. *Pennsylvania Inquirer*, 26 September 1836, in *Washington (DC) Daily National Intelligencer*, 28 September 1836; *Washington (DC) Daily National Intelligencer*, 4 October 1836; and Heale, *Presidential Quest*, 114.

7. *Frankfort (KY) Argus*, 26 October 1836; *Louisville (KY) Public Advertiser*, n.d., in the *Augusta (ME) Age*, 19 October 1836; and William C. Rives to Martin Van Buren, 13 October 1836, VLC.

8. Niven, *Martin Van Buren*, 398; Cole, *Martin Van Buren*, 278; and *Boston Daily Advertiser and Patriot*, 10 September 1835.

9. *Alexandria (VA) Gazette*, 24 November 1835; *Schenectady (NY) Cabinet*, 2 December 1835; and *New York Evening Post*, 10 January 1834.

10. *Alexandria (VA) Gazette*, 8 July 1836; *Albany (NY) Advertiser*, n.d., in *Columbian Centinel* (Boston), 16 September 1835; *Norwich (CT) Courier*, 13 July 1836; *Illinois Weekly State Journal* (Springfield), 23 January 1836; *Richmond (VA) Whig*, 2 February 1836; *North-Carolina Standard* (Raleigh), 11 February 1836; *Arkansas Times and Advocate* (Little Rock), 11 July 1836; *New Bedford (MA) Gazette*, 1 June 1835; *Haverhill (MA) Gazette*, 20 June 1835; *Portland (ME) Daily Advertiser*, 17 November 1835; and *National Banner and Nashville (TN) Whig*, 4 January 1836.

11. Howe, *What Hath God Wrought*, 326–27, 426; David Grimsted, *American Mobbing, 1828–1861: Toward Civil War* (New York: Oxford University Press, 1998), 4, 17; and Leonard L. Richards, *"Gentlemen of Property and Standing": Anti-Abolition Mobs in Jacksonian America* (New York: Oxford University Press, 1970), 51–52.

12. Shade, "Martin Van Buren, Slavery, and the Election of 1836," 466.

13. Martin Van Buren to William Schley, 10 September 1835, in *Saratoga (NY) Sentinel*, 20 September 1835; Russell K. Brown, "William Schley," *New Georgia Encyclopedia*, last edited 6 August 2013, http://www.georgiaencyclopedia.org/articles /government-politics/william-schley-1786–1858; and Junius Amis et al. to Martin Van Buren, 23 February 1836, and Martin Van Buren to Junius Amis et al., 6 March 1836, in *Niles' Weekly Register* 50 (16 April 1836): 126–28.

14. *Washington (DC) Globe*, 6 October 1835; and *United States Telegraph*, 16 October 1835.

15. Hugh L. White to John B. D. Smith, 17 March 1836, in *Niles' Weekly Register* 50 (16 April 1836): 128; statement undersigned by James Park et al., 30 September 1836, in *Niles' Weekly Register* 51 (5 November 1836): 150; John H. Pleasants to William H. Harrison, 15 September 1836, in *Niles' Weekly Register* 51 (8 October 1836): 94; William H. Harrison to John H. Pleasants, 15 September 1836, in *Niles' Weekly Register* 51 (8 October 1836): 94; and William H. Harrison to a committee of York, Penn., citizens, 8 October 1836, in *Niles' Weekly Register* 51 (5 November 1836): 151.

16. Benjamin W. Dudley et al. to Henry Clay, 12 October 1836, in *Niles' Weekly Register* 51 (5 November 1836): 151; Henry Clay to Benjamin W. Dudley et al., 13 October 1836, in *PHC*, 8:867; John Tyler to the editors of the *Whig*, *Niles' Weekly Register* 51 (17 September 1836): 44–45; *Niles' Weekly Register* 51 (17 September 1836): 45–46; and Edward P. Crapol, *John Tyler: The Accidental President* (Chapel Hill: University of North Carolina Press, 2006), 58–60.

17. Brown, "Miscegenation of Richard Mentor Johnson," 18–21; Thomas J. Pew to the editor, 6 June 1835, in *Albany (NY) Argus*, 6 June 1835; Thomas Henderson to unknown, 22 June 1835, in *Hartford (CT) Times*, 13 July 1835; and Richard M. Johnson to unknown, 10 October 1836, in *Newark (NJ) Daily Advertiser*, 5 November 1836.

18. *Adams Sentinel* (Gettysburg, PA), 3 October 1836; *Haverhill (MA) Gazette*, 9 August 1834; *Hagerstown (MD) Torch Light and Public Advertiser*, 3 November 1836; and *Weekly Raleigh (NC) Register*, 3 September 1838. The politicians identified in the lyrics to "King Andrew" were well-recognized Jackson associates: Secretary of War Lewis Cass, Postmaster General William T. Barry, former secretary of the Treasury Roger B. Taney, *Washington (DC) Globe* editor Francis P. Blair, former New Hampshire editor Isaac Hill, presidential advisers William B. Lewis and Amos Kendall, Attorney General Benjamin F. Butler, and Secretary of the Treasury Levi Woodbury. Lawrence, *Music for Patriots*, 248–49.

19. *Pennsylvanian* (Philadelphia), 3 October 1836; and *Albany (NY) Argus*, 14 October 1836.

20. Fischer, *Tippecanoe and Trinkets Too*, 18–21.

21. Ibid., 21–23.

22. *New-Hampshire Patriot and State Gazette* (Concord), 13 July 1835; *Daily Pennsylvanian* (Philadelphia), 1 October 1836; John H. Eaton to Richard M. Johnson, 30 June 1836, in *Washington (DC) Globe*, n.d., in *New York American*, 19 July 1836; and Richard M. Johnson to John H. Eaton [ca. 30 June 1836], in *Washington (DC) Globe*, n.d., in *New York American*, 19 July 1836.

23. *New York American*, 19 July 1836; *Alexandria (VA) Gazette*, 8 September 1836; *Newark (NJ) Daily Advertiser*, 5 October 1836; and *Columbian Register* (New Haven, CT), 22 October 1836.

24. Cheathem, *Old Hickory's Nephew*, 107–8; and Smith, *Press, Politics, and Patronage*, 139.

25. *United States Telegraph*, 24 June 1835.

26. *United States Telegraph*, 6 September 1836; and Cole, *Martin Van Buren*, 10–13.

27. William Miles, *The Image Makers: A Bibliography of American Presidential Campaign Biographies* (Metuchen, NJ: Scarecrow Press, 1979), 8–12; [William Emmons], *Authentic Biography of Col. Richard M. Johnson, of Kentucky* (Boston: Langworthy, 1834), 85; and [William Emmons], *Biography of Martin Van Buren, Vice President of the United States* (Washington, DC: Gideon Jr., 1835), 44.

28. J. D. Wade, "The Authorship of David Crockett's 'Autobiography,'" *Georgia Historical Quarterly* 6 (September 1922): 265–68; David Crockett [Augustin S. Clayton?], *The Life of Martin Van Buren* [. . .] (Philadelphia: Robert Wright, 1835), 19–20, 7; Robert J. Brugger, *Beverly Tucker: Heart over Head in the Old South* (Baltimore, MD: Johns Hopkins University Press, 1978); and [Nathaniel] Beverley Tucker, *The Partisan Leader: A Novel* (1836; Richmond: West and Johnston, 1862), 23, http://docsouth.unc.edu/imls/tucker/tucker.html.

29. [Henry K. Strong], *A Brief History of the Public Services of Gen. William Henry Harrison* [. . .] (Harrisburg, PA: n.p., 1835), 16; Richard Smith Elliott, *Notes Taken in Sixty Years* (St. Louis, MO: Studley, 1883), 55–56; and James Hall, *A Memoir of the Public Services of William Henry Harrison of Ohio* (Philadelphia: Edward C. Biddle, 1836), 322–23.

30. Alan R. Miller, "American's First Political Satirist: Seba Smith of Maine," *Journalism Quarterly* 47 (Autumn 1970): 491; John H. Schroeder, "Major Jack Downing and American Expansionism: Seba Smith's Political Satire, 1847–1856," *New England Quarterly* 50 (June 1977): 214–17; Henry Ladd Smith, "The Two Major Downings: Rivalry in Political Satire," *Journalism Quarterly* 41 (Winter 1964): 76; and [Seba Smith], *The Life and Writings of Major Jack Downing, of Downingville, Away Down East in the State of Maine* (Boston: Lilly, Wait, Colman, and Holden, 1834), 151.

31. Smith, "The Two Major Downings," 77–78; Schroeder, "Major Jack Downing," 217; [Charles Augustus Davis], *Letters of J. Downing, Major, Downingville Militia, Second Brigade, to His Old Friend Mr. Dwight, of the New-York Daily Advertiser* (London: John Murray, 1835), 99; and Edwin A. Miles, "The Whig Party and the Menace of Caesar," *Tennessee Historical Quarterly* 27 (Winter 1968): 361–79.

32. *King Andrew the First*, 1833, Prints and Photographs Division, Library of Congress, http://www.loc.gov/pictures/item/2008661753/.

33. Cohen, "Sport for Grown Children," 1301–18; *All Fours—Important State of the Game—The Knave about to Be Lost*, 1836, Prints and Photographs Division, Library of Congress, http://www.loc.gov/pictures/item/2008661283/; *Grand Match Between the Kinderhook Poney and the Ohio Ploughman*, 1836, Prints and Photographs Division, Library of Congress, http://www.loc.gov/pictures/item/2008661286/; and *Set-to between the Champion Old Tip & the Swell Dutcheman of Kinderhook*, 1836, Prints and Photographs Division, Library of Congress, http://www.loc.gov/pictures/item/2008661284/. For the use of "Salt River" as a metaphorical reference to political disaster, see Liz Hutter, "'Ho for Salt River!' Politics, Loss, and Satire," *Common-Place* 7 (April 2007), http://www.common-place.org/vol-07/no-03/hutter/.

34. *An Affecting Scene in Kentucky*, 1836?, Prints and Photographs Division, Library

of Congress, http://www.loc.gov/pictures/item/2008661287/; and Tanisha C. Ford and Carl R. Weinberg, "Slavery, Interracial Marriage, and the Election of 1836," *OAH Magazine of History* 23 (April 2009): 57–61. There is some uncertainty about whether this lithograph appeared during the 1836 or the 1840 election. I have followed the Library of Congress's logic in assigning it to 1836.

35. Piola, "Rise of Early American Lithography," 128–31; John Carbonell, "Anthony Imbert. New York's Pioneer Lithographer," in Tatham, *Prints and Printmakers of New York State*, 27; Cohen, "Sport for Grown Children," 1301–18; and Brandon Inabinet, "Democratic Circulation: Jacksonian Lithographs in U.S. Public Discourse," *Rhetoric and Public Affairs* 15 (Winter 2012): 659–66.

36. Lydia Maria Child, *The History of the Condition of Women, in Various Ages and Nations*, 2 vols. (London: Simpkin, Marshall, 1835), 2:265.

37. *Phoenix Civilian* (Cumberland, MD), 10 September 1836.

38. *Nashville (TN) National Banner and Daily Advertiser*, 31 August 1836.

39. *Portland (ME) Advertiser*, 12 July 1836; *Greensboro (NC) Patriot*, 20 July 1836; and *Montpelier (VT) Watchman*, 21 July 1835.

40. *Arkansas Gazette* (Little Rock), 19 July 1836; *Gloucester (MA) Democrat*, 15 January 1836; and *Columbia (TN) Democrat*, n.d., in *Frankfort (KY) Argus*, 28 September 1836.

41. Elizabeth R. Varon, *We Mean to Be Counted: White Women and Politics in Antebellum Virginia* (Chapel Hill: University of North Carolina Press, 1998), 74; and Lucy Kenney, *Description of a Visit to Washington* [. . .] (n.p., 1835), 3, 2, 8, 11.

42. Celia Morris Eckhardt, *Fanny Wright: Rebel in America* (Cambridge, MA: Harvard University Press, 1984), 118–20, 244–55; *Philadelphia Inquirer*, 26 July 1836 and 1 August 1836; and *Pawtucket (RI) Chronicle and Rhode-Island and Massachusetts Register*, 28 October 1836.

43. Roderick S. French, "Liberation from Man and God in Boston: Abner Kneeland's Free-Thought Campaign, 1830–1839," *American Quarterly* 32 (Summer 1980): 202–13; *Boston Investigator*, 24 October 1834, in *Niles' Weekly Register* 47 (22 November 1834): 178; *Jamestown (NY) Journal*, 22 June 1836; *Scioto Gazette* (Chillicothe, OH), 16 November 1836; *Salem (MA) Gazette*, 11 November 1836; *Baltimore (MD) Chronicle*, n.d., quoted in *New-Hampshire Sentinel* (Keene), 18 June 1835; and *Portland (ME) Advertiser*, 27 September 1836. "Loco focos" was the name given to a faction of pro-labor, egalitarian New York Democrats. It originated during an October 1835 meeting at Tammany Hall, the state headquarters of the New York Democrats. During a heated debate over a congressional appointment, one group of Democrats turned off the gaslights in the meeting hall to stop its proceedings. The "radical" faction used "loco foco" matches to provide light, giving them their nickname. Mark R. Cheatham and Terry Corps, eds., *Dictionary of Jacksonian Era and Manifest Destiny*, 2nd ed. (Lanham, MD: Rowman and Littlefield, 2017) 224–25.

44. Lori D. Ginzberg, "'The Hearts of Your Readers Will Shudder': Fanny Wright, Infidelity, and American Freethought," *American Quarterly* 46 (June 1994): 195; and *Ladies' Morning Star* (New York), n.d., in *New York Advocate of Moral Reform*, 1 August 1836, 112.

45. Hickey, *War of 1812*, 126–27; "William Allen," *BDUSC*, accessed 24 January

2017, http://bioguide.congress.gov/scripts/biodisplay.pl?index=a000150; and *Elyria (OH) Republican*, 11 February 1836.

46. *Scioto Gazette* (Chillicothe, OH), 10 February 1836, 20 January 1836, and 28 September 1836; and *Nashville (TN) National Banner and Daily Advertiser*, 24 August 1836.

47. Dubin, *United States Presidential Elections*, 61–71.

48. Shade, "Martin Van Buren, Slavery, and the Election of 1836," 479–80; and Dubin, *United States Presidential Elections*, 61.

49. Howe, *What Hath God Wrought*, 487; 8 February 1837, 13 Reg. Deb. 738–39 (1837); and James Graham to William Alexander Graham, 29 December 1836, in J. G. de Roulhac Hamilton, Max R. Williams, and Mary Reynolds Peacock, eds., *The Papers of William A. Graham*, 8 vols. (Raleigh: North Carolina Division of Archives and History, 1957–92), 1:472.

CHAPTER 10: **He Will Be a Party President**

1. Thomas Brown, "From Old Hickory to Sly Fox: The Routinization of Charisma in the Early Democratic Party," *Journal of the Early Republic* 11 (Autumn 1991): 339–69; James Buchanan to Benjamin Carpenter et al., 17 December 1836, in John Bassett Moore, ed., *The Works of James Buchanan, Comprising His Speeches, State Papers, and Private Correspondence*, 12 vols. (Philadelphia: J. B. Lippincott, 1908–11), 3:130; diary entry, 4 March 1837, in Bayard Tuckerman, ed., *The Diary of Philip Hone*, 2 vols. (New York: Dodd, Mead, 1889), 1:245–46; John C. Calhoun to Samuel D. Ingham, 18 December 1836, and John C. Calhoun to James E. Colhoun, 22 March 1837, in Robert L. Meriwether, W. Edwin Hemphill, Clyde N. Wilson, et al., eds., *The Papers of John C. Calhoun*, 28 vols. (Columbia: University of South Carolina Press, 1959–2003), 13:309, 499; and Edward Everett to Daniel Webster, 16 December 1836, in PDW, 4:165–66.

2. Cole, *Martin Van Buren*, 289; 1st inaugural address, 4 March 1837, in Richardson, *M&P*, 3:316–19; and Wilson, *Presidency of Martin Van Buren*, 41, 38–39.

3. Richardson, *M&P*, 3:315.

4. Jessica M. Lepler, *The Many Panics of 1837: People, Politics, and the Creation of a Transatlantic Financial Crisis* (New York: Cambridge University Press, 2013), 4.

5. Wilson, *Presidency of Martin Van Buren*, 45–46; Lepler, *Many Panics of 1837*, 18–23; and Howe, *What Hath God Wrought*, 502–3.

6. Wilson, *Presidency of Martin Van Buren*, 46–47, 50; and Howe, *What Hath God Wrought*, 500, 503–5.

7. Wilson, *Presidency of Martin Van Buren*, 52–54; Cole, *Martin Van Buren*, 295–96; Martin Van Buren to William C. Rives, 8 April 1837, VLC; and Lepler, *Many Panics of 1837*, 191–218.

8. Wilson, *Presidency of Martin Van Buren*, 55; Lepler, *Many Panics of 1837*, 117–19, 122, 152–54; *Washington (DC) Globe*, 22 April 1837; and *Washington (DC) Daily National Intelligencer*, 24 April 1837.

9. Cole, *Martin Van Buren*, 296–303, Wilson, *Presidency of Martin Van Buren*, 57–79; Lepler, *Many Panics of 1837*, 218–21; Howe, *What Hath God Wrought*, 506–7; message to special session, 4 September 1837, in Richardson, *M&P*, 3:328, 334; and *Washington (DC) Globe*, 5 September 1837.

10. Wilson, *Presidency of Martin Van Buren*, 61; Cole, *Martin Van Buren*, 309–12; and diary entry, 10 October 1837, in Adams, ed., *Memoirs of John Quincy Adams*, 9:399.

11. Cole, *Martin Van Buren*, 330–39; and Jeffrey L. Pasley, "Minnows, Spies, and Aristocrats: The Social Crisis of Congress in the Age of Martin Van Buren," *Journal of the Early Republic* 27 (Winter 2007): 632–49.

12. Wilson, *Presidency of Martin Van Buren*, 123–27, 138–41; Cole, *Martin Van Buren*, 359–60; and *Washington (DC) Globe*, 3 July 1840.

13. Cole, *Martin Van Buren*, 318–21; and Wilson, *Presidency of Martin Van Buren*, 148–52.

14. Wilson, *Presidency of Martin Van Buren*, 157–69; and Cole, *Martin Van Buren*, 321–27.

15. Cole, *Martin Van Buren*, 364–66; Wilson, *Presidency of Martin Van Buren*, 181–87; 1st annual message, 5 December 1837, 2nd annual message, 3 December 1838, and 3rd annual message, 2 December 1839, in Richardson, *M&P*, 3:391, 498, 537; and Cheathem, *Andrew Jackson, Southerner*, 158–59.

16. Shade, "Martin Van Buren, Slavery, and the Election of 1836," 481; inaugural address, 4 March 1837, in Richardson, *M&P*, 3:317–19; Cole, *Martin Van Buren*, 329, 361–64; and Wilson, *Presidency of Martin Van Buren*, 201–2.

17. Cole, *Martin Van Buren*, 363–64; Wilson, *Presidency of Martin Van Buren*, 154–57; Cong. Globe, 25th Cong., 2d Sess. 55 (1837); and Niven, *Martin Van Buren*, 468.

CHAPTER 11: Bring Out the Hurra Boys

1. Norma Lois Peterson, *The Presidencies of William Henry Harrison and John Tyler* (Lawrence: University Press of Kansas, 1989), 24–25; and William N. Chambers, "Election of 1840," in Schlesinger and Israel, *History of American Presidential Elections*, 1:659.

2. Chambers, "Election of 1840," 660–61; and Millard Fillmore to G. W. Patterson, 6 February 1839, in Frank Severance, ed., *Millard Fillmore Papers*, 2 vols. (Buffalo, NY: Buffalo Historical Society, 1907), 2:185.

3. Remini, *Daniel Webster*, 483–84; Timothy D. Johnson, *Winfield Scott: The Quest for Military Glory* (Lawrence: University Press of Kansas, 1998), 136–37; Robert Gray Gunderson, *The Log-Cabin Campaign* (Lexington: University of Kentucky Press, 1957), 51–53; and Winfield Scott to Henry Clay, 5 February 1839, in *PHC*, 9:277.

4. *Springfield (IL) Sangamo Journal*, 3 November 1838.

5. Gunderson, *Log-Cabin Campaign*, 48–51; William Henry Harrison to Harmar Denny, 2 December 1838, in the Richmond (VA) *Yeoman*, 29 January 1840; William Henry Harrison to William Ayres, 22 August 1838, William Henry Harrison Papers and Documents, 1791–1864 (DC050), Indiana Historical Society, Indianapolis; and John Bradley to Thurlow Weed, 29 August 1839, Thurlow Weed Papers, Department of Rare Books, Special Collections, and Preservation, River Campus Libraries, University of Rochester, New York.

6. Chambers, "Election of 1840," 657–58.

7. Ibid., 662–63; Gunderson, *Log-Cabin Campaign*, 57–62; and Henry Clay to Thomas Metcalfe et al., 20 November 1839, in *PHC*, 9:359.

8. Michael F. Holt, "The Election of 1840, Voter Mobilization, and the Emergence of the Second American Party System: A Reappraisal of Jacksonian Voting Behavior,"

in *A Master's Due: Essays in Honor of David Herbert Donald*, ed. William J. Cooper Jr., Michael F. Holt, and John McCardell (Baton Rouge: Louisiana State University Press, 1985), 54; Holt, *Rise and Fall of the American Whig Party*, 103–4; Heidler and Heidler, *Henry Clay*, 307–9; and Remini, *Henry Clay*, 549–52.

9. Dan Monroe, *The Republican Vision of John Tyler* (College Station: Texas A&M University Press, 2003), 57–65; Gunderson, *Log-Cabin Campaign*, 64–66; and *New York Spectator*, 9 March 1840.

10. *Niles' Weekly Register* 58 (9 May 1840): 152, 150; diary entry, 11 May 1840, in Tuckerman, ed., *Diary of Philip Hone*, 2:26; and Chambers, "Election of 1840," 666–67, 722–23.

11. Chambers, "Election of 1840," 667; unknown to Amos Kendall, 12 August 1839, VLC; and Andrew Jackson to Francis P. Blair, 22 May 1840, in *CAJ*, 6:61.

12. Chambers, "Election of 1840," 667; diary entry, 11 May 1840, in Tuckerman, ed., *Diary of Philip Hone*, 2:26; *Niles' Weekly Register* 58 (9 May 1840): 151; *Portland (ME) Advertiser*, 19 November 1832; and *Louisville (KY) Journal*, n.d., in *Massachusetts Spy* (Worcester), 21 October 1840.

13. Corey M. Brooks, *Liberty Power: Antislavery Third Parties and the Transformation of American Politics* (Chicago: University of Chicago Press, 2016), 9–10, 36; and Reinhard O. Johnson, *The Liberty Party, 1840–1848: Antislavery Third-Party Politics in the United States* (Baton Rouge: Louisiana State University Press, 2009), 12, 14.

14. Brooks, *Liberty Power*, 38–39; and Johnson, *Liberty Party*, 326–27, 339.

15. Gunderson, *Log-Cabin Campaign*, 95–96.

16. Cole, *Martin Van Buren*, 345; Gunderson, *Log-Cabin Campaign*, 101; and Charles Ogle, *Speech of Mr. Ogle, of Pennsylvania, on the Regal Splendor of the President's Palace* (Washington, DC: n.p., 1840), 1–32.

17. *Portland (ME) Advertiser*, 1 September 1840; *Wabash Courier* (Terre Haute, IN), 19 September 1840; *Ohio State Journal* (Columbus), 8 February 1840; *Richmond (VA) Whig*, 10 July 1840; and A Workingman, *More Than One Hundred Reasons Why William Henry Harrison Should and Will Have the Support of the Democracy* [. . .] (Boston: Tuttle, Dennett and Chisholm, 1840), 8.

18. Peterson, *Presidencies of Harrison and Tyler*, 23–24.

19. Cole, *Martin Van Buren*, 361–64; "Thomas Morris," BDUSC, accessed 24 January 2017, http://bioguide.congress.gov/scripts/biodisplay.pl?index=M000989; *Wilmington (NC) Advertiser*, n.d., in *Augusta (GA) Chronicle*, 8 October 1840; *Richmond (VA) Whig*, 14 January 1840; and *Charleston (SC) Southern Patriot*, 11 June 1840.

20. Horsman, "William Henry Harrison," 134–35, 142; *Western Carolinian* (Salisbury, NC), 20 March 1840; *Washington (DC) Globe*, 25 September 1840; Thomas Ritchie to William Allen, 16 February 1840, William Allen Papers, Library of Congress; and Andrew Jackson to Charles F. M. Dancy and Thomas B. M. Murphy, 3 July 1840, in *CAJ*, 6:67.

CHAPTER 12: Hard Cider, Coons, Log Cabins, and Big Balls

1. See, for example, Ronald G. Shafer, *The Carnival Campaign: How the Rollicking 1840 Campaign of "Tippecanoe and Tyler Too" Changed Presidential Elections Forever* (Chicago: Chicago Review Press, 2016), vii, 236.

2. Fischer, *Tippecanoe and Trinkets Too*, 29–49.

3. *New York Log Cabin*, 2 May 1840; Elliott, *Notes Taken in Sixty Years*, 121; Chambers, "Election of 1840," 669; and diary entry, 10 April 1840, in Tuckerman, ed., *Diary of Philip Hone*, 2:22.

4. Chambers, "Election of 1840," 669; Robert G. Gunderson, "Thurlow Weed's Network: Whig Party Organization in 1840," *Indiana Magazine of History* 48 (June 1952): 113; diary entry, 4 May 1840, in St. George L. Sioussat, ed., "Diaries of S. H. Laughlin of Tennessee, 1840, 1843," *Tennessee Historical Magazine* 2 (1916): 54–55; and Virginia Campbell to Mary Campbell, 11 October 1840, David Campbell Papers, Tennessee State Library and Archives (TSLA), Nashville.

5. Chambers, "Election of 1840," 644; William Coleman, "Music in the American Democratic Process: The 1840 and 2008 Presidential Elections," *Australasian Journal of American Studies* 29 (December 2010): 9; and diary entry, 20 April 1840, in Sioussat, "Diaries of S. H. Laughlin," 49–50.

6. Gunderson, "Thurlow Weed's Network," 114; *Norwich (CT) Aurora*, 17 June 1840; *Woodstock (VT) Spirit of the Age*, 7 November 1840; *Washington (DC) Globe*, 10 July 1840 and 3 July 1840; and *Hartford (CT) Times*, 30 May 1840.

7. Chambers, "Election of 1840," 668; 13 Reg. Deb. 391 (1837); Fischer, *Tippecanoe and Trinkets Too*, 31–32; *Concord (NH) Republican*, 31 July 1840; and *The Harrison Medal Minstrel* (Philadelphia: Grigg and Elliott, 1840), 161–62.

8. Fischer, *Tippecanoe and Trinkets Too*, 34–44; *Rock River Express* (Rockford, IL), 23 June 1840 and 10 October 1840; *Newark (NJ) Daily Advertiser*, 19 May 1840; and *Albany (NY) Argus*, 30 June 1840.

9. Fischer, *Tippecanoe and Trinkets Too*, 45–48; *Albany (NY) Argus*, 30 July 1839; *Boston Post*, 16 June 1840; and *Cleveland (OH) Herald*, 2 July 1840.

10. *Ohio Statesman* (Columbus), 12 June 1840; and Andrew Jackson to Martin Van Buren, 31 July 1840, in *CAJ*, 6:68.

11. Alexander, "Presidential Campaign of 1840," 26–27, 33–34; Joe L. Kincheloe Jr., "Similarities in Crowd Control Techniques of the Camp Meeting and Political Rally: The Pioneer Role of Tennessee," *Tennessee Historical Quarterly* 37 (Summer 1978): 155–69; Ronald Formisano, "The New Political History and the Election of 1840," *Journal of Interdisciplinary History* 23 (Spring 1993): 682; Richard Carwardine, "Evangelicals, Whigs, and the Election of William Henry Harrison," *Journal of American Studies* 17 (April 1983): 47–75; and Elizabeth R. Varon, "Tippecanoe and the Ladies, Too: White Women and Party Politics in Antebellum Virginia," *Journal of American History* 82 (September 1995): 504–5.

12. Daniel Walker Howe, "The Market Revolution and the Shaping of Identity in Whig-Jacksonian America," in *The Market Revolution in America: Social, Political, and Religious Expressions, 1800–1880*, ed. Melvyn Stokes and Stephen Conway (Charlottesville: University Press of Virginia, 1996), 274; and James Campbell to William Bowen Campbell, 4 February 1840, and [?] Martin to William Bowen Campbell, 10 February 1840, David Campbell Papers, TSLA.

13. Carwardine, "Evangelicals, Whigs," 55–57; Isaac R. Jackson, *The Life of William Henry Harrison, (of Ohio,) The People's Candidate for the Presidency: With a History of the Wars with the British and Indians on Our North-Western Frontier* (Philadelphia: Marshall, Williams and Butler, 1840), 211; An Old Democrat [Jacob Bailey Moore], *The Contrast: Or, Plain Reasons Why William Henry Harrison Should Be Elected President*

of the United States, and Why Martin Van Buren Should Not Be Re-Elected (New York: Giffing, 1840), 5; and Harmon Kingsbury to William Henry Harrison, 12 November 1840, William Henry Harrison Papers, Library of Congress.

14. Carwardine, "Evangelicals, Whigs," 59–60; and [Moore], *The Contrast*, 6.

15. Andrew Jackson to John F. Schermerhorn, 12 June 1832, in *PAJ*, 10:301–2; Richard R. John, "Taking Sabbatarianism Seriously: The Postal System, the Sabbath, and the Transformation of American Political Culture," *Journal of the Early Republic* 10 (Winter 1990): 557–62; report on Sunday mails, 19 January 1829, in *American State Papers: Post Office* (Washington, DC: Gales and Seaton, 1834), 211; Carwardine, "Evangelicals, Whigs," 64; *Worcester (MA) National Aegis*, 26 August 1840; [Moore], *The Contrast*, 11; and *Newark (NJ) Centinel of Freedom*, 1 September 1840.

16. Jayne Crumpler DeFiore, "'COME, and Bring the Ladies': Tennessee Women and the Politics of Opportunity during the Presidential Campaigns of 1840 and 1844," *Tennessee Historical Quarterly* 51 (Winter 1992): 201; *Springfield (IL) Sangamo Journal*, 5 June 1840; Chambers, "Election of 1840," 679; Kincheloe, "Similarities in Crowd Control Techniques," 157–58; and Skaggs, *William Henry Harrison*, 165–72.

17. Cole, *Martin Van Buren*, 368, 373–74.

18. T. H. Breen, *George Washington's Journey: The President Forges a New Nation* (New York: Simon and Schuster, 2016); Moats, "The Limits of 'Good Feelings,'" 155–91; Sandra Moats, *Celebrating the Republic: Presidential Ceremony and Popular Sovereignty, from Washington to Monroe* (DeKalb: Northern Illinois University Press, 2009); Fletcher M. Green, "On Tour with President Jackson," *New England Quarterly* 36 (June 1963): 209–28; Ellis, *Presidential Travel*, 59–69; Martin Van Buren to Henry Fitts et al., 25 March 1839, in *Newark (NJ) Daily Advertiser*, 25 March 1839; James K. Polk to Andrew Jackson, 7 February 1839, in *CJKP*, 5:52–54; and Martin Van Buren to Andrew Jackson, 29 May 1839, VLC.

19. *New York Daily Herald*, 25 June 1839; *Trenton (NJ) Emporium and True American*, 18 October 1839; and *Baltimore (MD) Patriot*, n.d., in *North American* (Philadelphia), 28 June 1839.

20. *Newark (NJ) Daily Advertiser*, 5 July 1839. These numbers are based on an extensive analysis of speeches published in newspapers and Van Buren's personal papers, which contain drafts of several speeches that he gave or had published.

21. Address to Judge Turrill et al., 30 August 1839, in *Richmond (VA) Enquirer*, 17 September 1839; and address to M. D. Burnet et al., 10 September 1839, in *New-Hampshire Patriot and State Gazette* (Concord), 21 October 1839.

22. *Madisonian for the Country* (Washington, DC), 29 June 1839; *Washington (DC) Daily National Intelligencer*, 8 July 1839; *Haverhill (MA) Gazette*, 5 July 1839; and *Hudson River Chronicle* (Ossining, NY), 16 July 1839.

23. *Trenton (NJ) Emporium and True American*, 28 June 1839; and *Albany (NY) Argus*, 2 August 1839.

24. *Albany (NY) Argus*, 3 September 1839, 20 September 1839, and 12 July 1839.

25. Martin Van Buren to William A. Tennille et al., 17 June 1840, and Martin Van Buren to Samuel S. Wandell et al. [29 June 1840], in West, Ferree, and Franz, *Papers of Martin Van Buren*, reel 35.

26. Gerald L. Leonard, "Party as a 'Political Safeguard of Federalism': Martin Van Buren and the Constitutional Theory of Party Politics," *Rutgers Law Review* 54 (Fall

2001): 221–81; Leonard, *The Invention of Party Politics: Federalism, Popular Sovereignty, and Constitutional Development in Jacksonian Illinois* (Chapel Hill: University of North Carolina Press, 2002), 177–82; John L. Brooke, *Columbia Rising: Civil Life on the Upper Hudson from the Revolution to the Age of Jackson* (Chapel Hill: University of North Carolina Press, 2010), 448–52; and Martin Van Buren, "Thoughts on New York" [March 1840], 1, 6, 74, VLC. Because of the many additions, deletions, and emendations in Van Buren's draft, the text here has been edited for clarity, and page numbers for each manuscript page, not present in the draft, have been included.

    27. Remini, *Andrew Jackson*, 3:454–59; Andrew Jackson to Andrew J. Donelson, 10 December 1839, in *CAJ*, 6:41; and *Washington (DC) Globe*, 22 January 1840, 29 January 1840, and 30 January 1840.

    28. Gunderson, *Log-Cabin Campaign*, 237–46; Alexander, "Presidential Campaign of 1840," 32–33; Chambers, "Election of 1840," 671; *Nashville (TN) Republican Banner*, 19 May 1841; and James Campbell to William Bowen Campbell, 16 June 1840, David Campbell Papers, TSLA.

    29. Robert V. Friedenberg, *Notable Speeches in Contemporary Presidential Campaigns* (Westport, CT: Praeger, 2002), 14–18.

    30. Jeffrey Bourdon, "Symbolism, Economic Depression, and the Specter of Slavery: William Henry Harrison's Speaking Tour for the Presidency," *Ohio History* 118 (2011): 5–23.

    31. *Ohio State Journal* (Columbus), 17 June 1840.

    32. *Newark (NJ) Centinel of Freedom*, 23 June 1840; *Portland (ME) Advertiser*, 1 September 1840; and Owens, *Mr. Jefferson's Hammer*, 23, 27–32.

    33. *Log Cabin* (Dayton, OH), 18 September 1840.

    34. *New York Log Cabin*, 17 October 1840; and *Log Cabin* (Dayton, OH), 18 September 1840.

    35. Gunderson, *Log-Cabin Campaign*, 201–18; *Washington (DC) Daily National Intelligencer*, 15 June 1840; *Washington (DC) Globe*, 20 June 1840; *Log Cabin* (Dayton, OH), 21 March 1840; *Ohio State Journal* (Columbus), 29 February 1840; and *Springfield (IL) Sangamo Journal*, 15 May 1840.

    36. *New York Log Cabin*, 5 September 1840; and *Washington (DC) Daily National Intelligencer*, 27 August 1840.

    37. Thomas Ritchie to Martin Van Buren, 1 June 1840, VLC; and Andrew Jackson to Francis P. Blair, 26 September 1840, in *CAJ*, 6:78.

    38. Gunderson, "Thurlow Weed's Network," 109–11; *Richmond (VA) Enquirer*, 8 May 1840; *Washington (DC) Extra Globe*, 26 October 1840, 414; and William H. Harrison to James Lyons, 1 June 1840, in *Niles' National Register* 58 (20 June 1840): 247.

    39. *Ohio State Journal* (Columbus), 26 March 1839 and 22 April 1840; and *Richmond (VA) Whig*, 24 July 1840.

    40. *Mobile (AL) Chronicle*, n.d., in *Newark (NJ) Centinel of Freedom*, 9 June 1840; *Alexandria (VA) Gazette*, 24 April 1840; and *Newark (NJ) Centinel of Freedom*, 31 March 1840.

    41. *Richmond (VA) Whig*, 24 July 1840; *Albany (NY) Argus*, 25 September 1840; and *New York Evening Post*, 30 July 1840.

    42. *Hartford (CT) Times*, 30 March 1839 and 26 September 1840; and *Galena (Ill.) Gazette*, n.d., in *Connecticut Courant* (Hartford), 30 May 1840.

43. John B. Cary et al. to Martin Van Buren, 12 June 1840, and Martin Van Buren to John B. Cary et al., 31 July 1840, in *Charleston (SC) Courier*, 17 August 1840 and 18 August 1840; and Martin Van Buren to John M. McCalla et al., 4 July 1840, in *New-Hampshire Patriot and State Gazette* (Concord), 3 August 1840.

44. William Henry Harrison to James Lyons, 1 June 1840, in *Niles' National Register* 58 (20 June 1840): 247; Walter F. Leak to Martin Van Buren, 21 March 1840, and Martin Van Buren to Walter F. Leak, 27 March 1840, in Elizabeth Gregory McPherson, "Unpublished Letters from North Carolinians to Van Buren," *North Carolina Historical Review* 15 (April 1938): 131–32; *North Carolina Standard* (Raleigh), 29 April 1840; and *Western Carolinian* (Salisbury, NC), n.d., in *Camden (SC) Journal*, 25 April 1840.

CHAPTER 13: **Doggerel Rhymes and Vulgar Pictures**

1. Brooke, "Press, Party, and Public Sphere," 61–62, 88, 99.

2. Chambers, "Election of 1840," 675–76; Brooke, "Press, Party, and Public Sphere," 61–62; Congleton, "George D. Prentice," 94; *Louisville (KY) Daily Journal*, 24 December 1839; and Alexander, "Presidential Campaign of 1840," 29–30.

3. Kenneth R. Stevens, *William Henry Harrison: A Bibliography* (Westport, CT: Greenwood Press, 1998), 59–60, 68–73; and Alexander, "Presidential Campaign of 1840," 29–30.

4. Chambers, "Election of 1840," 670; Donald B. Cole, *A Jackson Man: Amos Kendall and the Rise of American Democracy* (Baton Rouge: Louisiana State University Press, 2004), 227–28; Amos Kendall, *Mr. Kendall's Address to the People of the United States* (n.p., 1840), 1–2; and Andrew Jackson to Amos Kendall, 2 June 1840, in *CAJ*, 6:63.

5. Richard Hildreth, *The People's Presidential Candidate* [. . .] (Boston: Weeks, Jordan, 1839), 194–95, 197; and Jackson, *Life of William Henry Harrison*, v, 209–10.

6. Gunderson, *Log-Cabin Campaign*, 131; and Charles S. Todd and Benjamin Drake, *Sketches of the Civil and Military Services of William Henry Harrison* (Cincinnati, OH: U. P. James, 1840), 12, 161.

7. Captain Miller, *"Hero of Tippecanoe": Or the Story of the Life of William Henry Harrison* (New York: Giffing, 1840), 5, 7.

8. Moses Dawson, *Sketches of the Life of Martin Van Buren, President of the United States* (Cincinnati, OH: J. W. Ely, 1840), 3, 7, 207, 205; Dawson, *A Historical Narrative of the Civil and Military Services of Major-General William H. Harrison* [. . .] (Cincinnati, OH: Moses Dawson, 1824); and Cleaves, *Old Tippecanoe*, 255, 327.

9. A Harrison Democrat [Robert Mayo], *A Word in Season; or Review of the Political Life and Opinions of Martin Van Buren: Addressed to the Entire Democracy of the American People*, 2nd ed. (Washington, DC: W. M. Morrison, 1840), 2, 46; and [Anonymous], *A Brief Account of the Life and Political Opinions of Martin Van Buren, President of the United States: From the Most Authentic Sources* (n.p., 1840), 6.

10. Diary entry, 21 March 1843, in Tuckerman, ed., *Diary of Philip Hone*, 2:177.

11. *Log Cabin* (Dayton, OH), 23 October 1840; and "Old Tip, and the Penitent Loco" [1840], American Song Sheets, Rare Books and Special Collections, Library of Congress, accessed 15 March 2015, https://www.loc.gov/item/amss.as110400/.

12. *Tarboro' Press* (Tarborough, NC), 11 April 1840; and *Wellsboro (PA) Tioga Eagle*, 12 August 1840.

13. *Ottawa (IL) Free Trader*, 21 August 1840; "Good Hard Cider," 1840, Music

Division, Library of Congress, http://www.loc.gov/item/sm1840.371420/; and *The Harrison and Log Cabin Song Book* (Columbus, OH: I. N. Whiting, 1840), 8.

14. Kirsten E. Wood, "'Join with Heart and Soul and Voice': Music, Harmony, and Politics in the Early American Republic," *American Historical Review* 119 (October 2014): 1114.

15. *Fifty Cents. Shin Plaster*, 1837, Prints and Photographs Division, Library of Congress, http://www.loc.gov/pictures/item/2008661307/; *Uncle Sam Sick with La Grippe*, 1837, Prints and Photographs Division, Library of Congress, http://www.loc .gov/pictures/item/2008661302/; Lepler, *Many Panics of 1837*, 152; and Sam W. Haynes, *Unfinished Revolution: The Early American Republic in a British World* (Charlottesville: University of Virginia Press, 2010), 291–92.

16. *Granny Harrison Delivering the Country of the Executive Federalist*, 1840, Prints and Photographs Division, Library of Congress, http://www.loc.gov/pictures/item /2008661374/; and *A Political Movement*, 1840, Prints and Photographs Division, Library of Congress, http://www.loc.gov/pictures/item/2008661372/.

17. *The North Bend Farmer and His Visitors*, 1840, Prints and Photographs Division, Library of Congress, http://www.loc.gov/pictures/item/2008661371/.

18. *Independence Declared 1776. The Union Must Be Preserved*, 1839, Prints and Photographs Division, Library of Congress, http://www.loc.gov/pictures/item/2003 690781/; *Martin Van Buren*, 1840, Prints and Photographs Division, Library of Congress, http://www.loc.gov/pictures/item/89707962/; and executive order, 31 March 1840, in Peters and Woolley, *The American Presidency Project*, accessed 17 April 2015, http://www.presidency.ucsb.edu/ws/?pid=67312.

19. *Going Up Salt River*, 1840, Prints and Photographs Division, Library of Congress, http://www.loc.gov/pictures/item/2008661384/.

20. Ronald P. Formisano, "The 'Party Period' Revisited," *Journal of American History* 86 (June 1999): 114–15; Varon, "Tippecanoe and the Ladies, Too," 81–82, 498; and Paula Baker, "The Midlife Crisis of the New Political History," *Journal of American History* 86 (June 1999): 164–65.

21. Diary entry, 10 September 1840, in Tuckerman, ed., *Diary of Philip Hone*, 2:42.

22. Varon, "Tippecanoe and the Ladies, Too," 501; and speech, 5 October 1840, in [James W. McIntyre], ed., *The Writings and Speeches of Daniel Webster*, 18 vols. (Boston: Little, Brown, 1903), 3:105–7.

23. *New York Commercial Advertiser*, 15 October 1840; *Alexandria (VA) Gazette*, 12 October 1840; and *Richmond (VA) Whig*, 9 October 1840.

24. Alexander, "Presidential Campaign of 1840," 36; *Alexandria (VA) Gazette*, 14 August 1840; and *Auburn (NY) Journal and Advertiser*, 26 August 1840.

25. Virginia Campbell to Mary Campbell, 11 October 1840, David Campbell Papers, TSLA.

26. Varon, "Tippecanoe and the Ladies, Too," 500–501; Sarah Pendleton Dandridge to Martha Taliaferro Hunter, 18 April 1840, box 6, Hunter Family Papers, Virginia Historical Society, Richmond; Mrs. Roger A. Pryor [Sara Agnes Rice Pryor], *My Day: Reminiscences of a Long Life* (New York: Macmillan, 1909), 47, http:// docsouth.unc.edu/fpn/pryor/pryor.html; and Mary Pendleton Cooke Steger to Sarah Apphia Hunter, 13 September 1840, box 25, Correspondence, Series 13, Hunter Family Papers.

27. *New-Bedford (MA) Mercury*, 26 June 1840; and Eliza Davis to John Davis, 18 July [June] 1840, John Davis Papers, American Antiquarian Society, Worcester, Massachusetts.

28. Ronald J. Zboray and Mary Saracino Zboray, "Whig Women, Politics, and Culture in the Campaign of 1840: Three Perspectives from Massachusetts," *Journal of the Early Republic* 17 (Summer 1997): 296; Henry Varnum Poor to Mary Pierce, 1 November 1840, Poor Family Papers, 1791–1921, A-132, Schlesinger Library, Radcliffe Institute, Harvard University, Cambridge, MA, https://iiif.lib.harvard.edu/manifests /view/drs:424807495$130i; and Mary Pierce to Henry Varnum Poor, 9 November 1840, Poor Family Papers, 1791–1921, A-132, https://iiif.lib.harvard.edu/manifests/view/drs: 424807495$133i.

29. Lucy Kenney, *A Pamphlet Showing How Easily the Wand of a Magician May Be Broken* [. . .] (n.p., 1838), 10, 1, 2; and Kenney, *Description of a Visit*, 9.

30. Kenney, *A Pamphlet*, 2, 16; Wilson, *Presidency of Martin Van Buren*, 177; and Lucy Kenney, *A Letter Addressed to Martin Van Buren, President of the United States, in Answer to the Late Attack upon the Navy, by the Official Organ of the Government* (n.p., 1838), 7.

31. Eliza B. Runnells, *A Reply to a Letter Addressed to Mr. Van Buren, President of the United States; Purporting to be Written by Miss Lucy Kenny, the Whig Missionary* (n.p., 1838), 3; and Lucy Kenney, *A Satire: Being a Rejoinder to a Reply by Mrs. E. Runnells to My Letter in Vindication of the Navy* (n.p., 1838), 6.

32. Lucy Kenney, *An Address to the People of the United States* (n.p., 1840), 1, 3, 9, 11; and J. S. Buckingham, *The Eastern and Western States of America*, 3 vols. (London: Fisher, Son, 1842), 2:135.

33. Varon, *We Mean to Be Counted*, 81–84; Charles G. Sellers Jr., *James K. Polk*, 2 vols. (Princeton, NJ: Princeton University Press, 1957, 1966), 1:372; and *Richmond (VA) Enquirer*, 15 October 1840 and 15 September 1840.

34. Andrew Jackson to Martin Van Buren, 12 November 1840, in *CAJ*, 6:82; and diary entry, 3 November 1840, in Tuckerman, ed., *Diary of Philip Hone*, 2:48.

35. Dubin, *United States Presidential Elections*, 71–82; US Senate, "Party Division," United States Senate website, accessed 24 January 2017, http://www.senate.gov/page layout/history/one_item_and_teasers/partydiv.htm; and US House, "Party Divisions of the House of Representatives," History, Art and Archives: United States House of Representatives, accessed 24 January 2017, http://history.house.gov/Institution/Party -Divisions/Party-Divisions/.

36. Dubin, *United States Presidential Elections*, 71–82; and Andrew Jackson to Martin Van Buren, 24 November 1840, in *CAJ*, 6:83–84.

37. "The Late Election," *United States Magazine and Democratic Review* 8 (1840): 395–96; and Fitzpatrick, *Autobiography of Martin Van Buren*, 394.

38. *New York Log Cabin*, 5 December 1840.

EPILOGUE

1. Cleaves, *Old Tippecanoe*, 331–32; and "Diary of John Findlay Torrence 1841," *Register of the Kentucky State Historical Society* 7 (January 1909): 59–61.

2. Cleaves, *Old Tippecanoe*, 332–34; Peterson, *Presidencies of Harrison and Tyler*, 33–35; and diary entry, 2 March 1841, in Tuckerman, ed., *Diary of Philip Hone*, 2:66.

3. Bonney, *A Legacy of Historical Gleanings*, 2:160; Howe, *What Hath God Wrought*, 570; Peterson, *Presidencies of Harrison and Tyler*, 35–36; and inaugural address, 4 March 1841, in Richardson, *M&P*, 4:16, 19.

4. Peterson, *Presidencies of Harrison and Tyler*, 37–41; Holt, *Rise and Fall of the American Whig Party*, 124–27; and Henry Clay's draft of a proposed proclamation, n.d., William Henry Harrison to Henry Clay, 13 March 1841, and Henry Clay to William Henry Harrison, 15 March 1841, in *PHC*, 9:514, 515n2, 516–17.

5. Cleaves, *Old Tippecanoe*, 341–42; and Thomas Miller, "Case of the Late William H. Harrison, President of the United States," *Boston Medical and Surgical Journal* 24 (2 June 1841): 261–67. Harrison may have actually died from enteric fever. On this point, see Jane McHugh and Philip A. Mackowiak, "What Really Killed William Henry Harrison?" *New York Times*, 31 March 2014.

6. *Niles' National Register* 60 (10 April 1841): 83; diary entry, 5 April 1841, in Tuckerman, ed., *Diary of Philip Hone*, 2:71; and Carwardine, "Evangelicals, Whigs," 75.

7. Henry Horn to Andrew Jackson, 9 April 1841, and Andrew Jackson to Francis P. Blair, 19 April 1841, in *CAJ*, 6:103, 105.

8. Howe, *What Hath God Wrought*, 589–95. On the 1844 election, see Charles G. Sellers Jr., "Election of 1844," in Schlesinger and Israel, *History of American Presidential Elections*, 1:745–861.

9. Holt, *Rise and Fall of the American Whig Party*, 673–985. On the 1848 election, see Joel H. Silbey, *Party Over Section: The Rough and Ready Presidential Election of 1848* (Lawrence: University Press of Kansas, 2009). On the Taylor and Fillmore presidencies, see Elbert B. Smith, *The Presidencies of Zachary Taylor and Millard Fillmore* (Lawrence: University Press of Kansas, 1988).

10. Michael P. McDonald, "National General Election VEP Turnout Rates, 1789–Present," *United States Elections Project*, University of Florida, last updated 11 June 2014, http://www.electproject.org/national-1789-present.

Bibliography

PRIMARY SOURCES

Manuscript Collections

Allen, William. Papers. Library of Congress, Washington, DC.

American Song Sheets. Rare Books and Special Collections. Library of Congress, Washington, DC. https://www.loc.gov/collections/nineteenth-century-song-sheets.

America on Stone: 19th Century American Lithographs. The Harry T. Peters Collection. Smithsonian National Museum of American History, Washington, DC. http://amhistory.si.edu/petersprints/lithograph.cfm.

Campbell, David. Papers. Tennessee State Library and Archives, Nashville.

Cook, William C., War of 1812 in the South Collection. The Historic New Orleans Collection. Williams Research Center, New Orleans, LA. http://hnoc.minisisinc.com/thnoc/catalog/3/9575.

Davis, John. Papers. American Antiquarian Society, Worcester, MA.

Documenting the American South. University of North Carolina at Chapel Hill. http://docsouth.unc.edu.

Founders Online. National Archives, College Park, MD. https://founders.archives.gov.

Harrison, William Henry. Papers. Library of Congress, Washington, DC.

———. Papers and Documents, 1791–1864. Indiana Historical Society, Indianapolis.

Hunter Family Papers. Virginia Historical Society, Richmond.

Jackson, Andrew. Papers. Library of Congress, Washington, DC.

Jefferson, Thomas. Papers. Library of Congress, Washington, DC.

Madison, James. Papers. Library of Congress, Washington, DC.

Poor Family Papers, 1791–1921. Schlesinger Library, Radcliffe Institute, Harvard University, Cambridge, MA.

Prints and Photographs Division. Library of Congress, Washington, DC. http://www.loc.gov/pictures.

Van Buren, Martin. Papers. Cumberland University, Lebanon, TN. http://vanburenpapers.org.

———. Papers. Library of Congress, Washington, DC.

Weed, Thurlow. Papers. Department of Rare Books, Special Collections, and Preservation. River Campus Libraries, University of Rochester, NY.

Newspapers and Other Periodicals

Adams Sentinel (Gettysburg, PA)
Albany (NY) Advertiser
Albany (NY) Argus
Albany (NY) Register
Alexandria (VA) Gazette
American Advocate (Hallowell, ME)
Arkansas Gazette (Little Rock)
Arkansas Times and Advocate (Little
   Rock)
Auburn (NY) Journal and Advertiser
Augusta (GA) Chronicle
Augusta (ME) Age
Baltimore (MD) Daily Intelligencer
Baltimore (MD) Federal Gazette
Baltimore (MD) Gazette and Daily
   Advertiser
Baltimore (MD) Patriot
Baltimore (MD) Republican
Berks and Schuylkill Journal (Reading,
   PA)
Boston Commercial Gazette
Boston Courier
Boston Daily Advertiser & Patriot
Boston Daily American Statesman
Boston Independent Chronicle
Boston Post
Boston Weekly Messenger
Bridgeport (CT) Spirit of the Times
Camden (SC) Journal
Carlisle (PA) Gazette
Carolina Sentinel (Newbern, NC)
Castine (ME) Eagle
Charleston (SC) Courier
Charleston (SC) Southern Patriot
Charles Town (VA) Farmers' Repository
Cincinnati (OH) Daily Gazette
Cleveland (OH) Herald
Columbian Centinel (Boston)
Columbian Register (New Haven, CT)
Concord (NH) Republican
Connecticut Courant (Hartford)
Connecticut Herald (New Haven)
Crawfordsville (IN) Record
Daily Cincinnati (OH) Republican

Daily Georgian (Savannah)
Daily Pennsylvanian (Philadelphia)
Eastern Argus (Portland, ME)
Easton (MD) Gazette
Elyria (OH) Republican
Federal Intelligencer and Baltimore (MD)
   Daily Gazette
Frankfort (KY) Argus
Frederick (MD) Republican Gazette and
   General Advertiser
Gazette of Maine (Portland)
Gazette of the United States
   (Philadelphia)
Gloucester (MA) Democrat
Gloucester (MA) Telegraph
Greensboro (NC) Patriot
Hagerstown (MD) Torch Light and Public
   Advertiser
Hallowell (ME) Gazette
Hartford (CT) Times
Haverhill (MA) Gazette
Hudson River Chronicle (Ossining, NY)
Illinois Weekly State Journal (Springfield)
Independent Chronicle and Boston
   Patriot
Ithaca (NY) Journal
Jamestown (NY) Journal
Jefferson Democrat and Farmers' and
   Mechanics' Advocate (Steubenville,
   OH)
Jerseyman (Morristown, NJ)
Kennebec Journal (Augusta, ME)
Kentucky Gazette (Lexington)
Literary Cadet and Saturday Evening
   Bulletin (Providence, RI)
Log Cabin (Dayton, OH)
Louisville (KY) Daily Journal
Lynchburg Virginian
Madisonian for the Country (Washington,
   DC)
Massachusetts Spy (Worcester)
Middletown (CT) Sentinel and Witness
Miller's Weekly Messenger (Pendleton,
   SC)

Milton (NC) Gazette and Roanoke
   Advertiser
Montpelier (VT) Watchman
N. Carolina Chronicle (Murfreesboro)
Nashville (TN) Republican
Nashville (TN) Republican Banner
Nashville (TN) Whig
National Banner and Nashville (TN) Whig
Newark (NJ) Centinel of Freedom
Newark (NJ) Daily Advertiser
New Bedford (MA) Gazette
New-Bedford (MA) Mercury
Newbern (NC) Sentinel
New-Hampshire Patriot and State Gazette
   (Concord)
New-Hampshire Sentinel (Keene)
New Orleans (LA) Argus
Newport (RI) Mercury
New York Advocate of Moral Reform
New York American
New York Commercial Advertiser
New York Daily Herald
New York Evening Post
New York Herald
New York Log Cabin
New York National Advocate
New York Register of the Times
New York Spectator
New York Statesman
Niles' Weekly Register (Baltimore, MD)
North American (Philadelphia)
North-Carolina Standard (Raleigh)
Norwich (CT) Aurora
Norwich (CT) Courier
Ohio State Journal (Columbus)
Ohio Statesman (Columbus)
Ottawa (IL) Free Trader
Paul Pry (Washington, DC)
Pawtucket (RI) Chronicle and Rhode-
   Island and Massachusetts Register
Philadelphia Inquirer
Philadelphia National Gazette
Phoenix Civilian (Cumberland, MD)
Portland (ME) Advertiser
Portsmouth (NH) Journal of Literature
   and Politics

Potomak Guardian and Berkeley Adver-
   tiser (Shepherdstown, VA)
Poulson's American Daily Advertiser
   (Philadelphia)
Providence (RI) Gazette
Providence (RI) Gazette and Country
   Journal
Providence (RI) Journal
Rhode Island American (Providence)
Richmond (VA) Enquirer
Richmond (VA) Whig
Richmond (VA) Yeoman
Rock River Express (Rockford, IL)
Salem (MA) Gazette
Salem (MA) Register
Salisbury (NC) Journal
Saratoga (NY) Sentinel
Schenectady (NY) Cabinet
Scioto Gazette (Chillicothe, OH)
Signs of the Times (Albany, NY)
Springfield (IL) Sangamo Journal
Springfield (MA) Republican
Tarboro' Press (Tarborough, NC)
Trenton (NJ) Emporium and True
   American
Truth's Advocate and Monthly Anti-
   Jackson Expositor
United States Magazine and Democratic
   Review
United States Telegraph (Washington,
   DC)
United States Telegraph Extra (Washing-
   ton, DC)
Vermont Gazette (Bennington)
Vincennes (IN) Gazette
Virginia Gazette and Alexandria
   Advertiser
Wabash Courier (Terra Haute, IN)
Washington (DC) Daily National
   Intelligencer
Washington (DC) Daily National Journal
Washington (DC) Extra Globe
Washington (DC) Federalist
Washington (DC) Globe
Washington (PA) Herald of Liberty
Washington (PA) Review and Examiner

Weekly Raleigh (NC) Register
Wellsboro (PA) Tioga Eagle
Western Carolinian (Salisbury, NC)

We the People (Washington, DC)
Woodstock (VT) Spirit of the Age
Worcester (MA) National Aegis

Government Documents

American State Papers: Post Office. Washington, DC: Gales and Seaton, 1834.
Biographical Directory of the United States Congress, 1774–Present. http://bioguide
   .congress.gov.
Congressional Globe. 25th Congress, 2nd Session (1837).
*Journal of the House of Representatives of the State of Tennessee, at the Twenty-first
   General Assembly, Held at Nashville*. Knoxville, TN: Ramsey and Craighead, 1836.
Register of Debates. 21st Congress, 1st Session (1830).
Register of Debates. 23rd Congress, 1st Session (1834).
Register of Debates. 24th Congress, 2nd Session (1837).
US House. "Party Divisions of the House of Representatives." History, Art and
   Archives: United States House of Representatives. Accessed 24 January 2017. http://
   history.house.gov/Institution/Party-Divisions/Party-Divisions/.
US Senate. "Party Division." United States Senate website. Accessed 24 January 2017.
   http://www.senate.gov/pagelayout/history/one_item_and_teasers/partydiv.htm.
US Statutes at Large. Vol. 1, 239 (1792).
US Statutes at Large. Vol. 5, 721 (1845).

Published Works

Adams, Charles Francis, ed. *Memoirs of John Quincy Adams, Comprising Portions of
   His Diary from 1795 to 1848*. 12 vols. Philadelphia: J. B. Lippincott, 1876.
Adams, John Quincy, comp. *The Duplicate Letters, the Fisheries and the Mississippi:
   Documents Relating to Transactions at the Negotiation of Ghent*. Washington:
   Davis and Force, 1822.
[Anonymous]. *A Brief Account of the Life and Political Opinions of Martin Van Buren,
   President of the United States: From the Most Authentic Sources*. N.p., 1840.
Bassett, John Spencer, and J. Franklin Jameson, eds. *Correspondence of Andrew
   Jackson*. 7 vols. Washington, DC: Carnegie Institute of Washington, 1926–35.
Bishop, Abraham. *Connecticut Republicanism: An Oration, on the Extent and Power
   of Political Delusion, Delivered in New-Haven, on the Evening Preceding the Public
   Commencement, September 1800*. Philadelphia: William Carey, 1800. http://quod
   .lib.umich.edu/e/evans/N27748.0001.001?rgn=main;view=fulltext.
Bonney, Catharina V. R., ed. *Legacy of Historical Gleanings*. 2 vols. Albany, NY:
   J. Munsell, 1875.
Brown, Everett S., ed. *The Missouri Compromises and Presidential Politics, 1820–1825,
   From the Letters of William Plumer, Junior, Representative from New Hampshire*.
   St. Louis: Missouri Historical Society, 1926.
Brunhouse, Robert L., ed. "David Ramsay, 1749–1815: Selections from His Writings."
   Transactions of the American Philosophical Society 55 (August 1965): 1–250.
Buckingham, J. S. *The Eastern and Western States of America*. 3 vols. London: Fisher,
   Son, 1842.

Captain Miller. *"Hero of Tippecanoe"; Or the Story of the Life of William Henry Harrison.* New York: Giffing, 1840.

Chevalier, Michel. *Society, Manners and Politics in the United States; Being a Series of Letters on North America.* Boston: Weeks, Jordan, 1839.

Child, Lydia Maria. *The History of the Condition of Women, in Various Ages and Nations.* 2 vols. London: Simpkin, Marshall, 1835.

Clinton, DeWitt. *An Address Delivered before Holland Lodge, December 24, 1793.* New York: Childs and Swaine, 1794.

Colton, Calvin, ed. *The Works of Henry Clay, Comprising His Life, Correspondence and Speeches.* 10 vols. New York: Henry Clay Publishing, 1904.

Crockett, David [Augustin S. Clayton?]. *The Life of Martin Van Buren* [. . .]. Philadelphia: Robert Wright, 1835.

Cunningham, Noble E., Jr., ed. *The Making of the American Party System, 1789–1809.* Englewood Cliffs, NJ: Prentice-Hall, 1965.

[David, Charles Augustus]. *Letters of J. Downing, Major, Downingville Militia, Second Brigade, to His Old Friend Mr. Dwight, of the New-York Daily Advertiser.* London: John Murray, 1835.

Dawson, Moses. *A Historical Narrative of the Civil and Military Services of Major-General William H. Harrison* [. . .]. Cincinnati, OH: Moses Dawson, 1824.

———. *Sketches of the Life of Martin Van Buren, President of the United States.* Cincinnati, OH: J. W. Ely, 1840.

[Eaton, John H.]. *The Letters of Wyoming, to the People of the United States, on the Presidential Election, and in Favour of Andrew Jackson.* Philadelphia: S. Simpson and J. Conrad, 1824.

Elliott, Richard Smith. *Notes Taken in Sixty Years.* St. Louis, MO: Studley, 1883.

[Emmons, William]. *Authentic Biography of Col. Richard M. Johnson, of Kentucky.* Boston: Langworthy, 1834.

———. *Biography of Martin Van Buren, Vice President of the United States.* Washington, DC: Gideon, Jr., 1835.

[Erwin, Andrew]. *Gen. Jackson's Negro Speculations, and His Traffic in Human Flesh, Examined and Established by Positive Proof.* N.p, 1828.

Fitzpatrick, John C., ed. *The Autobiography of Martin Van Buren.* Vol. 2 of the *Annual Report of the American Historical Association for the Year 1918.* Washington, DC: GPO, 1920.

A Free Man [William J. Snelling]. *A Brief and Impartial History of the Life and Actions of Andrew Jackson, President of the United States.* Boston: Stimpson and Clapp, 1831.

Gibbs, George, ed. *Memoirs of the Administrations of Washington and John Adams, Edited from the Papers of Oliver Wolcott, Secretary of the Treasury.* 2 vols. New York: n.p., 1846.

Goodwin, Philo A. *A Biography of Andrew Jackson.* Hartford, CT: Clapp and Benton, 1832.

Hall, James. *A Memoir of the Public Services of William Henry Harrison of Ohio.* Philadelphia: Edward C. Biddle, 1836.

Hamilton, J. G. de Roulhac, ed. *The Papers of Thomas Ruffin.* 2 vols. Raleigh, NC: Edwards and Broughton, 1918.

Hamilton, J. G. de Roulhac, and Henry M. Wagstaff, eds. "Letters to Bartlett Yancey." *James Sprunt Historical Publications* 10, no. 2 (1911): 23–76.

Hamilton, J. G. de Roulhac, Max R. Williams, and Mary Reynolds Peacock, eds. *The Papers of William A. Graham.* 8 vols. Raleigh: North Carolina Division of Archives and History, 1957–92.

The Harrison and Log Cabin Song Book. Columbus, OH: I. N. Whiting, 1840.

A Harrison Democrat [Robert Mayo]. *A Word in Season; or Review of the Political Life and Opinions of Martin Van Buren: Addressed to the Entire Democracy of the American People.* 2nd ed. Washington, DC: W. M. Morrison, 1840.

The Harrison Medal Minstrel. Philadelphia: Grigg and Elliott, 1840.

Hildreth, Richard. *The People's Presidential Candidate; or The Life of William Henry Harrison, of Ohio.* Boston: Weeks, Jordan, 1839.

Hillard, G. S., ed. *Memoirs of Jeremiah Mason.* 1873. Reprint, Boston: Boston Law Book, 1917.

Hopkins, James F., Robert Seager II, and Melba Porter Hay, eds. *The Papers of Henry Clay.* 11 vols. Lexington: University Press of Kentucky, 1959–92.

Humphrey, Carol Sue, ed. *The Revolutionary Era: Primary Documents on Events from 1776 to 1800.* Westport, CT: Greenwood, 2003.

Jackson, Isaac R. *The Life of William Henry Harrison, (of Ohio,) The People's Candidate for the Presidency: With a History of the Wars with the British and Indians on Our North-Western Frontier.* Philadelphia: Marshall, Williams and Butler, 1840.

Kendall, Amos. *Mr. Kendall's Address to the People of the United States.* N.p., 1840.

Kennedy, John P., ed. *Memoirs of the Life of William Wirt, Attorney General of the United States.* 2 vols. Philadelphia: Lea and Blanchard, 1849, 1856.

Kenney, Lucy. *An Address to the People of the United States.* N.p., 1840.

——. *Description of a Visit to Washington* [. . .]. N.p., 1835.

——. *A Letter Addressed to Martin Van Buren, President of the United States, in Answer to the Late Attack upon the Navy, by the Official Organ of the Government.* N.p., 1838.

——. *A Pamphlet Showing How Easily the Wand of a Magician May Be Broken* [. . .]. N.p., 1838.

——. *A Satire: Being a Rejoinder to a Reply by Mrs. E. Runnells to My Letter in Vindication of the Navy.* N.p., 1838.

A Letter from the Jackson Committee of Nashville, in Answer to One from a Similar Committee at Cincinnati, Upon the Subject of Gen. Jackson's Marriage: Accompanied by Documents in an Appendix, Thereto Annexed (Nashville: Hall and Fitzgerald, 1827). Reprinted in Major L. Wilson, ed., *Mississippi Valley Collection Bulletin* 1 (Summer 1968).

Livermore, Harriet. *A Narration of Religious Experience.* Concord, NH: Jacob B. Moore, 1826.

Longmoor, W. W. "Diary of John Findlay Torrence 1841." *Register of the Kentucky State Historical Society* 7 (May 1909): 57, 59–65.

McClure, James P., ed. *The Papers of Thomas Jefferson.* 42 vols. to date. Princeton, NJ: Princeton University Press, 1950–. https://jeffersonpapers.princeton.edu.

McDonald, Michael P. "National General Election VEP Turnout Rates, 1789–Present." *United States Elections Project,* University of Florida. Last updated 11 June 2014. http://www.electproject.org/national-1789-present.

McGrane, Reginald C., ed. *The Correspondence of Nicholas Biddle Dealing with National Affairs, 1807–1844.* Boston: Houghton Mifflin, 1919.

[McIntyre, James W.], ed. *The Writings and Speeches of Daniel Webster.* 18 vols. Boston: Little, Brown, 1903.

McPherson, Elizabeth Gregory. "Unpublished Letters from North Carolinians to Van Buren." *North Carolina Historical Review* 15 (April 1938): 131–55.

Meriwether, Robert L., W. Edwin Hemphill, Clyde N. Wilson, and Shirley Bright Cook, eds. *The Papers of John C. Calhoun.* 28 vols. Columbia: University of South Carolina Press, 1959–2003.

Miller, Thomas. "Case of the Late William H. Harrison, President of the United States." *Boston Medical and Surgical Journal* 24 (2 June 1841): 261–67.

Moore, John Bassett, ed. *The Works of James Buchanan, Comprising His Speeches, State Papers, and Private Correspondence.* 12 vols. Philadelphia: J. B. Lippincott, 1908–11.

Murray, Judith Sargent. *The Gleaner.* 3 vols. Boston: I. Thomas and E. T. Andrews, 1798.

Nevins, Allan, ed. *The Diary of John Quincy Adams, 1794–1845.* New York: Scribner's, 1951.

A New-England Farmer [John Lowell]. *Mr. Madison's War: A Dispassionate Inquiry into the Reasons Alleged by Mr. Madison for Declaring an Offensive and Ruinous War against Great Britain; Together with Some Suggestions as to a Peaceable and Constitutional Mode of Averting that Dreadful Calamity.* Boston: Russell and Cutler, 1812.

Ogle, Charles. *Speech of Mr. Ogle, of Pennsylvania, on the Regal Splendor of the President's Palace.* Washington, DC: n.p., 1840.

An Old Democrat [Moore, Jacob Bailey]. *The Contrast: Or, Plain Reasons Why William Henry Harrison Should Be Elected President of the United States, and Why Martin Van Buren Should Not Be Re-Elected.* New York: Giffing, 1840.

Peters, Gerhard, and John T. Woolley. *The American Presidency Project.* Last accessed 17 April 2015. http://www.presidency.ucsb.edu.

Prentice, George D. *Biography of Henry Clay.* Hartford, CT: Hanmer and Phelps, 1831.

Preston, Daniel, Marlena C. DeLong, and Cassandra Good, eds. *The Papers of James Monroe.* 6 vols. to date. Westport, CT: Greenwood Press, 2003–.

[Pryor, Sara Agnes Rice]. *My Day: Reminiscences of a Long Life.* New York: Macmillan, 1909.

Reid, John, and John Henry Eaton. *The Life of Andrew Jackson.* Edited by Frank L. Owsley Jr. Tuscaloosa: University of Alabama Press, 1974.

Richardson, James D., ed. *The Messages and Papers of the Presidents, 1789–1897.* 10 vols. Washington, DC: GPO, 1896–99.

Runnells, Eliza B. *A Reply to a Letter Addressed to Mr. Van Buren, President of the United States; Purporting to be Written by Miss Lucy Kenny, the Whig Missionary.* N.p., 1838.

Severance, Frank, ed. *Millard Fillmore Papers.* Buffalo, NY: Buffalo Historical Society, 1907.

Sioussat, St. George L., ed. "Diaries of S. H. Laughlin of Tennessee, 1840, 1843." *Tennessee Historical Magazine* 2 (March 1916): 43–85.

Smith, Margaret Bayard. *The First Forty Years of Washington Society*. Edited by
Gaillard Hunt. New York: Charles Scribner's Sons, 1906.
Smith, Sam B., Harriet Chappell Owsley, Harold D. Moser, Sharon Macpherson,
David H. Roth, George H. Hoemann, Daniel Feller, Thomas Coens, and Laura-
Eve Moss, eds. *The Papers of Andrew Jackson*. 10 vols. to date. Knoxville: University
of Tennessee Press, 1980–.
[Smith, Seba]. *The Life and Writings of Major Jack Downing, of Downingville, Away
Down East in the State of Maine*. Boston: Lilly, Wait, Colman, and Holden, 1834.
[Strong, Henry K.]. *A Brief History of the Public Services of Gen. William Henry
Harrison, Commander in Chief of the North-Western Army in the War of 1812, The
Hero of the Battles of Tippecanoe, Fort Meigs, and the Thames*. Harrisburg, PA: n.p.,
1835.
Todd, Charles S., and Benjamin Drake. *Sketches of the Civil and Military Services of
William Henry Harrison*. Cincinnati, OH: U. P. James, 1840.
Tucker, Nathaniel Beverley. *The Partisan Leader: A Novel*. 1836. Richmond, VA: West
and Johnston, 1862.
Tuckerman, Bayard, ed. *The Diary of Philip Hone*. 2 vols. New York: Dodd, Mead,
1889.
Twohig, Dorothy, ed. *The Papers of George Washington*. Presidential Series, vol. 2,
1 April 1789–15 June 1789. Charlottesville: University Press of Virginia, 1987.
Washburne, E. B., ed. *The Edwards Papers*. Chicago: Fergus Printing, 1884.
Weaver, Herbert, Wayne Cutler, Tom Chaffin, and Michael David Cohen, eds. *Cor-
respondence of James K. Polk*. 12 vols. to date. Knoxville: University of Tennessee
Press, 1969–.
West, Lucy Fisher, Walter L. Ferree, and George W. Franz, eds. *The Papers of Martin
Van Buren*. Microfilm ed. Alexandria, VA: Chadwyck-Healey, 1987.
Wiltse, Charles M., and Harold D. Moser, ed. *The Papers of Daniel Webster: Corre-
spondence*. 7 vols. Hanover, NH: University Press of New England, 1974–86.
A Workingman. *More Than One Hundred Reasons Why William Henry Harrison
Should and Will Have the Support of the Democracy, for President of the United
States, in Preference to Martin Van Buren*. Boston: Tuttle, Dennett and Chisholm,
1840.

SECONDARY SOURCES

Adams, Henry. *The Life of Albert Gallatin*. Philadelphia: J. B. Lippincott, 1879.
Alexander, Thomas B. "The Presidential Campaign of 1840 in Tennessee." *Tennessee
Historical Quarterly* 1 (March 1942): 21–43.
Allgor, Catherine. "Margaret Bayard Smith's 1809 Journey to Monticello and Mont-
pelier: The Politics of Performance in the Early Republic." *Early American Studies*
10 (Winter 2012): 30–68.
———. *Parlor Politics: In Which the Ladies of Washington Help Build a City and a
Government*. Charlottesville: University Press of Virginia, 2000.
Atkins, Jonathan M. *Parties, Politics, and the Sectional Conflict in Tennessee, 1832–1861*.
Knoxville: University of Tennessee Press, 1997.
———. "The Presidential Candidacy of Hugh Lawson White in Tennessee, 1832–1836."
Journal of Southern History 58 (February 1992): 27–56.

Baker, Jean H. "Politics, Paradigms, and Public Culture." *Journal of American History* 84 (December 1997): 894–99.

Baker, Paula. "The Midlife Crisis of the New Political History." *Journal of American History* 86 (June 1999): 158–66.

Basch, Norma. "Marriage, Morals, and Politics in the Election of 1828." *Journal of American History* 80 (December 1993): 890–918.

Belko, W. Stephen. *The Invincible Duff Green: Whig of the West.* Columbia: University of Missouri Press, 2006.

——. *Philip Pendleton Barbour in Jacksonian America: An Old Republican in King Andrew's Court.* Tuscaloosa: University of Alabama Press, 2016.

——. "Toward the Second American Party System: Southern Jacksonians, the Election of 1832, and the Rise of the Democratic Party." *Ohio Valley History* 14 (Spring 2014): 28–50.

Bernstein, R. B. *Thomas Jefferson.* New York: Oxford University Press, 2005.

Bourdon, Jeffrey N. "Compassionate Protector: The Symbolism of Old Hickory in a Jackson Woman's Mind." *American Nineteenth Century History* 12 (June 2011): 177–201.

——. "Symbolism, Economic Depression, and the Specter of Slavery: William Henry Harrison's Speaking Tour for the Presidency." *Ohio History* 118 (2011): 5–23.

Breen, T. H. *George Washington's Journey: The President Forges a New Nation.* New York: Simon and Schuster, 2016.

Brooke, John L. "Ancient Lodges and Self-Created Societies: Voluntary Association and the Public Sphere in the Early Republic." In *Launching the "Extended Republic": The Federalist Era,* edited by Ronald Hoffman and Peter J. Albert, 273–377. Charlottesville: University of Virginia Press, 1996.

——. *Columbia Rising: Civil Life on the Upper Hudson from the Revolution to the Age of Jackson.* Chapel Hill: University of North Carolina Press, 2010.

——. "To Be 'Read by the Whole People': Press, Party, and Public Sphere in the United States, 1789–1840." *Proceedings of the American Antiquarian Society* 110 (April 2000): 41–118.

Brooks, Corey M. *Liberty Power: Antislavery Third Parties and the Transformation of American Politics.* Chicago: University of Chicago Press, 2016.

Brown, Everit, and Albert Strauss. *A Dictionary of American Politics.* New York: A. L. Burt, 1892.

Brown, Norman D. "Webster-Jackson Movement for a Constitution and Union Party in 1833." *Mid-America* 46 (July 1964): 147–71.

Brown, Thomas. "The Miscegenation of Richard Mentor Johnson as an Issue in the National Election Campaign of 1835–1836." *Civil War History* 39 (March 1993): 5–30.

Brugger, Robert J. *Beverly Tucker: Heart over Head in the Old South.* Baltimore, MD: Johns Hopkins University Press, 1978.

Burke, Pauline Wilcox. *Emily Donelson of Tennessee.* Edited by Jonathan M. Atkins. Knoxville: University of Tennessee Press, 2001.

Carbonell, John. "Anthony Imbert: New York's Pioneer Lithographer." In *Prints and Printmakers of New York State, 1825–1940,* edited by David Tatham, 11–42. Syracuse, NY: Syracuse University Press, 1986.

Carwardine, Richard. "Evangelicals, Whigs, and the Election of William Henry Harrison." *Journal of American Studies* 17 (April 1983): 47–75.

Cayton, Andrew R. L. "The Debate over the Panama Congress and the Origins of the Second American Party System." *Historian* 47 (February 1985): 219–38.

Chambers, William N. "Election of 1840." In *History of American Presidential Elections*, vol. 1, edited by Arthur M. Schlesinger and Fred L. Israel, 643–744. New York: Chelsea House, 1971.

Chase, James S. *Emergence of the Presidential Nominating Convention, 1789–1832*. Urbana: University of Illinois Press, 1973.

Cheathem, Mark R. *Andrew Jackson, Southerner*. Baton Rouge: Louisiana State University Press, 2013.

———. *Andrew Jackson and the Rise of the Democrats*. Santa Barbara, CA: ABC-CLIO, 2015.

———. *Old Hickory's Nephew: The Political and Private Struggles of Andrew Jackson Donelson*. Baton Rouge: Louisiana State University Press, 2007.

Cheathem, Mark R., and Terry Corps, eds. *Dictionary of Jacksonian Era and Manifest Destiny*. 2nd. ed. Lanham, MD: Rowman and Littlefield, 2017.

Clapp, Elizabeth J. *A Notorious Woman: Anne Royall in Jacksonian America*. Charlottesville: University of Virginia Press, 2016.

Clayton, W. W. *History of Davidson County, Tennessee*. Nashville, TN: J. W. Lewis, 1880.

Cleaves, Freeman. *Old Tippecanoe: William Henry Harrison and His Time*. New York: Scribner's, 1939. Reprint, Norwalk, CT: Easton Press, 1986.

Coens, Thomas M. "The Formation of the Jackson Party, 1822–1825." PhD diss., Harvard University, 2004.

Cohen, Kenneth. "'Sport for Grown Children': American Political Cartoons, 1790–1850." *International Journal of the History of Sport* 28 (May–June 2011): 1301–18.

Cole, Donald B. *A Jackson Man: Amos Kendall and the Rise of American Democracy*. Baton Rouge: Louisiana State University Press, 2004.

———. *Martin Van Buren and the American Political System*. Princeton, NJ: Princeton University Press, 1984.

———. *The Presidency of Andrew Jackson*. Lawrence: University Press of Kansas, 1993.

———. *Vindicating Andrew Jackson: The 1828 Election and the Rise of the Two-Party System*. Lawrence: University Press of Kansas, 2009.

Coleman, William. "Music in the American Democratic Process: The 1840 and 2008 Presidential Elections." *Australasian Journal of American Studies* 29 (December 2010): 1–23.

Congleton, Betty C. "George D. Prentice: Nineteenth Century Southern Editor." *Register of the Kentucky Historical Society* 65 (April 1967): 94–119.

Cook, William C. "The Coffin Handbills—America's First Smear Campaign." *Imprint* 27 (Spring 2002): 23–37.

Countryman, Edward. *The American Revolution*. New York: Hill and Wang, 1985.

Crapol, Edward P. *John Tyler: The Accidental President*. Chapel Hill: University of North Carolina Press, 2006.

Davison, Nancy R. "E. W. Clay and the American Political Caricature Business." In *Prints and Printmakers of New York State, 1825–1940*, edited by David Tatham, 91–110. Syracuse, NY: Syracuse University Press, 1986.

DeFiore, Jayne Crumpler. "'COME, and Bring the Ladies': Tennessee Women and the Politics of Opportunity during the Presidential Campaigns of 1840 and 1844." *Tennessee Historical Quarterly* 51 (Winter 1992): 197–212.

Dubin, Michael J. *United States Presidential Elections, 1788–1860: The Official Results by County and State.* Jefferson, NC: McFarland, 2002.

Dupre, Daniel. "Barbecues and Pledges: Electioneering and the Rise of Democratic Politics in Antebellum Alabama." *Journal of Southern History* 60 (August 1994): 479–528.

Dzurec, David. "Of Salt Mountain, Prairie Dogs, and Horned Frogs: The Louisiana Purchase and the Evolution of Federalist Satire, 1803–1812." *Journal of the Early Republic* 35 (Spring 2015): 79–108.

Eckhardt, Celia Morris. *Fanny Wright: Rebel in America.* Cambridge, MA: Harvard University Press, 1984.

Edel, Charles N. *Nation Builder: John Quincy Adams and the Grand Strategy of the Republic.* Cambridge, MA: Harvard University Press, 2014.

Ellis, Richard E. *The Union at Risk: Jacksonian Democracy, States' Rights, and the Nullification Crisis.* New York: Oxford University Press, 1987.

Ellis, Richard J. *Presidential Travel: The Journey from George Washington to George W. Bush.* Lawrence: University Press of Kansas, 2008.

Emch, Lucille B. "An Indian Tale by William J. Snelling." *Minnesota History* 26 (September 1945): 211–21.

Fischer, Roger A. *Tippecanoe and Trinkets Too: The Material Culture of American Presidential Campaigns, 1828–1984.* Champaign: University of Illinois Press, 1988.

Forbes, Robert Pierce. *The Missouri Compromise and Its Aftermath: Slavery and the Meaning of America.* Chapel Hill: University of North Carolina Press, 2007.

Ford, Tanisha C., and Carl R. Weinberg. "Slavery, Interracial Marriage, and the Election of 1836." *OAH Magazine of History* 23 (April 2009): 57–61.

Formisano, Ronald P. "Deferential-Participant Politics: The Early Republic's Political Culture, 1789–1840." *American Political Science Review* 48 (June 1974): 473–87.

———. "The New Political History and the Election of 1840." *Journal of Interdisciplinary History* 23 (Spring 1993): 661–82.

———. "The 'Party Period' Revisited." *Journal of American History* 86 (June 1999): 93–120.

French, Roderick S. "Liberation from Man and God in Boston: Abner Kneeland's Free-Thought Campaign, 1830–1839." *American Quarterly* 32 (Summer 1980): 202–21.

Friedenberg, Robert V. *Notable Speeches in Contemporary Presidential Campaigns.* Westport, CT: Praeger, 2002.

Gaines, Pierce W. "Political Writings in the Young Republic." *Proceedings of the American Antiquarian Society* 76 (October 1966): 262–92.

Gammon, Samuel Rhea, Jr. *The Presidential Campaign of 1832.* Baltimore, MD: Johns Hopkins University Press, 1922.

Ginzberg, Lori D. "'The Hearts of Your Readers Will Shudder': Fanny Wright, Infidelity, and American Freethought." *American Quarterly* 46 (June 1994): 195–226.

Gordon-Reed, Annette. *Thomas Jefferson and Sally Hemings: An American Controversy.* Charlottesville: University Press of Virginia, 1997.

Green, Fletcher M. "On Tour with President Jackson." *New England Quarterly* 36 (June 1963): 209–28.

Grimsted, David. *American Mobbing, 1828–1861: Toward Civil War.* New York: Oxford University Press, 1998.

Gunderson, Robert Gray. *The Log-Cabin Campaign.* Lexington: University of Kentucky Press, 1957.

——. "Thurlow Weed's Network: Whig Party Organization in 1840." *Indiana Magazine of History* 48 (June 1952): 107–18.

Haley, James L. *Sam Houston.* Norman: University of Oklahoma Press, 2002.

Hay, Robert P. "The Case for Andrew Jackson in 1824: Eaton's *Wyoming Letters.*" *Tennessee Historical Quarterly* 29 (Summer 1970): 139–51.

Haynes, Sam W. *Unfinished Revolution: The Early American Republic in a British World.* Charlottesville: University of Virginia Press, 2010.

Heale, M. J. *The Presidential Quest: Candidates and Images in American Political Culture, 1787–1852.* New York: Longman, 1982.

Heidler, David S., and Jeanne T. Heidler. *Henry Clay: The Essential American.* New York: Random House, 2010.

——. *Old Hickory's War: Andrew Jackson and the Quest for Empire.* Mechanicsburg, PA: Stackpole, 1996.

Henderson, Archibald. *Washington's Southern Tour, 1791.* Boston: Houghton Mifflin, 1923.

Hickey, Donald R. *Glorious Victory: Andrew Jackson and the Battle of New Orleans.* Baltimore, MD: Johns Hopkins University Press, 2015.

——. *The War of 1812: A Forgotten Conflict.* Urbana: University of Illinois Press, 2012.

——. "'What We Know That Ain't So': Myths of the War of 1812." In *The Battle of New Orleans in History and Memory*, edited by Laura Lyons McLemore, 10–27. Baton Rouge: Louisiana State University Press, 2016.

Holt, Michael F. "The Election of 1840, Voter Mobilization, and the Emergence of the Second American Party System: A Reappraisal of Jacksonian Voting Behavior." In *A Master's Due: Essays in Honor of David Herbert Donald*, edited by William J. Cooper Jr., Michael F. Holt, and John McCardell, 16–58. Baton Rouge: Louisiana State University Press, 1985.

——. *The Rise and Fall of the American Whig Party: Jacksonian Politics and the Onset of the Civil War.* New York: Oxford University Press, 1999.

Horsman, Reginald. "William Henry Harrison: Virginia Gentleman in the Old Northwest." *Indiana Magazine of History* 96 (June 2000): 124–49.

Howe, Daniel Walker. "The Market Revolution and the Shaping of Identity in Whig-Jacksonian America." In *The Market Revolution in America: Social, Political, and Religious Expressions, 1800–1880*, edited by Melvyn Stokes and Stephen Conway, 259–81. Charlottesville: University Press of Virginia, 1996.

——. *What Hath God Wrought: The Transformation of America, 1815–1848.* New York: Oxford University Press, 2007.

Huston, Reeve. "Rethinking the Origins of Partisan Democracy in the United States, 1795–1840." In *Practicing Democracy: Popular Politics in the United States from the Constitution to the Civil War*, edited by Daniel Peart and Adam I. P. Smith, 46–71. Charlottesville: University of Virginia Press, 2015.

Hutson, James L. "Thomas Jefferson's Letter to the Danbury Baptists: A Controversy Rejoined." *William and Mary Quarterly* 56 (October 1999): 775–90.

Hutter, Liz. "'Ho for Salt River!' Politics, Loss, and Satire." *Common-Place* 7 (April 2007). http://www.common-place.org/vol-07/no-03/hutter/.

Inabinet, Brandon. "Democratic Circulation: Jacksonian Lithographs in U.S. Public Discourse." *Rhetoric amd Public Affairs* 15 (Winter 2012): 659–66.

John, Richard R. *Spreading the News: The American Postal System from Franklin to Morse.* Cambridge, MA: Harvard University Press, 1998.

———. "Taking Sabbatarianism Seriously: The Postal System, the Sabbath, and the Transformation of American Political Culture." *Journal of the Early Republic* 10 (Winter 1990): 517–67.

Johnson, Reinhard O. *The Liberty Party, 1840–1848: Antislavery Third-Party Politics in the United States.* Baton Rouge: Louisiana State University Press, 2009.

Johnson, Timothy D. *Winfield Scott: The Quest for Military Glory.* Lawrence: University Press of Kansas, 1998.

Kaplan, Fred. *John Quincy Adams: American Visionary.* New York: HarperCollins, 2014.

Keyssar, Alexander. *The Right to Vote: The Contested History of Democracy in the United States.* New York: Basic Books, 2000.

Kincheloe, Joe L., Jr. "Similarities in Crowd Control Techniques of the Camp Meeting and Political Rally: The Pioneer Role of Tennessee." *Tennessee Historical Quarterly* 37 (Summer 1978): 155–69.

Larson, John Lauritz. *Internal Improvement: National Public Works and the Promise of Popular Government in the Early United States.* Chapel Hill: University of North Carolina, 2001.

———. *The Market Revolution in America: Liberty, Ambition, and the Eclipse of the Common Good.* New York: Cambridge University Press, 2010.

Lawrence, Vera Brodsky. *Music for Patriots, Politicians, and Presidents.* New York: Macmillan, 1975.

Leonard, Gerald L. *The Invention of Party Politics: Federalism, Popular Sovereignty, and Constitutional Development in Jacksonian Illinois.* Chapel Hill: University of North Carolina Press, 2002.

———. "Party as a 'Political Safeguard of Federalism': Martin Van Buren and the Constitutional Theory of Party Politics." *Rutgers Law Review* 54 (Fall 2001): 221–81.

Lepler, Jessica M. *The Many Panics of 1837: People, Politics, and the Creation of a Transatlantic Financial Crisis.* New York: Cambridge University Press, 2013.

Marszalek, John F. *The Petticoat Affair: Manners, Mutiny, and Sex in Andrew Jackson's White House.* New York: Free Press, 1997.

Martin, Robert W. T. *Government by Dissent: Protest, Resistance, and Radical Democratic Thought in the Early American Republic.* New York: New York University Press, 2013.

Maxeiner, Andrea. "Sing America! Using Folk Songs to Teach American History." *Common-Place* 5 (July 2005). http://www.common-place-archives.org/vol-05/no-04/school/.

McCormick, Richard P. "Was There a 'Whig Strategy' in 1836?" *Journal of the Early Republic* 4 (Spring 1984): 47–70.

Middlekauff, Robert. *The Glorious Cause: The American Revolution, 1763–1789*. New York: Oxford University Press, 1982.

Miles, Edwin A. "President Adams' Billiard Table." *New England Quarterly* 45 (March 1972): 31–43.

———. "The Whig Party and the Menace of Caesar." *Tennessee Historical Quarterly* 27 (Winter 1968): 361–79.

Miles, William. *The Image Makers: A Bibliography of American Presidential Campaign Biographies*. Metuchen, NJ: Scarecrow Press, 1979.

Miller, Alan R. "American's First Political Satirist: Seba Smith of Maine." *Journalism Quarterly* 47 (Autumn 1970): 488–92.

Moats, Sandra. *Celebrating the Republic: Presidential Ceremony and Popular Sovereignty, from Washington to Monroe*. DeKalb: Northern Illinois University Press, 2009.

———. "The Limits of 'Good Feelings': Partisan Healing and Political Futures during James Monroe's Boston Visit of 1817." *Proceedings of the American Antiquarian Society* 118 (April 2008): 155–91.

Monroe, Dan. *The Republican Vision of John Tyler*. College Station: Texas A&M University Press, 2003.

Mooney, Chase C. *William H. Crawford, 1772–1834*. Lexington: University Press of Kentucky, 1974.

Morgan, William G. "The Decline of the Congressional Nominating Caucus." *Tennessee Historical Quarterly* 24 (Fall 1965): 245–55.

———. "The Origin and Development of the Congressional Nominating Caucus." *Proceedings of the American Philosophical Society* 113 (April 1969): 184–96.

New Georgia Encyclopedia. Atlanta: Georgia Humanities Council and University of Georgia Press, 2004–17. http://www.georgiaencyclopedia.org.

Niven, John C. *John C. Calhoun and the Price of Union: A Biography*. Baton Rouge: Louisiana State University Press, 1988.

———. *Martin Van Buren: The Romantic Age of American Politics*. New York: Oxford University Press, 1983.

Owens, Robert M. *Mr. Jefferson's Hammer: William Henry Harrison and the Origins of American Indian Policy*. Norman: University of Oklahoma Press, 2007.

Parsons, Lynn Hudson. *The Birth of Modern Politics: Andrew Jackson, John Quincy Adams, and the Election of 1828*. New York: Oxford University Press, 2009.

Parton, James. *Life of Andrew Jackson*. 3 vols. New York: Mason Brothers, 1859–61.

Pasley, Jeffrey L. "The Devolution of 1800: Jefferson's Election and the Birth of American Government." In *America at the Ballot Box: Elections and Political History*, edited by Gareth Davies and Julian E. Zelizer, 13–35. Philadelphia: University of Pennsylvania Press, 2015.

———. *The First Presidential Contest: 1796 and the Founding of American Democracy*. Lawrence: University Press of Kansas, 2013.

———. "Minnows, Spies, and Aristocrats: The Social Crisis of Congress in the Age of Martin Van Buren." *Journal of the Early Republic* 27 (Winter 2007): 599–653.

Pasley, Jeffrey L., Andrew W. Robertson, and David Waldstreicher, eds. *Beyond the Founders: New Approaches to the Political History of the Early American Republic*. Chapel Hill: University of North Carolina Press, 2004.

Peart, Daniel. *Era of Experimentation: American Political Practices in the Early Republic*. Charlottesville: University of Virginia Press, 2014.

Peterson, Norma Lois. *The Presidencies of William Henry Harrison and John Tyler*. Lawrence: University Press of Kansas, 1989.

Piola, Erika. "The Rise of Early Lithography and Antebellum Visual Culture." *Winterthur Portfolio* 48 (Summer/Autumn 2014): 125–38.

Ratcliffe, Donald J. *The One-Party Presidential Contest: Adams, Jackson, and 1824's Five-Horse Race*. Lawrence: University Press of Kansas, 2015.

——. "Popular Preferences in the Presidential Election of 1824." *Journal of the Early Republic* 34 (Spring 2014): 45–77.

Remini, Robert V. *Andrew Jackson*. 3 vols. New York: Harper and Row, 1977–84.

——. *Andrew Jackson and His Indian Wars*. New York: Viking Penguin, 2001.

——. *Andrew Jackson and the Bank War*. New York: Norton, 1967.

——. *Daniel Webster: The Man and His Time*. New York: Norton, 1997.

——. *The Election of Andrew Jackson*. New York: J. B. Lippincott, 1963.

——. *Henry Clay: Statesman for the Union*. New York: Norton, 1991.

Richards, Leonard L. *"Gentlemen of Property and Standing": Anti-Abolition Mobs in Jacksonian America*. New York: Oxford University Press, 1970.

Robertson, Andrew W. "Jeffersonian Parties, Politics, and Participation: The Tortuous Trajectory of American Democracy." In *Practicing Democracy: Popular Politics in the United States from the Constitution to the Civil War*, edited by Daniel Peart and Adam I. P. Smith, 99–122. Charlottesville: University of Virginia Press, 2015.

——. "'Look at this Picture . . . And on This!' Nationalism, Localism, and Partisan Images of Otherness in the United States, 1787–1820." *American Historical Review* 106 (October 2001): 1263–80.

Roediger, David R. *The Wages of Whiteness: Race and the Making of the American Working Class*. Rev. ed. Brooklyn, NY: Verso, 1999.

Satz, Ronald N. *American Indian Policy in the Jacksonian Era*. Lincoln: University of Nebraska Press, 1975.

Schlesinger, Arthur M. "Liberty Tree: A Genealogy." *New England Quarterly* 25 (December 1952): 435–58.

Schoenbachler, Matthew. "Republicanism in the Age of Democratic Revolution: The Democratic-Republican Societies of the 1790s." *Journal of the Early Republic* 18 (Summer 1998): 237–61.

Schroeder, John H. "Major Jack Downing and American Expansionism: Seba Smith's Political Satire, 1847–1856." *New England Quarterly* 50 (June 1977): 214–33.

Sellers, Charles G., Jr. "Election of 1844." In *History of American Presidential Elections*, vol. 1, edited by Arthur M. Schlesinger and Fred L. Israel, 745–861. New York: Chelsea House, 1971.

——. *James K. Polk*. 2 vols. Princeton, NJ: Princeton University Press, 1957, 1966.

Shade, William G. "'The Most Delicate and Exciting Topics': Martin Van Buren, Slavery, and the Election of 1836." *Journal of the Early Republic* 18 (Fall 1998): 459–84.

Shafer, Ronald G. *The Carnival Campaign: How the Rollicking 1840 Campaign of "Tippecanoe and Tyler Too" Changed Presidential Elections Forever*. Chicago: Chicago Review Press, 2016.

Shalev, Eran. "Ancient Masks, American Fathers: Classical Pseudonyms during the American Revolution and Early Republic." *Journal of the Early Republic* 23 (Summer 2003): 151–72.

Sharp, James Roger. *The Deadlocked Election of 1800: Jefferson, Burr, and the Union in the Balance.* Lawrence: University Press of Kansas, 2010.

Silbey, Joel H. "Election of 1836." In *History of American Presidential Elections*, vol. 1, edited by Arthur M. Schlesinger and Fred L. Israel, 575–640. New York: Chelsea House, 1971.

———. *Party Over Section: The Rough and Ready Presidential Election of 1848.* Lawrence: University Press of Kansas, 2009.

Skaggs, David Curtis. *William Henry Harrison and the Conquest of the Ohio Country: Frontier Fighting in the War of 1812.* Baltimore, MD: Johns Hopkins University Press, 2014.

Smith, Culver H. *Press, Politics, and Patronage: The American Government's Use of Newspapers, 1789–1875.* Athens: University of Georgia Press, 1977.

———. "Propaganda Techniques in the Jackson Campaign of 1828." *East Tennessee Historical Society's Publications* 6 (1934): 44–66.

Smith, Elbert B. *The Presidencies of Zachary Taylor and Millard Fillmore.* Lawrence: University Press of Kansas, 1988.

Smith, Henry Ladd. "The Two Major Downings: Rivalry in Political Satire." *Journalism Quarterly* 41 (Winter 1964): 74–78, 127.

Sprague, William B. *The Life of Jedidiah Morse, D.D.* New York: Anson D. F. Randolph, 1874.

Stevens, Kenneth R. *William Henry Harrison: A Bibliography.* Westport, CT: Greenwood Press, 1998.

Sullivan, John. "The Case of 'A Late Student': Pictorial Satire in Jacksonian America." *Proceedings of the American Antiquarian Society* 83 (October 1973): 277–86.

———. "Jackson Caricatured: Two Historical Errors." *Tennessee Historical Quarterly* 31 (Spring 1972): 39–44.

Taylor, Alan. "'The Art of Hook and Snivey': Political Culture in Upstate New York during the 1790s." *Journal of American History* 79 (March 1993): 1371–96.

Terry, Roderick. "The History of the Liberty Tree of Newport, Rhode Island." *Bulletin of the Newport Historical Society* 27 (October 1918): 1–35.

Teute, Fredrika J. "Roman Matron on the Banks of Tiber Creek: Margaret Bayard Smith and the Politicization of Spheres in the Nation's Capital." In *A Republic for the Ages: The United States Capitol and the Political Culture of the Early Republic*, edited by Donald R. Kennon, 89–121. Charlottesville: University of Virginia Press, 1999.

Van Atta, John R. *Wolf by the Ears: The Missouri Crisis, 1819–1821.* Baltimore, MD: Johns Hopkins University Press, 2015.

Varon, Elizabeth R. "Tippecanoe and the Ladies, Too: White Women and Party Politics in Antebellum Virginia." *Journal of American History* 82 (September 1995): 494–521.

———. *We Mean to Be Counted: White Women and Politics in Antebellum Virginia.* Chapel Hill: University of North Carolina Press, 1998.

Wade, J. D. "The Authorship of David Crockett's 'Autobiography.'" *Georgia Historical Quarterly* 6 (September 1922): 265–68.

Waldstreicher, David. *In the Midst of Perpetual Fetes: The Making of American Nationalism, 1776–1820*. Chapel Hill: University of North Carolina Press, 1997.

Ward, John William. *Andrew Jackson: Symbol for an Age*. New York: Oxford University Press, 1955.

Watson, Harry L. *Liberty and Power: The Politics of Jacksonian America*. 2nd. ed. New York: Hill and Wang, 2006.

Wilentz, Sean. *The Rise of American Democracy: Jefferson to Lincoln*. New York: Norton, 2005.

Wilson, Major. *The Presidency of Martin Van Buren*. Lawrence: University Press of Kansas, 1984.

Wood, Gordon S. *The Creation of the American Republic, 1776–1787*. Chapel Hill: University of North Carolina Press, 1993.

———. *Empire of Liberty: A History of the Early Republic, 1789–1815*. New York: Oxford University Press, 2009.

Wood, Kirsten E. "'Join with Heart and Soul and Voice': Music, Harmony, and Politics in the Early American Republic." *American Historical Review* 119 (October 2014): 1083–1116.

Wooldridge, John L., ed. *History of Nashville, Tenn [. . .]*. Nashville: H. W. Crew, 1890.

Zagarri, Rosemarie. "Gender and the First Party System." In *Federalists Reconsidered*, edited by Doron Ben-Atar and Barbara B. Oberg, 118–34. Charlottesville: University of Virginia Press, 1998.

———. *Revolutionary Backlash: Women and Politics in the Early American Republic*. Philadelphia: University of Pennsylvania Press, 2007.

———. "Women and Party Conflict in the Early Republic." In *Beyond the Founders: New Approaches to the Political History of the Early American Republic*, edited by Jeffrey L. Pasley, Andrew W. Robertson, and David Waldstreicher, 107–28. Chapel Hill: University of North Carolina Press, 2004.

Zboray, Ronald J., and Mary Saracino Zboray. "Whig Women, Politics, and Culture in the Campaign of 1840: Three Perspectives from Massachusetts." *Journal of the Early Republic* 17 (Summer 1997): 277–315.

Index